China

Rise, Repression & Resistance

Adrian Budd

b

Bookmarks
Publications

China: Rise, Repression & Resistance
by Adrian Budd

Published 2024 by Bookmarks Publications
c/o 1 Bloomsbury Street, London WC1B 3QE
© Bookmarks Publications

Cover design by Ben Windsor
Typeset by Ben Windsor
Printed by Halstan, Amersham HP6 6HJ

ISBN paperback 978-1-917020-16-9
Kindle 978-1-917020-17-6
ePub 978-1-917020-18-3
PDF 978-1-917020-19-0

Cover photograph: Workers protest outside a
factory in Shenzen, October 2007 (Getty Images)

About the author

Adrian Budd has taught Politics and International Relations at London South Bank University for over 30 years. He is an activist in the University and College Union and has served as a branch officer for much of his time at LSBU. He is the author of *Class, States and International Relations: a critical appraisal of Robert Cox and neo-Gramscian theory* (2013) and numerous other chapters and articles. He is a member of the *International Socialism* editorial board.

Acknowledgements

In researching and writing on China I have benefitted from friendship and discussion with many people. Aside from my general debt to those writing in the International Socialist tradition, I would like to thank Jane Hardy for encouraging me to co-write an article with her for *International Socialism* in 2012. Sally Campbell encouraged me to work on the *China in Focus* series in 2018-19 when she was editor of *Socialist Review*. Phil Marfleet has been a source of encouragement over nearly four decades while challenging me to provide more convincing answers to complex questions. I have also benefitted from my membership of an online group of revolutionary socialists from a variety of backgrounds (including the International Socialist and Fourth International traditions) – my thanks go to all the members but to Kevin Lin in particular for establishing and convening the group.

For help and support to complete the book my thanks go to Camilla Royle and Mark Thomas of Bookmarks, and to Carol Williams for her attention to detail (and commitment to comprehensible sentences) as copy editor. Thanks also to Simon Gilbert, Rob Hoverman, Jane Hardy, Joseph Choonara and Alex Callinicos for their comments on the chapters in draft. The finished product is greatly improved as a result of their efforts.

Shaminder Takhar lived with the writing of this book during and after a six-month sabbatical from my usual work for London South Bank University in 2023. My deepest gratitude is to her for her forbearance, support, and love.

Contents

China's neighbours

China's regions

Abbreviations

ACFTU All-China Federation of Trade Unions (state controlled)

ACWF All-China Women's Federation

BWAF Beijing Workers Autonomous Federation

CCCDR Central Commission for Comprehensively Deepening Reform

CCDI Central Commission for Discipline Inspection

CCP Chinese Communist party

CDOs Collateralised Debt Obligations

CHIPS Clearing House Interbank Payments System

CHIPS US Creating Helpful Incentives to Produce Semiconductors (CHIPS) and Science Act

CICIIF China Integrated Circuit Investment Industry Fund

Comintern Communist International

FDI Foreign Direct Investment

GDP Gross Domestic Product

GMD Guomindang nationalist party

HKCTU Hong Kong Confederation of Trade Unions (more radical than HKFTU)

HKFTU Hong Kong Federation of Trade Unions (pro-regime)

ILO International Labour Organisation

LGFVs Local Government Financing Vehicles

MIC Made in China 2025 industrial policy

NGOs Non-Governmental Organisations

OECD Organisation for Economic Co-operation and Development

PLA People's Liberation Army

RMB Renminbi (Chinese currency)

SASAC State-owned Assets Supervision and Administration Commission

SOE State-owned enterprises

SEZs Special Economic Zones

SMIC Semiconductor Manufacturing International Corporation

SWIFT Society for Worldwide Interbank Financial Telecommunications

TSMC Taiwan Semiconductor Manufacturing Company

TVEs Township and Village Enterprises

USSR Union of Soviet Socialist Republics (Soviet Union)

XPCC Xinjiang Production and Construction Corps (or *Bingtuan*)

WTO World Trade Organisation

Chinese terms

Guanxi beneficial social and business connections

Hukou geographical residency permit

Nongmingong "peasant workers", migrants who work part in industry and part on the land

Shuanggui "double designation"; practice where someone accused of a crime must report at a designated time and designated place for investigation

Tongzhi "comrade"; a word used by LGBT+ people themselves when referring to each other

Tuanpai Chinese Communist Youth League

Yizu, shuzu "ant tribe", "mouse tribe"; disparaging words used to describe workers living in the worst urban housing

Zhuada fangxiao "grasp the big, release the small" economic restructuring programme

Timeline

1911 Qing dynasty overthrown, birth of republican era

1919 First republican leader Sun Yat-sen establishes Guomindang (GMD) nationalist party

1921 Chinese Communist Party (CCP) formed, inspired by 1917 Russian Revolution

1925-1927 Major worker struggles. Pre-revolutionary situation ended by massacre of Shanghai workers by Chiang Kai-shek's GMD troops

1927-1949 CCP-GMD Civil War. Periods of cooperation against Japanese imperialism 1937-45

1934-6 CCP's Long March to escape GMD and regroup

1949 Revolution. Nationalists flee to Formosa/Taiwan

1958-1961 Great Leap Forward and famine

1966-76 Cultural Revolution. Threat of descent into civil war

1972 US takes advantage of deepening Sino-Soviet split to seek détente with China

1976 9 Sep Mao dies. 11 Oct Gang of Four arrested. Deng Xiaoping wins ensuing power struggle

1978-88 Initial stages of reform of Mao's self-reliant statist economic model

1989 Tiananmen Square protests and massacre

1992 Deng's "southern tour" re-starts reform. Aims to build a "socialist market economy with Chinese characteristics"

1997 Hong Kong returned to China by UK

2001 China joins WTO. Massive increase in exports and inward investment

2008-9 China's huge stimulus package maintains economic growth and helps prevent global economic collapse

2009 China becomes the world's largest exporter (was 21st in 1978)

2012 Xi Jinping becomes CCP leader and (2013) president of China

2013 Belt and Road Initiative launched

2016 On purchasing power parity basis, China becomes world's largest economy

Post-2016 Sharp authoritarian turn, including more strident nationalism. Crackdown on corruption in CCP. Response to 2007-2016 strike wave, Hong Kong "umbrella movement" (2014), declining growth rates and other challenges to CCP legitimacy. Repression of Uyghur Muslims, feminists, labour activists etc intensifies. Rising tensions with US, including over Taiwan, and in South China Sea

Introduction

The developmental model that Mao built after the 1949 revolution that established the People's Republic of China was geared towards self-reliance and semi-autarky. For most of the following forty years, the world's writers and broadcasters mirrored Mao's inward-lookingness and largely ignored the country. When they did focus on China it was often to ridicule its eccentricities, including the wild pseudo-revolutionism of the Red Guards unleashed by Mao in the Cultural Revolution. Occasionally, when the US sought détente with Mao for instance, there were more positive statements about "the great helmsman" and his country, but for the most part serious analysis of China, let alone understanding, was in short supply. That began to change in the late spring and early summer of 1989 when the Tiananmen Square protests and the massacre of protesters captured the world's attention, encouraging tens of thousands to protest in support of the victims of state repression. For the Left, the realisation that "we are part of China and China is part of us" began to shatter the separation of China from the rest of the world, though in practical terms the connections remained flimsy, limited to expressions of solidarity from afar.[1] China's economic connections with the rest of the world were increasing however. Between Mao's death in 1976 and 1989, after a decade of tentative reform and the beginnings of the opening to the world economy under Mao's successor Deng Xiaoping, China's exports rose from less than $7 billion to $52.5 billion (in current dollars). By 1989 China's practical relevance to the outside world was greater than at any time in the previous forty years, but while during the postwar era the phrase "when the US sneezes the rest of the world catches a cold" was often heard, even as late as 1989 a Chinese sneeze barely registered. Today, when its exports are over $3.6 trillion, sixty-five times more than in 1989, China matters.

This book aims to provide a Marxist understanding of contemporary China and explain why it matters to the international Left. Unlike much writing on China, it does not explore how Western business can benefit from the opportunities China offers. Nor does it echo the concerns of mainstream writers over the perceived threat China poses to Western values. Western values are generally invoked to promote the interests of the major imperialist powers and their ruling capitalist classes. These values and interests were expressed in 2023 and 2024 by the mildness of the major Western powers' suggestions, in the face of global demands for a ceasefire, that Israel slow down and make less visible its assault on Gaza using Western-supplied weapons.

The values expressed by China's leading politicians and state officials are no better. A dwindling number of people on the Left still believe the claim of Article 1 of the Chinese constitution that China has "a socialist state under the people's democratic dictatorship led by the working class and based on the alliance of workers and peasants" and that "the exploiting classes as such have been abolished in our country".[2] The Chinese Communist Party (CCP) today is a party of millionaire and billionaire businesspeople, courted by the current president Xi Jingping as "a group of individuals from the business world who are determined to march with the Party".[3] That party has transformed China's economy while presiding over a massive increase in inequality in the last three decades, making China one of the most unequal countries in the world. Nevertheless, some of China's defenders claim that it remains socialist because it has a state-planned economy that is fundamentally different to Western forms of capitalism. In reality the five-year plans set annual growth targets and broad policy guidelines that are then interpreted by local authorities, producing duplication, waste, and under-utilisation of infrastructure in what MIT professor Yasheng Huang calls "one country, thirty-two economies".[4] Some believe that state-owned enterprises (SOEs) dominate the economy, yet they produce only around 30 percent of total output. In any case, isolating the legal form of property ownership as the key difference between capitalism and socialism obscures the real relations of class exploitation that exist within SOEs and more generally in China today.[5] Some see in the CCP a leadership committed to the long-term development of the national economy in a socialist direction, yet its own internal documents describe the party as inspired by neoliberalism and it presides over a vast system of class exploitation.[6] Some highlight state control over finance, which allows state-owned banks to exercise a decisive influence over the allocation of investment resources. But these banks feed off the huge savings rate of China's workers who are ruthlessly exposed to markets: they cannot rely on state support in the privatised housing market or for their welfare needs – nor, in the case of millions of migrant workers, for support in educating their children. Furthermore, the state-owned banks' activities are supplemented by a large deregulated shadow finance system. Defenders of Chinese "socialism" adjust their definition of socialism each time the evidence undermines their earlier definition, as did defenders of the USSR under Stalin. The Russian Revolution had destroyed the Tsarist capitalist state and begun the process of building a new workers' state (albeit with significant weaknesses that could not be overcome without the assistance of the wider European revolution). Under Lenin, Russia, and later the USSR, was socialist because the working class organised in Soviets (workers' councils) governed the country. When Stalinism destroyed the last remnants of workers' power and ruthlessly subordinated the working class to the interests of a new class of party-state managers, defenders of Stalin came up with a new definition – state control over the means of production. Some defenders of China now see state control over finance as key to the definition of socialism. With the criteria becoming ever narrower, the logic of clinging to an impossible label could lead to a definition of socialism as "state control of the commanding heights of the state"!

Others on the Left recognise that in the absence of workers' democracy and democratic planning China is not socialist, but they nevertheless argue that the system of economic planning and the role of state firms make China a non-capitalist economy or a transitional economy situated between capitalism and socialism. This is the view of Carchedi and Roberts in their important Marxist analysis of contemporary global capitalism. But as we have seen, claims about planning and the role of SOEs are misplaced. The absence of planning was highlighted in 2023 when the Chinese property sector, which comprises 25 percent of the economy, went into freefall as giant developers such as Evergrande faced insolvency, undermining the wider domestic market for household goods. Despite repeated official commitments to rebalancing the economy towards domestic consumption, household spending as a proportion of GDP today stubbornly refuses to rise in line with these plans. The post-Mao transformation reinforced the centrality of profitability as the key yardstick of economic activity and the subordination of planning to markets.

After forty years of global neoliberal attacks on trade unions, wages and working conditions, an impending climate catastrophe driven by capitalism's logic of competitive capital accumulation, and endless imperialist wars, wishful thinking that there is an existing, albeit imperfect, alternative to Western power is understandable. This is particularly true in the international sphere, where some regard China's rhetoric of development and "win-win" agreements with countries of the Global South, including via the Belt and Road Initiative (see chapter six), as a progressive alternative to the decades of West-imposed structural adjustment. But China's contribution to the global climate emergency, its own imperialist designs – particularly on the Global South where its banks charge higher interest rates than the World Bank and many Western lenders – the harsh exploitation of labour, and the gender, religious and other oppressions imposed on China's citizens, all suggest that popular hopes for the future should not be placed in China's state-capitalist rulers. As Ho-fung Hung writes:

> [T]he underlying principle and basic dynamics of capitalism as an economic system are universal, though capitalism is always enmeshed in historically and nationally specific sociopolitical structures that enable the release of its productive forces at some times and fetter its reproduction at other times. There is no such thing as Chinese capitalism that is fundamentally different from American capitalism, Japanese capitalism, or German capitalism.... [albeit that] capitalism in China is combined with China's particular social relations, state institutions, and geopolitical interests to present a particular face and to bring particular consequences to the global order.[7]

China's capitalism carries all the pathologies of other variants of capitalism, but it also carries the seeds of an alternative. Both the pathologies and grounds for optimism were highlighted by important events in October-December 2022. In October, a mass break-out of thousands of migrant workers from Foxconn's 250,000-worker iPhone production complex in Zhengzhou took place after rumours of new deaths from Covid-19 began to spread.[8] Foxconn's draconian factory regime, the closed-loop system that is shared by Tesla and others, involved the lock-down of workers between workshops and inadequate dormitories in order to maintain production. Workers testing positive were quarantined, with inadequate food, water or medicines. Seldom has the argument of the *Communist Manifesto* that under capitalism workers are a mere appendage to a machine, their lives subordinated to the drive for production and profits, been more accurate. In response to the break-out the local authorities initially supplied Foxconn with their own staff to maintain production and then recruited replacement workers with promises of bonus payments. When these promises were broken, worker riots were repressed by the local police. The complicity of the local state, the police and giant corporations contrasted starkly with the solidarity the escapees received as they walked to their home towns and villages. Local villagers left food by the roadside to sustain them, fearful of contracting Covid-19 via direct contact.

The events of the following month underlined the contrast between state repression and elementary popular solidarity with those facing oppression and persecution. On 24 November a fire in a tower-block, which was locked from the outside under the strict Covid regulations, killed a dozen Uyghur Muslims in Urumchi, capital of Xinjiang. Xinjiang's Uyghurs and other Turkic minorities have long endured a settler-colonial regime of mass surveillance, detention, relocation and cultural repression, and the anti-lockdown protests that erupted in Urumchi mainly involved Han Chinese (the ethnic majority). The Han have been criticised for their silence on Uyghur oppression, but they protested because they understood that Uyghur protests would face severe police repression. Inter-ethnic solidarity with people that the state labels terrorists was a turning point and recognition that Han people also face state repression.[9] Overseas Han student groups also protested, demanding the closure of the concentration camps in which perhaps hundreds of thousands of Uyghurs have been incarcerated.[10] China's surveillance state censors blocked social media images of the protests, yet they quickly spread to other cities, including Beijing and

Shanghai, where protesters' awareness of the threat of repression was demonstrated by the creativity they used to try to avoid arrest. Words from China's national anthem "rise up, those who refuse to be slaves" were heard while, more famously, protesters held up blank sheets of paper representing "everything we want to say but cannot say".[11] For the first time since the Tiananmen protests of 1989, generalised political demands were raised in a few places where chants of "Down with the CCP! Down with Xi Jinping!" were heard, along with calls for freedom and democracy and denunciations of authoritarianism.[12]

The protests increased pressure for the relaxation of China's zero-Covid regime that had begun in early November.[13] But the main driver behind the relaxation announced in early December was the growing opposition to lockdowns from corporations. In early December a letter from Foxconn's founder to the party-state leadership warned that lockdowns threatened China's position as an investment location. According to the *Wall Street Journal*, this "played a major role" in the easing of zero-Covid restrictions.[14] Protesters since then have been arrested and face further repression under a surveillance regime strengthened by the contact-tracing apps developed during the Covid pandemic.

Measured by comparative death rates, zero-Covid was successful – 10 per million in China, 3,130 per million in Britain – albeit that the repeated lockdowns lead to increased suicide rates and mental-health and domestic-violence crises along with shortages of food and medical services.[15] But the motivation behind zero-Covid was less about securing the lives of Chinese citizens than "securing the life of the party".[16] The party-state feared that the under-resourced health-care system would be unable to cope with mass hospitalisation (it has 10 percent of the USA's intensive-care beds per capita), which would pose a challenge to regime legitimacy. Despite that fear, regime nationalism inhibited the purchase of Western vaccines even though they were superior to Chinese vaccines.[17]

The Foxconn escape and the protests following the Urumchi fire highlighted many of the issues that this book will address. They showed the inter-relationships of the state and big business, posed questions about the legitimacy of the increasingly authoritarian and repressive CCP regime, highlighted the oppression of Uyghur Muslims (as well as Hong Kong activists who also showed solidarity with the Uyghurs) and exposed the under-funding of the state welfare system.[18] They also revealed the build-up of anger at the base of society, including among young women who played a prominent role in the protests, underlining the importance of feminist criticism of all aspects of contemporary life for women in China. The regime's vaccine-nationalism also pointed to the inter-imperialist rivalry with the West. But these events also demonstrated the potential power of protest and of the millions of workers in China's factories.

The protests and their aftermath also exploded what remained of the myth that China is socialist. As Yuri Prasad asked at the time, "what sort of 'socialist' society sends in heavily armed cops to break up students' anti-lockdown demonstrations...uses force against workers striking for health and safety at a firm making phones for a giant US multinational?"[19] Understanding contemporary China requires a Marxist analysis rather than misplaced hopes or wishes. Such an analysis was developed in Tony Cliff's critique of Stalinist state capitalism in the USSR, which forms the essential theoretical bedrock of the current book.[20] For Cliff, Marxist theory was not a set of ready-made slogans, a "frozen orthodoxy" that merely repeated existing theoretical formulations and mechanically applied them to the world. The world is in motion, constantly throwing up novel phenomena, and orthodoxy "cannot lead us through the labyrinth of reality as it has no dynamism and does not recognise its complexity".[21] Mobilising Marxism as a living and dynamic theory, Cliff argued that the new phenomenon he sought to explain, the consolidation of Stalinism under the first Five Year Plan of 1928, represented a counter-revolution. This was carried out by a new and increasingly self-conscious ruling class after the decimation of the working class during Soviet Russia's post-1917 civil war and the wars of foreign intervention. The social power of this ruling class derived not from personal property, as in other capitalist societies, but from ownership (understood as effective control) of nationalised property.[22] One of Cliff's crucial insights was that the Soviet Union could not be understood in isolation but had to be placed in the context of the pressure from capitalism's global dynamic of competitive accumulation, expressed in the military threat from other states.

Within this international framework, the new state capitalist ruling class was interested not in supporting socialist revolution but in protecting what it saw as the national interests of the USSR, and therefore its own power. The Communist International, established under Lenin in 1919 to promote world revolution, became equally Stalinised as the Soviet state and the world's communist parties became tools of the Soviet ruling class. In all essentials this national-developmental model under a bureaucratic ruling class was emulated after 1949 in China.

Structure

In China's 1949 revolution Mao's Communists swept Chiang Kai-shek's nationalist Guomindang (GMD) government from power. The revolution was of global significance. For most on the Left it represented the enlargement of the non-capitalist area of the world, a complement to the Red Army's advance into Eastern Europe at the end of the Second World War. For millions in China and the wider Global South, the revolution offered hope, ended a century of humiliation suffered by China at the hands of imperialism, and was a key moment in the postwar wave of decolonisation that began in India in 1947. Chapter one provides the historical background to the later chapters on contemporary developments that are likely to be of most interest to readers. It contains some historical detail, but this has been kept to the minimum required to illustrate the nature and evolution of China's state-capitalist regime. It outlines the history of the CCP, explains the Stalinist roots of Maoism, and explores the origins and events of the 1949 national-developmental revolution. It then analyses the construction and development of state capitalism under Mao, including the mass campaigns of the Great Leap Forward and Cultural Revolution, whose voluntarism contrasted with the sclerosis and bureaucratism of the USSR and pro-Soviet Stalinist parties and generated considerable support on the international Left. History does not provide neat periodisation, and to set the scene for the rest of the book chapter one takes the story into the early years of the post-Mao transition, including the 1989 Tiananmen protests and massacre. It was only in the early 1990s that the ruling class launched itself fully onto the path of major economic reform.

Chapter two covers the contemporary Chinese economy that developed from the restructuring and opening to the world since the early 1990s. Private capital contributed almost nothing in 1978 but today accounts for 60 percent of GDP. Many superlatives have been written about the economic take-off in the post-Mao reform period, including the lifting of millions of people out of extreme poverty. China has indeed been transformed economically. But on what basis? David Harvey's argument that the party-state has constructed a "neoliberalism with Chinese characteristics" captures the experience of many. Delivering some 280-300 million migrant workers to the coastal Special Economic Zones (SEZs), where minimal workers' rights, low wages, low or non-existent corporate taxes and customs duties, and simplified procedures for establishing production sites attracted foreign capital and subsequently generated vast pools of surplus value and profits. The state remains an active player in the economy and SOEs remain important, including in the modernisation of economic infrastructures, local authorities promote growth in their competitive relations with each other, and finance remains substantially in state hands. But China's hybrid of state capitalism and neoliberalism is no more able to escape the contradictions of capitalism that Marx identified in the nineteenth century than capitalism in the West.

Workers' struggles (allied to labour shortages as the working-age population shrinks and the flow of migration slows to a trickle) have lead to wage rises. Growth rates have slowed but have been propped up by huge and unsustainable injections of debt. Asset-price and property bubbles have begun to burst in various cities and regions. Youth unemployment hovers around 20 percent. Xi's Made in China 2025 (MIC) industrial policy announced in 2015, and the later dual circulation strategy, have continued the reorientation of the economy away from dependence on exports but have run up against capital's resistance to higher wages and had only modest success in boosting domestic consumption. China's economy remains dangerously dependent on over-accumulation and state spending on infrastructure. As the early signs of economic crisis multiply, ruling-class concerns over social stability and regime legitimacy have grown.

The focus of chapter three is captured by a comment from the exiled novelist Ma Jian: China may have "a new coat of prosperity, but inside it's become more brutal than ever…[a] venomous combination of extreme authoritarianism and extreme capitalism".[23] There has been a heavy-handed crack-down on non-governmental organisations (NGOs), particularly those providing support for workers, new national security and intelligence laws that demand that every citizen, corporation and institution cooperate with the state security apparatus, and a heightened nationalism alongside other conservative invocations of tradition, including Confucianism. Superficial commentary argues that these developments reflect Xi's personal hostility to Western values and fear of political instability, but the real explanation has deeper roots. The CCP has become a party dominated by and serving the interests of the mega-rich and, as its own internal documents proclaim, geared towards neoliberal economic management. The consequences of this (including greater inequality, environmental devastation, and corruption) pose long-term threats to both social stability and the legitimacy of the party-state and state-capitalist regime. The intensified repression under Xi is part of a strategy to shore up party rule in the face of the challenges he inherited when he assumed office in 2012 and those that the party-state elite anticipates in the future as the promise of prosperity on the back of continued economic growth begins to fade.

Popular challenges to CCP power ebb and flow, as elsewhere, but are a permanent worry for the ruling class. These challenges are the focus of the next two chapters. Chapter four looks at China's draconian labour regimes and the response of Chinese workers, particularly in the strike wave of 2007-16. Intensified repression after 2015 brought an end to the strike wave before an independent national labour movement could develop, and the 800-million strong working class remains poorly organised and weaker than its numbers suggest it should be. But the resilience, combativity and embryonic grassroots organisation that began to by-pass the official state-run unions up to 2016 give grounds for optimism about the future. Chapter five extends this analysis to those suffering under other pathologies of contemporary capitalism. Whether it involves national and religious oppression (Uyghur Muslims, Tibetans, Hong Kongers), gender violence and oppression, or environmental degradation, ordinary Chinese people have demonstrated their capacity for collective resistance, even in the face of severe surveillance and repression, and to lay down sediments of collective memory. As the May 1968 events in France and the Arab Spring of 2011 revealed, revolutionary movements rooted in resistance at the base of society can develop when we least expect them.

Mobilising the perspective of inter-imperialist rivalry developed during the First World War by the Russian Marxists Lenin and Bukharin, chapter six places China's contemporary problems in the wider context of the increasingly unstable and hostile global system. Forty years of growth and modernisation have transformed China from a relatively inward-looking power into a growing imperialist force. China's imperialism is concentrated in but not limited to Asia, but it poses a growing challenge to the world's major imperialist power, the US. The response of the US and its allies – containment, strengthening and potential expansion of alliances like the QUAD and NATO, moves towards high-tech decoupling of the Chinese and Western economies in order to limit China's economic and military development – have greatly intensified the rivalry and the possibility of military conflict. The consequences for all of humanity are potentially devastating, reinforcing the impacts of the wider crises facing global society.

The book concludes with a call to arms. We cannot accurately predict the precise form of the economic crisis that seems set to engulf China in the coming years, but Cliff's prediction in 1948, rooted in classical Marxism, of the probable form of the economic crisis of the Stalinist regime, stagnation, proved to be remarkably accurate and serves as a warning for China. Stagnation already afflicts China's state-owned sector, which contains many zombie firms on debt-powered life support. Falling growth rates reinforce these problems and the crisis of stagnation is likely to be accompanied by a traditional crisis of over-production and falling profit rates in the coming years. The gathering contradictions strengthen the case for radical change, but Xi's repression has, for now at least, narrowed the space for workers' activism and social protest. Class contradictions do not automatically produce working class revolution, but they do produce struggle and revolt. If the working class is to achieve its own liberation, its self-emancipation, it will need to build on its history of activism and struggle. Historical experience indicates that there is one essential ingredient that is currently missing in China, a revolutionary socialist party rooted in the struggles of workers and the oppressed. I hope that this book makes a small contribution towards the building of such a party. Conditions are hard, the risk of repression is high, but it is no exaggeration to say that the interests of all the world's workers and the future of the planet depend on it.

Chapter 1
The 1949 revolution, Maoism and the post-Mao transition

Introduction

China's tumultuous twentieth-century history produced revolutionary changes of global significance. The rule of the Qing dynasty had been punctuated by rebellions in the second half of the nineteenth century, and by the end of that century the Qing hold on power was so weak that the 1899-1901 anti-colonial Boxer Rebellion was only defeated with the help of eight foreign armies.[1] A decade later, the 1911 Wuchang Uprising sparked the Xinhai revolution that overthrew the dynasty and ushered in the Republican era. The revolutionary atmosphere was heightened when the 1917 Russian Revolution provided a beacon of hope for the colonial and semi-colonial countries of the Global South. In 1919, the May Fourth Movement emerged from protests against the perpetuation of China's dependence when the Versailles Treaty handed German territories in China to Japan.[2] It was against this backdrop that the Chinese Communist Party was established in 1921.

The first leader of the republican era, Sun Yat-sen, had established the Guomindang (GMD, the Nationalist People's Party) in 1919 as a vehicle to secure central control over a fragmented society in which regional warlords dominated large parts of the country. But fragmentation continued, and the problems facing China's rulers (and would-be rulers) were soon magnified by the rise of the labour movement. In 1926-27 socialist revolution based on the concentrated power of the working class in the cities was firmly on the agenda. That this was squandered was chiefly due to the strategy of the increasingly Stalinised Communist Party – itself subject to the dominance of the USSR and the Communist International (Comintern).

The next twenty years were dominated by a civil war between the CCP and GMD. Japan took advantage of the chaos to invade

Manchuria in 1931 and from 1937 extended its control to much of the rest of China. The civil war was periodically suspended as the CCP and GMD focused their energies on national liberation from Japanese imperialism but was renewed after Japan's defeat in the Second World War. US support for the corrupt and brutal GMD could not prevent its defeat, and on 1 October Mao Zedong proclaimed the formation of the People's Republic.

The impact of this seismic event was greatest on the rural landlords, warlords and GMD government, which fled to Taiwan. But as China's old order was swept away so too was subjugation to external powers. The revolution was not socialist, the working class played no significant part, but it held the promise of national liberation and development. In 1820 the Chinese economy was the largest in the world, producing one-third of total global output. But the rise of industrial capitalism, initially in Western Europe, swept away pre-capitalist limits to development and provided the economic and military means for Britain and others to impose a century of humiliation on China after the Opium War (1839-42). Britain forced open the Chinese market and imposed the first of the unequal treaties that China had to endure, gaining the first of the Western concessions of coastal territories, including the villages that later developed into Hong Kong and the city of Shanghai. Humiliation continued at the end of the nineteenth century with the first Sino-Japanese war of 1894-95. By 1900 China represented just 11 percent of the global economy. China's revolutionary twentieth century unfolded against the background of humiliation and the 1917 Russian Revolution and its consequences.

The CCP, Stalinism and permanent revolution

By the early 1920s the revolutionary working class in the USSR had been decimated by starvation and disease and demobilised by years of civil war and defence of the Soviet republic from the invading armies of the capitalist powers. On the ruins of working-class power, the increasingly Stalinised bureaucracy tightened its grip on the state, before finally consolidating itself as a new state-capitalist ruling class with the first five-year plan in 1928. Stalinism represented not the continuation of the 1917 revolution but its brutal annihilation and negation. The Comintern, launched by the Bolsheviks in 1919 to promote world socialist revolution, was also progressively transformed and turned into an instrument for promoting Moscow's interests. Henceforth, the defence of the USSR against imperialism would not involve support for socialist revolution but the construction of alliances with any mainstream political forces whose interests might clash with those of the major capitalist states. In China, the nationalist GMD was identified as the political force most capable of resisting the growth of Japanese power in Asia, and from 1924 Soviet advisers began to help build the GMD's party organisation and discipline and train its armed forces. When Sun Yat-sen died in 1925 and his successor as party leader, Chiang Kai-shek, moved the party to a more aggressively pro-capitalist position, the Comintern continued to insist on CCP acquiescence to GMD leadership of the national struggle.

Throughout his political life Lenin had insisted upon the independence of the revolutionary party and in mid-1917 had adopted Trotsky's views on permanent revolution. Developed after Russia's 1905 Revolution, Trotsky's theory of permanent revolution argued that in less developed and semi-dependent countries such as Russia and China, the weakness of the capitalist classes rendered them incapable of defeating reaction and completing the bourgeois revolution. The defeat of Russian Tsarism would require the support of the masses. In a predominantly rural society, albeit with pockets of advanced industry and concentrated workers movements, much of the anger driving change would come from the peasants. But their geographical dispersion and the divisions between rich and poor peasants made them unable to unite and carry the revolution forward. This task would require the concentrated power and organisation of the working class. This posed a problem for the small national capitalist class, for once mobilised the working class's own interests would begin to come to the fore. If, as Trotsky argued, the bourgeois revolution could only be completed by the working class, the revolution would rapidly grow over into the socialist revolution. The revolution would become "permanent".

The Russian Revolution of October 1917 confirmed Trotsky's analysis. Tragically, the Chinese events of 1925-27 provided a negative confirmation. The Comintern failed to promote independent working-class interests, fostered the illusion that the GMD could lead a successful struggle for socialism and against imperialism and instructed the CCP to work closely with the GMD. This strategic orientation was given a theoretical window-dressing by a sharp retreat from the Marxist understanding of irreconcilable class antagonisms and an accommodation to what was later called Third World nationalism. In place of proletarian class struggle, the Comintern declared in March 1926 that the GMD was "a revolutionary bloc of the workers, peasants, intellectuals and urban bourgeoisie", established "on the basis of a community of class interests…in the struggle against the imperialists and the whole militarist-feudal order".[3] The fanciful idea of common interests across the "bloc of four classes" entailed the CCP's subordination to the GMD and the abandonment of its radical land redistribution programme. The CCP became merely "the left-wing appendage" of the GMD.[4] This was shortly to have devastating consequences.

The groundwork for Stalinism's disastrous failure to prevent the rise of German (and later, Spanish) fascism was laid in China. Between 1925 and 1927 China was gripped by a wave of peasant revolts and major workers' struggles that involved millions of workers, including in a year-long general strike in British-controlled Hong Kong. Trade union membership mushroomed, workers became increasingly conscious of their class interests, strikes spread from foreign-owned to Chinese-owned firms, and the CCP's membership increased to somewhere between 30,000 and 50,000 by early 1927. The early stages of a workers' revolution were rapidly developing.

As national unity evaporated, the GMD's demand for unity was exposed as a thinly disguised cover for its defence of capitalist interests. In the countryside it supported the brutal reaction of the landlords, and in the industrial centres it rounded up many CCP members and attacked the Hong Kong strike headquarters in March 1926. Yet under Comintern orders the CCP remained committed to cooperation with the GMD – when Shanghai's unions called a general strike, involving three-quarters of a million workers, and workers' militias took control of the city for twelve days, the CCP instructed workers to give up their arms when GMD troops entered Shanghai. This provided an opportunity for Chiang Kai-shek to keep the promise he had made in meetings with Shanghai's capitalists. In April 1927 the GMD massacred 40,000 workers in Shanghai and destroyed their organisations. Tens of thousands were murdered elsewhere as the workers, disoriented by the CCP, proved ill-prepared for their self-defence. Only a handful of CCP leaders called for an end to the alliance with the GMD. Mao Zedong was not among them and supported the alliance to the bitter end.

The revolutionary class: workers or peasants?

The Shanghai massacre did not shift the CCP from its allegiance to Stalinism, and it switched its support to the left-GMD government in Wuhan until it too attacked the Wuhan workers, murdering thousands.[5] Another massacre followed in Quandong in December after an adventurist coup attempt by the CCP, part of a brief campaign of lightning attacks on key cities in the second half of 1927 ordered from Moscow as Stalin sought a victory with which to finally destroy the remaining Soviet opposition at December's up-coming fourteenth congress of the CPSU.[6] The CCP's depleted numbers now retreated to the remote Hunan-Jiangxi border in south-east China, where they were gradually joined by other CCP remnants. As numbers increased, the Jiangxi Soviet declared itself a state, the Chinese Soviet Republic, from where CCP forces mounted sporadic guerrilla attacks on the GMD and republic. But the CCP's forces were outnumbered and despite heroic resistance to a series of GMD encirclement campaigns, by late 1934 the military, material and personnel losses forced the leadership around Mao into a second strategic retreat – the heroic Long March.

Before the Shanghai massacre two-thirds of CCP members were workers, but by September 1930 workers made up less than 2 percent of the membership. Separation from the everyday disciplines and rhythms of working-class life was reinforced in the Long March to the remote Shaanxi province in the north-west. Survival in the face of constant hounding by the GMD's superior numbers as well as warlords aligned with the GMD, and the harsh conditions of the relatively barren hinterland, was a remarkable feat of endurance, but it took an enormous human toll. Of the 65-85,000 (estimates vary) who set off only around 8,000 arrived in Shaanxi in October 1935. Now firmly under Mao's leadership, the CCP used Shaanxi as a base to restore its military strength and deepen its roots among the peasantry, which Mao now proclaimed to be the revolutionary class. But this had to be juggled with the building of a cross-class alliance in the interest of national unity against Japan.

The CCP was never a straightforwardly peasant party but a party of professionals and bureaucrats, many of them ex-peasants now far removed from peasant agriculture. It had no clear peasant programme and its agrarian policy zig-zagged as circumstances demanded. The Jiangxi Soviet had nationalised the land under its control and distributed it for use among the peasants, but the later demands of the cross-class unity in the anti-Japanese struggle put an end to land confiscation and focused CCP efforts on the arbitration of rents and interest payments, Mao arguing that radical land reform was a sectional demand. After Japan's defeat in 1945, land expropriation returned to the CCP agenda, not out of commitment to the overthrow of private property but as a means to gain peasant support against landlords and rich peasants who favoured the GMD.

The CCP's relations with the peasantry meant a further break, if that were possible, with Marxism. For, however terrible its living conditions and poverty may be, and however much its struggles against landowners and the aristocracy may form an auxiliary to working-class struggles, even in predominantly peasant societies it is workers' collective organisations that pose the greatest threat to capital. Peasants' limited life experiences and education make them parochial, disinterested in universal questions, and politically fragmented and marginal and their goals remain limited by their commitment to private property. As Marx argued in *The 18th Brumaire of Louis Napoleon:*

> [I]nsofar as there is merely a local interconnection among these small-holding peasants, and the identity of their interests forms no community, no national bond, and no political organization among them, they do not constitute a class. They are therefore incapable of asserting their class interest in their own name...[7]

Nevertheless, China's peasants were capable of heroic acts of resistance to Japanese imperialism, which, combined with the CCP's efforts to improve their daily lives, drove millions towards the CCP. By 1940 CCP membership had reached 800,000 and there were similar numbers in the Red Army. But its perspective remained thoroughly Stalinist. In 1935-36 Mao proposed that the CCP and GMD form a second united front against Japan, in pursuit of which the CCP ditched its commitment to a "worker-peasant democratic dictatorship" and the dispossession of landlords. This was not a united front as understood by Lenin and Trotsky, unity in action between the parties of the left, but the sort of cross-class alliance promoted by Stalinism in the mid-1930s in France and elsewhere in Europe.[8]

Meanwhile, the GMD was riven by factions, mired in corruption and utterly incapable of either defeating imperialism or bringing about progressive change. Once Japan had been defeated, the CCP-GMD civil war was renewed with a vengeance. The CCP forces were withdrawn from the GMD-commanded national army in 1946 and reformed as the People's Liberation Army (PLA), which rapidly extended its control beyond the 10 percent of China it controlled in 1945 and became influential across much of the rest of the country. Meanwhile, in the areas under its control, the GMD inspired little commitment among the mass of the population, or even its own armies. The civil war lasted until October 1949, when Mao's communists took power with the promise of ejecting imperialism, developing the national economy and moving towards economic self-sufficiency. Workers self-emancipation was not part of the equation, and in the subsequent years workers' interests would be subordinated to a new ruling class built around the CCP leadership.

1949: the national revolution

The PLA took control of Manchuria and northern China in 1947-48 and on 31 January 1949 entered Beijing. It faced only sporadic resistance from the GMD's demoralised and disorganised troops. The GMD's capital, Nanjing, fell in April and over the rest of the spring and summer cities "fell to the PLA like ninepins".[9] Chiang Kai Shek meanwhile had been preparing the GMD's flight to Taiwan, moving the party's financial resources, troops and military equipment there in early 1949. The twenty-year civil war petered out relatively tamely and on 1 October Mao proclaimed the birth of the People's Republic of China in Beijing's Tiananmen Square.

Coming soon after the USSR's expansion into Eastern Europe after the Second World War, the Chinese revolution shook the West. In the United States, Republicans rounded on Truman's Democratic administration for the "loss of China", encouraging Senator Joseph McCarthy's hysterical anti-communist witch-hunts of the following years and contributing to the militarisation of the US strategy of the containment of communism in the Cold War. Yet, although the Chinese revolution strengthened the USSR and removed China from Western influence, it was not socialist. It was, rather, the culmination of "a military-territorial battle" in which working-class struggle "was no more than a supporting element".[10] As Michael Löwy put it, "there was no working-class uprising" and therefore no possibility of the self-emancipation of the working class, the cornerstone of the Marxist conception of socialism and socialist revolution.[11] As the PLA marched on the major cities, proclamations were issued that workers should stay at work. Nor was there a destruction of the state machinery as in Russia in 1917, when the workers councils (Soviets) replaced the crumbling Tsarist state. Rather the CCP took hold of the existing state machinery and absorbed the majority of GMD functionaries under CCP leadership. Another proclamation told GMD officials to "remain at their posts".[12]

Private capitalists were also spared. Shortly before October, Mao had assured businesspeople that the CCP aimed to reform capitalism and not overthrow it. In many places the bosses rejoiced as the CCP takeover promised to end the chaos and confusion they experienced under GMD rule. One Hong Kong business paper reported as the PLA entered Shanghai that "the hour of liberation struck... The oppressions and frustrations of the past shall now be forgotten... The nightmare is over".[13] The enthusiasm for Mao's take-over at the Shanghai Chamber of Commerce moved the US consul-general to write that "the rejoicing couldn't have been greater if the city had been liberated by American forces".[14]

Against Trotsky's perspective of permanent revolution, Stalinism adopted a mechanical theory of stages, under which only capitalist development was possible in under-developed countries, not socialism. This theory provided a justification for the conservatism of the world's communist parties and dovetailed with the USSR's opposition to social transformations in the colonial and semi-colonial countries that might imperil its quest for bourgeois allies abroad. Rhetorical flourishes aside, the CCP leadership was also firmly attached to this perspective, which treated the working class as an object of party strategy rather than a revolutionary agent for its own self-emancipation. The new state would, Mao argued, pursue "a policy of readjusting the relations between capital and labour", but "the theme of communist propaganda was not the struggle of labour against capital, but class harmony and national unity".[15]

Class harmony is a pipe-dream, but the revolution did strike a powerful blow at the humiliation of China at the hands of imperialism and provided the opportunity to realise the aspiration for national development. The size of the challenge was forcefully brought home the following year when the Korean War broke out. Known in China as the "war to resist US aggression and aid Korea", it underlined the external pressures on China and the imperative to industrialise as a basis for the construction of China's defence infrastructure. Mao supporters argue the assistance he gave to North Korea reflected his internationalist principles, but the evidence suggests that Mao was firmly focused on national development.

In January 1950 Stalin acceded to North Korea's Stalinist leader Kim Il Sung's request for permission to invade the South. Stalin hoped this might bog the US down in war and encourage armed challenges to pro-Western regimes across Asia. But according to Chinese historian Shen Zhihua, Stalin's key war aim was to gain access to Pacific warm-water ports.[16] Some were in South Korea, but Stalin ensured that a clause on sharing the Chinese port of Lushun (once known as Port Arthur) was included in the USSR-China alliance that Mao was desperate to conclude in spring 1950. This clause would be activated if either the USSR or China became involved in a war in Asia and, for Shen Zhihua, explains Stalin's support for Kim's plan to invade South Korea. The invasion came in June 1950.

Stalin had manoeuvred Mao into the war in defence of Soviet interests, but China's own interests were also involved. Mao sought to protect its north-eastern border and the energy resources and production of China's north-east, which would be threatened should the North lose the war. He also believed that failure to intervene would undermine Stalin's trust in Mao, which he believed was vital for the consolidation of the new China. Intervention, conversely, would lead to Soviet military and economic support. Although the end of the war in 1953 returned the Korean peninsula to the 1950 status quo, the US was prevented from fundamentally weakening North Korea and threatening China itself.

Troop numbers in the Korean War reveal the scale of the US commitment to its Asian empire. Presenting the intervention in Korea as a UN action, the US corralled fifteen of its allies to commit troops. Most were either current or soon-to-be NATO members or members of the British Commonwealth. These fifteen states sent a total of 40,000 troops. Over the three years of the war, 5,720,000 US troops served in Korea.[17] That China and North Korea were able, with Soviet support, to prevent a US victory bears testimony to their troops' commitment and heroism, but this should not disguise the wider issue of the enormous external pressure on China. Just as Soviet state-capitalist industrialisation reflected Stalin's argument that the USSR was between fifty and a hundred years behind the advanced countries and that the USSR must catch up in ten years or be crushed, so Mao also had to address the problem. The initial overtures to private capital were quickly supplemented by an inter-connected strategy of economic modernisation comprising agricultural reform, the development of heavy industry, and the subordination of workers' consumption to accumulation.

Under the 1950 Agrarian Reform Law the land of rich peasants, industrialists, merchants and landlords was confiscated and distributed among the peasants, while rents and interest payments were also reduced. The peasants' land gains were tiny (one-third of an acre on average) and to counter the economically regressive break-up of large holdings, the state also promoted mutual aid and producer cooperatives, in which small farmers would share tools and machinery and, where possible, farm separate small plots as if they were part of larger farms. By 1957 nearly all peasants belonged to cooperatives.

These measures were initially welcomed by the peasants, but it soon became clear that their interests were subordinate to the requirements of industrialisation. Their output was taxed arbitrarily, depending on the state's changing requirements, and from their perspective state taxation was no different to the rents previously paid to landlords. The state monopoly on grain purchases, established in November 1953 to increase food supplies to the cities, reinforced that subordination.[18] Grain prices were held down while prices of manufactured goods increased, a scissor movement representing a transfer of value from the countryside to industry. The peasants' response to the squeeze on their incomes was two-fold: they consumed more of the agricultural output themselves and also sold land to pay for major items such as weddings.

Land sales, including to high-ranking local party members, reinforced the social differentiation in the countryside. One consequence was that the CCP had to instruct members not to engage in the exploitation of poor peasants. Another consequence was a significant migration of surplus labour to the cities in search of work. This early wave of migrants was sent back by state security forces, as the cities were unable to absorb the extra labour – from April to October 1955 over 500,000 people returned from Shanghai to the rural areas.[19]

By the second half of the 1950s the developing crisis threatened the entire Maoist national development project. Facing huge strains in delivering surplus food from millions of peasant holdings to the cities to support industrialisation, Mao adopted Stalin's solution to a similar crisis in 1927-28 in the USSR: the rapid collectivisation of agriculture in the People's Communes. The state also imposed limits on migration by attaching rights to place of birth: the *hukou* (geographical residency permit) system. Without major industrialisation the party-state feared that migration would lead to unemployment and urban protest. The authoritarian *hukou* system enabled China to avoid the shanty towns that developed elsewhere, but the inequality and poverty experienced by hundreds of millions of Chinese workers and peasants, although less visible, were on a similar scale to other parts of the Global South.

State and private capital

In 1949 the CCP took over the state monopolies (in electricity, coal, cement, sugar, and banking) that existed in many areas under GMD control, with which the CCP shared a "vision of building a strong, autonomous, and centralised state to seek state-led urban-industrial development after the model of Germany, Japan, or Soviet Russia, where a centralised state extracted and concentrated scattered rural surplus to fuel primitive accumulation of industrial capital".[20] As Japanese capital had also been expropriated in 1945, Mao's revolution "inherited a completely state-owned industrial complex in Manchuria, and a large state-owned sector in China proper".[21]

Mao's embrace of the contribution of the national bourgeoisie to the new China lasted until at least 1956, when he reassured business circles that the "communist" state would not shy away from telling workers that class struggle would not be tolerated:

> [W]e cannot say the bourgeoisie is useless to us; it is useful, very useful. The workers do not understand this because in the past, they have had conflicts with the capitalists in the factory... We should therefore explain the situation to the workers... [who would then] change their attitude towards you.[22]

The relationship was not equal, however, and as early as 1951 the CCP's five-anti campaign (against bribery, tax evasion, leaking state economic secrets, theft of state assets and holding/cheating over labour and materials) was directed at both private and state capital. State inspectors carried out half a million investigations into private firms in China's nine major cities alone, imposing heavy fines on wrong-doers, as capitalists "were left in no doubt that private enterprise is a dependent of the state".[23]

This became clearer at the end of the 1950s. Despite Mao's accommodation to private capital, and higher growth rates than at any time previously in the twentieth century, external pressures and the rapid growth of China's rivals in the long postwar boom demanded that the pace of industrialisation increase. The mass of small private firms made this problematic, and from the mid-1950s the balance between the state and private capital tipped progressively in the former's favour. Starting with state-capitalist joint ventures, and reinforced by public purchases from private capitals (by 1955, 82 percent of their sales were to the state, which also took the lion's share of joint ventures' profits), the state's economic role expanded inexorably.[24] By the mid-1950s much private capital had been taken into state hands, albeit that previous owners were often recruited as managers.

The corollary of rapid industrialisation was the subordination of consumption to capital accumulation. In China's first five-year plan (1953-57), heavy industry was prioritised and light industry and agriculture downgraded, save for periodic re-adjustments to accommodate discontent. An associated corollary was intense labour discipline. This included the removal of the right to strike under the 1954 constitution and a draconian regulation on workplace dispute resolution.[25] In practice, the discipline exercised over workers was even worse. Mao had written in the early days of the revolution of the need for a ten-hour working day, but this was soon extended to twelve or even eighteen hours. Meanwhile, skilled workers' wages were lowered to those of the unskilled and labour productivity was increased with the imposition of a piece rate system.

The logic of China's entanglement in global processes of competitive capital accumulation and inter-state rivalry dominated leadership thinking. Industrialisation could not be left to the slow and random movement of market forces, and since only the state could achieve this, and it was simultaneously imposing a heavy discipline on workers, the party-state necessarily became increasingly separated from the masses. Exercising a vice-like grip on state power to promote economic advance, the state appropriated to itself the power to "judge where the people's real interests lie. A socio-political dictatorship is born".[26]

The form that this took was the very phenomenon that many on the left isolate as the key defining feature of socialism, namely, economic planning. As in the USSR, the state was mobilised as an economic force and a new ruling class of senior party bosses, industrial managers and military leaders emerged. Their subordination of consumption to accumulation, squeezing of the countryside to generate resources for industry, and draconian discipline over workers combined to produce some success in the 1950s. Between 1949 and 1957 industrial output increased by around 20 percent annually, but by this time the state-capitalist ruling class had a tight grip on power and the working class remained a mere object of its calculations. The ruling class was now able to launch new plans for society relatively insulated from social pressures from below, reinforcing the wilfulness and voluntarism latent in Maoism for the previous twenty-five years.

Mass campaigns directed from above

By the late-1950s the new ruling class was relatively secure and self-confident. The GMD had been defeated, peasants had largely accepted CCP rule, workers were either swept along with the promise of national development or cowed by the new labour regime (or simply exhausted by it). Women were beginning to benefit from the promotion of greater gender equality that provided a mechanism to uproot tradition in the countryside (the 1950 Marriage Law for instance gave them the right to consent to a marriage partner and to divorce). Internationally, the US threat had been successfully resisted in Korea, albeit that the US began to increase its role in Vietnam in 1956. But the rival national strategies of the USSR and China were producing a serious deterioration in their relations, including the 1960 withdrawal of Soviet technical advisers upon which China's industrialisation plans had rapidly become dependent after 1949. Meanwhile the problems of authoritarian communism had been demonstrated by the Hungarian uprising against Stalinist rule in 1956. It was in this context that Mao launched a campaign that he hoped would deepen the legitimacy of his regime among intellectuals and so head-off potential criticism that might generate a new Hungary.

In 1957 Mao proclaimed "let 100 flowers bloom, let 100 schools of thought contend". The top-down One Hundred Flowers campaign was designed to open a small space for criticism, which might also produce new policy initiatives to address emerging problems. Instead, academics and students in particular were soon calling for change, and the dissent quickly went beyond the limits the CCP would tolerate. When workers and peasants began to organise strikes and oppose agricultural taxes, the campaign was quickly closed down. Harsh repression followed and the blooming flowers wilted before the purges of the so-called anti-Rightist campaign, which affected hundreds of thousands of people. The regime vulnerability that had been exposed increased in late 1957 when the USSR's *Sputnik* satellite flight reminded Beijing that its economy lagged behind even the relatively under-developed USSR. Mao's response provided a powerful expression of the grandiosity and voluntarism that Maoism became associated with.

Mao now launched another mass campaign, the Great Leap Forward (1958-61), based on his belief that industrialisation and the progress of the 1950s must be accelerated. It was "a spectacular attempt to break through the limitations of backwardness, to ward off the pressing demands of the mass of the population for some improvements in their living standards, and to accelerate vastly the growth of all sectors of industry".[27] Other leaders wanted to address those pressing demands by increasing the supply of consumer goods, but the Great Leap Forward pointed in entirely the opposite direction. Accelerated industrialisation was now the order of the day, and the February 1958 party Congress formally endorsed the absurd targets of the Great Leap Forward. Electricity output was to rise by 18 percent in a year and steel output was to double. Industrial expansion would be underpinned by the rapid collectivisation of agriculture, peasant cooperatives were amalgamated into people's communes (effectively giant production units), and the whole society was mobilised behind grandiose efforts to transcend material necessity and the prevailing level of technological development. The plan was a disaster and as the Great Leap Forward progressed, economic output collapsed – by nearly 20 percent in 1961.

The catastrophic failure flowed not just from Mao's voluntarism, where aspiration triumphed over reality, but also from the absence of democracy. Local and national bureaucrats were given absurd output targets, for crop yields for instance, which they claimed to have met to avoid punishment. To double steel output peasants were persuaded to shift from planting crops to smelting tools and farm implements in the backyard steel mills which appeared across China but produced only low-grade steel. The consequence was the famine that gripped the country, believed to have claimed 20-50 million lives between 1959 and 1961.[28] Mao, like all subsequent leaders, including Xi Jinping today, blamed local party apparatchiks for slacking and failing to achieve targets, but others in the leadership understood that the real cause of failure rested with Mao. Mao reluctantly accepted some responsibility, and although still officially endorsed as the revolution's great thinker, he was subsequently marginalised as a largely ceremonial figure by a more pragmatic leadership, including Deng Xiaoping.[29] In agriculture there was a retreat from the giant communes and return to the old cooperatives, village-level organisation, and private plots. In industry local managers were given greater responsibility for implementing national instructions, and there was a limited opening to foreign trade. Growth rates recovered from 1962.

Mao was relatively silent for a few years, but in private he was cementing his relationships with senior military commanders and planning a comeback. In 1965 some new essays by Mao were published in an obscure Shanghai literary journal, having been refused in Beijing, and on this basis Mao proclaimed that China required a "cultural revolution", a revolution in propaganda, education and cultural fields. As Nigel Harris put it, "culture must be purged of diversity. The reality of life...must be eliminated [from film, literature, etc] to create simple sagas of moral heroes totally devoted to the interests of the state".[30]

Some on the left still claim that the Great Proletarian Cultural Revolution demonstrated Mao's revolutionism and anti-bureaucratism.[31] In reality, this was another top-down mobilisation designed to settle scores within the ruling class and restore Mao to the centre of power. To achieve this, he took advantage of an unintended consequence of his marginalisation – to preserve regime legitimacy the pragmatists had not renounced Mao but instead presented a narrative of continuity from 1949, yet by removing Mao from the mundane everyday they elevated him to the position of unquestioned moral leader. From this lofty perch Mao proclaimed, chiefly to students, that "it is right to rebel against reactionaries".[32]

In Mao's thinking the focus of this rebellion was limited to his rivals in the ruling class, who were now labelled "capitalist roaders". Secured by his close links to the military, in mid-1966 Mao encouraged the formation of Red Guards to pressurise those in regional and local governments who did not slavishly follow him. The space opened for dissent was supposed to be small, and focused on culture and teachers and lecturers, but in the coming months millions occupied it to criticise party-state officials and every aspect of life. Criticism rapidly turned into violent attacks, as capitalist roaders were forced to admit to crimes in public and many who were declared "enemies of the people" were beaten to death. So-called symbols of bourgeois culture, including libraries, were destroyed, while "backward" cultures in Tibet and elsewhere were also attacked: many of Tibet's monasteries were destroyed (see chapter five).

The students and Red Guards had slipped the leash that Mao believed he had them on. For students in particular, yet to face the routines and disciplines of work or the responsibilities of adulthood, the Cultural Revolution offered an intoxicating taste of freedom. Given the chance to "torment their tormentors, the local instruments of the national plan, teachers, headmaster, professors", they revered Mao, around whom a cult of personality rapidly deepened.[33] But their goals were frequently opposite to Mao's – many supported him precisely to challenge rapid capital accumulation and the intense work discipline it entailed. Within weeks, at the end of 1966, with the universities closed in order, ironically, that curricula be re-written "to accord with the need for accumulation", 11 million students visited Beijing to pay homage to Mao.[34]

Students were generally hostile to stale curricula and oppressive school and university regimes, but there was no single interpretation of Mao's vague and enigmatic pronouncements and the Red Guards soon began to fragment into rival factions. As Wu Yiching put it, the Red Guards' "relationships with the purportedly omnipotent Great Leader were highly fragile. Called to political activism by Mao, many of the rebels mobilised also in response to their own immediate social, economic, and political circumstances".[35] Rivalry sometimes resembled war and there were frequent pitched battles involving hundreds, and sometimes thousands, of guards. And, while some local CCP leaders reacted to criticism by ordering the security forces to fire at protesters, most simply declared fidelity to Mao and organised their own Red Guard groups, which now proliferated – in Wuhan alone there were over fifty.

Recognising the chaos he had caused, from late 1966 Mao moved to contain the movement. Attempting to seduce the Red Guards by conjuring up images of past heroism, Mao instructed students to leave Beijing and take a "long march" home. But the movement had its own momentum and the genie was not so easily put back in its bottle. By mid-1967 many parts of China were dangerously close to economic paralysis and civil war. Equally dangerous for the regime was that while the CCP had insisted, in the interests of production, that the Cultural Revolution should not enter workplaces, workers began to take advantage of the chaos and mobilise around their own grievances.[36] A substantial strike wave developed from late 1966. Most strikes were victorious and many were supported by new student groups intent not on settling scores with individual bureaucrats or lecturers but on elaborating a perspective of socialist transformation. Serious Marxist analysis now appeared, arguing that the Cultural Revolution's chaos flowed from a deeper class antagonism, between the "new bureaucratic bourgeoisie" and society, concluding that the solution lay in arming the workers to smash the state.

With the party hopelessly divided and facing its own paralysis, the only force capable of protecting the party-state, restoring order and bringing the Cultural Revolution to an end was the army. In the second half of 1967 it fought back, assuming control of many local governments, breaking strikes, shooting protesters and declaring an end to the Cultural Revolution in the localities. But such were the divisions and rivalries within the state machinery that the army was not always loyal to Beijing. In Wuhan the senior commanders mutinied, and when Mao sent gunboats and troops against them disaster was only narrowly avoided at the last minute when the two sides compromised. It took two more years and hundreds of thousands of deaths at the hands of the army before order was fully restored and the ninth CCP Congress could declare an end to the Cultural Revolution in 1969.

Transition

Having unleashed pent-up social anger to resolve a power struggle in the ruling class, Mao then moved to crush the resultant movements. As Wu Yiching argues, "Maoist politics cannibalized its own children and exhausted its once explosive energy".[37] Although the economic impact was less severe than that of the Great Leap Forward, the economy contracted by 10 percent in 1967 and 1968 combined, reinforcing the determination of reformists in the ruling class to relax state control and initiate a process of economic modernisation. The first steps were necessarily halting – too rapid a modernisation risked reinforcing resistance from ruling class conservatives or remobilising the recently retired Red Guards. The power of the increasingly senile Mao was diminished, allowing the modernisers to begin a limited opening to the world economy and make tentative overtures to Western capitalism, but Maoist loyalists, led by Mao's wife Jiang Qing and her key allies in the Gang of Four, prevented any more fundamental retreat from self-reliance and state control. In the first half of the 1970s the Gang of Four mounted a sustained attack on the reformers, notably premier Zhou Enlai, and when Zhou died in early 1976, they turned their attention to Deng Xiaoping.

External pressures for a change in economic direction were intensifying, however. Border skirmishes with the USSR in 1969 had underlined the need to modernise defence-related heavy industry and the emerging global economic crisis of the early 1970s highlighted the vulnerability of even the relatively self-contained Chinese economy to competitive pressures operating in the world political economy. The reformers' resolve was strengthened in April 1976 when Tiananmen Square erupted in protests after wreaths laid at a memorial to Zhou were removed by the police. The Gang of Four fought back by blaming Deng for the protests and arresting 100,000 people in Beijing, assumed to be Deng supporters. But when Mao died in September, the Gang of Four's days were numbered. They were arrested a month later, and over the next two years the reformers seized their chance. By 1978 Deng was (relatively) firmly in control and the stage was set for what he called the four modernisations: agriculture, industry, science and technology and defence.

Reducing state influence over economic actors was intended to restore regime legitimacy and generate a new economic upturn. Under Mao, exhortation and the fear of failure on the part of factory managers and local authorities had generated growth, but it had also produced waste, over-reporting and misallocation of resources and become a brake on innovation and rational economic calculation. A heavy industrial base had been built, but the well-being of the mass of people presented a contradictory picture. Per capita grain production and calorific intake were broadly the same in 1978 as in 1955, and oil seed output, the base for cooking oil, was a third lower. Nevertheless, largely thanks to the "barefoot doctor" system in rural areas – a low-cost health scheme using medical staff with only basic training in most areas – life expectancy had risen from forty-one in 1949 to sixty-five in 1978, while infant mortality fell from 195 to 52 per 1,000 in the same period.[38]

Internal modernisation was to be supported by an opening to the world economy, including the import of modern technology as a pre-condition for the development of export industries. The opening was not a success in the early years. Imported capital goods were more expensive than anticipated and imports were scaled back almost as soon as they began, the initial special economic zones (SEZs) on the south coast attracted only modest foreign investment, and exports increased but imports increased faster, leading to balance of payments problems. Opening exposed China to the fluctuations of the world economy and revealed its severe economic weakness.

Modernisation nevertheless produced some impressive gains. The agricultural communes were dismantled and replaced by the household responsibility system in which private plots of land were restored to the peasants. Although forced to sell a proportion of their crops to the state, peasant production for the market lead to a near doubling of output between 1978 and 1990. The downside was reduced state investment in agriculture and rural welfare spending, thereby increasing healthcare costs and producing a fall in school enrolments after 1978 as children were put to work on family plots. A second reform in the countryside involved the establishment of small-scale industry producing light consumer goods and processed foods. By the second half of the 1980s there were some 15 million township and village enterprises (TVEs) employing 20 percent of rural workers, predominantly peasants released from the land.

Industrial modernisation combined a drive for change with traditional state-capitalist instincts, and foreshadowing the work regimes that later dominated the SEZs one moderniser argued in 1978 that "no enterprise and no worker should be allowed to waste time, and not even a single minute, and both should be held responsible for losses caused by the waste of time".[39] Many of those released from the land became industrial workers and faced this harsh regime, but for the factory managers who controlled industry deregulation meant that they could retain profits and expand their firms. The surge in output was huge – up to 20 percent a year in the first half of the 1980s. Industrial advance provided the under-pinning, along with state investment in education and strategic industries, for the modernisation of science and technology and defence.

But reform produced contradictory results and by the mid-1980s was generating popular opposition. Firstly, rural inequality increased rapidly as the commune break-up weakened welfare support and produced both a new middle class based on small farms and TVEs and a mass of landless labourers and under-protected workers. Secondly, inequality was reinforced by sharply rising inflation as price controls were lifted, supply shortages developed as TVEs and urban industry expanded, and backward infrastructure struggled to cope with increased economic activity – energy prices and blackouts increased simultaneously, for instance. And when factory managers used their control of goods in short supply to inflate prices, workers responded by demanding, and frequently winning, higher wages.

The inflationary surge was addressed by state measures to limit price rises, but the alternation between expansionary liberalisation and contractionary conservatism was not just due to problems in the economy itself but also reflected continuing conflicts in the ruling class between modernisers and conservatives. These strategic differences were based on rival calculations of how to improve regime legitimacy – by risking greater exposure to the international economy in order to force the drive for competitiveness or preparing more gradually to face that risk via continued state economic management. But both wings of the ruling class were aware that the future of the party-state regime was dependent on economic success and rising living standards.

Incomes had risen since 1978 but real income growth was eroded by inflation, which reached nearly 20 percent in 1988. Meanwhile, market opening had increased both inequality and corruption, reinforcing a popular sense of powerlessness that had previously erupted in democratisation protests when ruling-class rivalries created a space for criticism and revolt. By the end of the 1980s, China's state-capitalist ruling class faced precisely the dilemma facing Gorbachev in the USSR. Gorbachev argued that openness (*glasnost*) and new thinking would reinvigorate the economy by providing ideas for restructuring (*perestroika*) while winning the support of intellectuals and workers. Deng thought this wrong-headed: openness would generate protest unless restructuring had already set the economy on an upward path. He and his ruling-class allies were soon to discover the depth of popular anger.

Tiananmen Square 1989: protest and massacre

On 15 April 1989 the death was announced of former CCP general secretary Hu Yaobang, a key reformer until he was sacked for his moderation towards student protests in 1984-86. Students responded by gathering in Tiananmen Square to re-state their support for change. Within days tens of thousands had occupied the square demanding press freedom and wider democratisation. The state responded with a ban on all demonstrations in Tiananmen Square, but at Hu's funeral on 22 April, 150,000 protesters, many singing *The Internationale* and denouncing the CCP leadership, filled the square. Deng demanded the suppression of the protests "by bloodshed if necessary", but within days there were demands from the streets for his resignation and over the next month protest on a vast scale swept across China.

The protests expressed the meagre results of the thirteen years of zig-zag between deeper reform and partial retreat, political relaxation and repression. Almost immediately after Deng had secured power, the Democracy Wall movement (1978-81) appeared and soon included hundreds of groups and magazines promoting radical change. The movement was crushed in 1981 and two years of repression followed. In 1984 and 1986 student protests again erupted and were again crushed. Deng's enigmatic phrase that it "doesn't matter whether the cat is black or white, so long as it catches mice", suggesting that the goal of national development need not follow a single state-led path, was not to apply to the state itself, which was to remain firmly in the hands of the CCP leadership.

Within a few days the Tiananmen protests had drawn in workers, notably young workers, who accounted for up to half of a 150,000 march in Beijing. Millions more joined protests in other cities in the following weeks, producing an exhilarating sense of freedom and popular power. Many students were initially hostile to workers' involvement, fearing that it would radicalise the limited changes they aimed for, produce undisciplined and violent protest, and provide an excuse for state repression. But many began to understand that working-class power was the one force that could overthrow the system. Many young workers were also groping towards this conclusion and within days of the April protests the Beijing Workers Autonomous Federation (BWAF) was formed and similar federations were soon established in Shanghai and elsewhere. Andrew Walder and Gong Xiaoxia noted that support for the BWAF came from numerous industries and, after initial anxiety about infiltration and state reprisals, the group played an increasingly important role in the Tiananmen protests.[40] Within a few weeks the BWAF claimed to have 20,000 members. Its initially moderate demands – improved working conditions, worker representation, and rights to monitor SOEs and their managements – were soon radicalised to include the publication of officials' income and the ending of discrimination against women in employment hiring decisions. The BWAF's significance is summed up by Promise Li, who argues that it "formed the backbone of the city's mobilization against the state".[41]

On 13 May Tiananmen students began a hunger strike in support of democratisation. Over 1,000 students joined in the first two days, believing that media focus on Beijing during a state visit by Gorbachev, which began on 15 May, would force the state into dialogue. Millions protested and struck in support, including hundreds of thousands of workers with banners from key workplaces across Beijing, and

Gorbachev's arrival was greeted by 500,000 protesters in Tiananmen Square. Two days later the figure was 2 million. On 18 May, as the hunger strikes had spread to other cities, Prime Minister Li Peng and other CCP leaders met the hunger strike leaders telling them they would address the single issue of student concerns. The response from one of the student leaders, the Uyghur Uerkesh Daolet, emphasised the growing confidence of the hunger strikers – as the protesters had demanded the talks, "it is for us to decide" the agenda! What's more, they demanded the dialogue be broadcast live on television. The state's offer of dialogue was a fig-leaf – the following day martial law was declared.

The 300,000 troops brought to Beijing in preparation for martial law over the previous days had been told they were defending Beijing from counter-revolutionary upheaval. The troops were met by students and workers who commandeered vehicles and built barricades to halt the army's advance and tube workers cut the tube system's power to prevent it being used to move troops. As the numbers of workers in the movement swelled, calls for a general strike increased. Social divisions began to evaporate as people from all walks of life protested on the streets in solidarity with the central core of protesters. Most of Beijing was now in the hands of protesting citizens. In the days following the declaration of martial law, huge numbers of troops came over to the rebellion, with one report claiming 80 percent of soldiers supported it. Power was now ebbing away from the state and towards the people. Over the weekend of 20-21 May, what had begun as a student revolt was rapidly developing into a revolution, with workers at its heart.

For two weeks the movement ebbed and flowed, but it was hamstrung by the absence of clear demands that could unify the students and workers. Although groups of worker-activists developed revolutionary demands, which they relayed to the protesters in open letters, compromise with the regime and the official unions dominated the movement. Proposals for a general strike were raised but then disappeared, weakening the possibility of a demonstration of workers' power that could have drawn students, and troops, towards revolutionary conclusions. Without a clear strategy to move forward, the movement was paralysed and for nearly two weeks was locked in a stalemate with the regime. Behind the scenes, however, Deng Xiaoping and the military were preparing the state's response.

On 3 June tanks and troops began the Tiananmen massacre, the bloody crushing of the protests. Within hours the state's indiscriminate violence saw hospitals inundated with injured bodies and bloody corpses. The death toll across the country was in the tens of thousands. The Chinese Red Cross estimated 2,600 dead in Tiananmen Square, a figure it later denied. Whatever the true figure, the mass murder of protesters was an assertion of ruling-class power. Its pretence to lead the Chinese people was in tatters and for now the regime rested on little more than naked military power.

When news came through of the massacre, workers across China responded. Protests and street fighting erupted in many cities, barricades were erected, military vehicles were attacked, and calls for a general strike were renewed. BWAF members were in the vanguard of resisting troops to protect students – unsurprisingly, on 8 June, the BWAF was declared a counter revolutionary organisation. Across China, the ruling-class message that it was the sole state authority was demonstrated by public executions and thousands of other protesters were shot in detention.

Conclusion

Deng's brutal dedication to ruling-class power was captured in his belief that "the gunshots will buy us twenty or more years of stability".[42] For added insurance the Tiananmen massacre was followed by three years of massive repression as the regime sought to avoid the revenge of history that the ruling classes of the Stalinist states of the USSR and Eastern Europe had faced.[43] But domestic repression left unresolved another central dilemma – how to articulate China with the global economy to reform its decrepit economic structures and backward technology. The conservatives temporarily had the upper hand, but the experience of Eastern Europe over the previous twenty years demonstrated that state repression provided no long-term solution to economic stagnation. Although there was no agreed ruling-class strategy, most understood that the Maoist model of a statised economy largely sealed-off from the world economy had run its course and that reform must continue. But reform was put on hold for three years as conservatives resisted the changes that they argued had led to Tiananmen. By 1992, however, Deng was ready to kick-start modernisation.

On a tour of Southern provinces Deng proclaimed a new wave of economic liberalisation, including the creation of new SEZs to accelerate the link to the world economy. Echoing his statement about black and white cats, Deng now argued that no economic model was sacrosanct and that there should be no preconceptions about whether the existing statised economy was better than the alternatives – China should "cross the river by feeling for the stones". His purpose was to set China's economy on a new growth path and thereby restore CCP legitimacy.

The Southern tour brought the transition to a close and opened the way for the massive expansion of China's economy that has been the preoccupation of ruling classes in the rest of the world ever since. The state-capitalist regime had tottered on the edge of the abyss, but when the dust settled it was clear that for all Maoism's crazy zig-zags and irrationality, China had remained independent. This was far from what most would regard as socialism, but Mao's drive for self-reliance after the humiliation at the hands of imperialism, and as a means towards national development, meant that, unlike many states in the Global South, China was not burdened by huge foreign debts and possessed a vast pool of literate, educated and healthy, albeit poorly paid, workers. The foundations had been laid for rapid economic transformation, largely on China's own terms, guided by a strong autonomous state that had proven capable of concentrating economic power, derived from the rural surplus, to build a relatively modern infrastructure and powerful state-owned heavy industries. The results have been spectacular. But no form of capitalism can escape the laws of capitalist development uncovered by Marx in the second half of the nineteenth century. As the next chapters show, the thirty years of growth since 1992 have generated new contradictions and there is mounting evidence that Chinese state capitalism faces serious crises in the coming years.

Chapter 2
Economic rise and emerging problems – the contradictions of authoritarian state capitalism

Introduction

Since 1978, the classical model of state capitalism developed under Mao has been progressively transformed as the economy has been restructured and opened to the world. Private capital contributed almost nothing in 1978, but today it accounts for 60 percent of GDP and 90 percent of exports. The contribution of SOEs to GDP has fallen below 30 percent, and the Chinese Communist Party (CCP) and the party-state now embraces, interacts with and accommodates private capitalist class interests (see chapter three).[1]

For three decades after 1978 when the reform process began, discussion in the West of China's economy was overwhelmingly positive. Benefitting from what Trotsky called the privileges of backwardness, enabling it to leap over stages of technological change that would not have been possible in isolation from the world capitalist system, China's economic transformation has been remarkable. Contrary to neoliberal myth, average growth rates of nearly 10 percent a year were achieved by a combination of state production and state orchestration of private capital. In 2009 China overtook Germany to become the world's largest exporter – having increased exports from $10 billion in 1978 to $2,100 billion – and second largest economy, and has surpassed the US to become the world's largest energy consumer. From just 1 percent in 1978, today China accounts for around 18 percent of the global economy.

China has accounted for around a quarter of global economic

growth in the weak recovery from the 2008 crisis. Nearly 300 million new workers have joined the labour force since 1978, drawn initially as low-paid rural migrants to the SEZs established under Deng. They produce masses of surplus value for the world's capitalists, thereby injecting a degree of dynamism into a system whose advanced heartland in the West remains relatively stagnant.

Under both the Made in China 2025 industrial policy, announced by the State Council in 2015 and incorporated in the 2017 five-year plan, and the 2020 dual circulation strategy China has encouraged indigenous innovation and self-sufficiency in a range of new technologies, including cloning, semi-conductors, the quantum internet, artificial intelligence and robotics. Xi Jinping sees science and technology as "the main battlefield of the economy", and in these sectors China has become a magnet for the world's brightest scientists – research spending increased over thirty-fold between 1995 and 2013. In 2016, one million patents were filed in China, 40 percent of the world total, albeit that cutting-edge patents are not the norm.[2] In 2022 China became the largest contributor to research articles published in top science journals.[3] China's digital payments' market is fifty times larger than America's.

An ultra-modern infrastructure is being rapidly developed under a $1 trillion spending programme. In 2008 China had no bullet trains or track suitable for them but by 2018 it had more track than the rest of the world combined. Similarly with motorway construction: in Guizhou province alone nearly as many miles were built between 2013 and 2018 as in Britain's entire network. Along the way China has radically restructured its SOEs which now operate as major competitors in global markets, in part thanks to state-orchestrated spending under Xi's Belt and Road Initiative.

The idea that China is a mere low-cost assembly plant for the rest of the world is hopelessly out of date. Its rulers have carefully managed the process of economic modernisation using, but not slavishly following, the advice of the Western bourgeois economists brought in to advise on the post-Mao transformation. This enabled China to avoid the economic collapse produced by "shock therapy" in post-Soviet Russia and Eastern Europe, to grow rapidly for nearly four decades and to pose a serious threat to dominant Western interests in the global economy.[4] But, as China's economy became increasingly inter-connected with the rest of the world, its capacity to insulate itself from capitalist crises declined. Even before the 2008 crisis former prime minister Wen Jiabao described China's economy as "unstable, unbalanced, uncoordinated and ultimately unsustainable".[5] China's significance in the global economy was underlined by the contribution its huge stimulus package made to the global system after the financial crisis. But in the last decade growth rates have slowed and the economy is beset by deepening problems. China may have experienced economic take-off, but it cannot escape the gravitational pull of the economic laws of capitalism that Marx identified.

This chapter outlines the transformation of the Chinese economy since the 1990s and explains the deepening of economic contradictions in the last decade. It explores the issues of the over-accumulation of capital, the role of SOEs, attempts to move China up the value chain and reduce vulnerability to world markets by developing the domestic economy, deepening problems in the financial system, massive inequality, and low profit rates. The response to these problems from workers, women, ethnic and religious minorities etc will be explored in later chapters.

China's economic take-off: external & internal drivers

Deng's post-1978 project had internal and external dimensions. Internally, the dismantling of the people's communes and establishment of TVEs, which released under-employed and inefficiently used rural resources, were followed by the restructuring of the vast state-owned industrial sector. SOEs shed labour on a colossal scale in the 1990s, especially after 1997 when, at the 15th CCP Congress, general secretary Jiang Zemin told SOE managers to cut jobs to increase efficiency. Sixty million workers lost their jobs between 1994 and 2005, simultaneously losing access to the "iron rice bowl" of employer-provided welfare services and on-site hospitals and schools. The benefits for China's rulers were not immediate, but over the twenty-five years from 1992, tens of millions of workers migrated to the new growth centres of the coastal cities. These in turn were central to the external aspect of reform. The SEZs initially attracted Chinese diasporic capital from the rest of

Asia but increasingly became bases for foreign capital searching for a production platform from which to export to richer countries. From the perspective of the CCP leadership and transnational capital, a virtuous circle was established – FDI would help upgrade industry via imports of new technology and production methods while the upgraded industry would access the low-wage labour released by internal reform.

FDI flooded in, rising from $3.4 billion in 1989 to $156 billion in 2008. It dipped under the impact of the financial crisis in 2009 but recovered to $291 billion in 2013 and reached $344 billion in 2021.[6] The exports that this FDI contributed to mushroomed from $10 billion in 1978 and $85 billion in 1992 to $3,590 billion in 2022.[7] Coastal SEZs such as the Pearl River Delta to the north of Hong Kong and Macau were transformed. In 1970 Shenzhen was a sleepy fishing town with a population of 30,000, but after being designated as the first SEZ in 1979, it grew into today's mega-city of 18 million people. The Greater Bay Area of which Shenzhen forms part has a population of 70 million and a GDP of over $2 trillion – the 12th biggest economy in the world. The SEZs attracted FDI by offering low taxes and customs duties and freedom for foreign firms to repatriate profits.

SOEs

Deng and other reformers recognised that the Mao model of semi-autarkic development had run out of steam by the time that he died, and by the 1980s and 1990s the big SOEs and nationalised banks were inefficient and frequently unprofitable. They were reformed, and from the 1990s transformed into profit-making corporations almost indistinguishable from private corporations elsewhere. The SOEs were listed on the Hong Kong stock exchange and gained an infusion of new funds, notably from Chinese diasporic capital in the first instance. The banks meanwhile, although remaining state-owned, were recapitalised. Table 1 shows that although FDI expanded dramatically, it formed only a small part of total investment, the rest being undertaken by Chinese domestic capitals, including SOEs.

Mainstream economists portray SOEs as inefficient and a drag on the economy, but Qi and Kotz show that the opposite is true:

Table 1: China – selected economic indicators				
	1989	2006	2013	Latest available*
% of global GDP	2	10	15	18.5
Inward FDI ($billions)	3.4	124	291	334
Inward FDI (% of GDP)	1	4.5	3	1.9
Outward FDI ($billions)	0.8	24	73	128
Exports ($billions)	10	992	2,354	3,550
Exports (% of GDP)	9	36	25	21
Capital accumulation (% of GDP)	26	39	45	42
Household consumption (% of GDP)	51	38	36	38
* In late 2023				
Sources: various, including World Bank Data https://data.worldbank.org/country/china				

"SOEs might be less profitable than private enterprises, [but] they can create economy-wide positive externalities that promote economic growth" – conversely the privatisation imposed on the Global South by Western institutions has had a negative impact on growth.[8] In industry, SOEs accounted for 39 percent of assets, 23 percent of sales revenue, 17 percent of profits, and 18 percent of employment in 2017.[9] Their importance to the Chinese model is underlined by the fact that they pay 63 percent of total business tax, in effect subsidising the low-tax regime of the SEZs despite their minority role in the economy and profit rates that are less than half those in the private sector.[10] They are particularly important in slower-growing areas like the north-east, where employment in SOEs contributes to social stability and development, while in the export-oriented coastal zones SOEs have almost no presence.

Although SOEs now represent less than 30 percent of GDP, their scale is so great that after partial-privatisation, where the state sold a proportion of the shares while retaining a controlling stake, they make up 80 percent of stock market value.[11] The core "national champion" SOEs are enormous: China has 124 corporations in the *Fortune* Global 500 (compared to the US's 121) and twenty of the top twenty-five are state-owned. It is estimated that SOEs also own about a third of all private companies. Since the CCP adopted the slogan of *"zhuada fangxiao"* (grasp the big, release the small) in 1999, many SOEs have closed and/or been involved in mega-mergers organised by the State-owned Assets Supervision and Administration Commission (SASAC), the dominant shareholder in the largest SOEs which occupy the most strategically important sectors, including defence, energy, railway, telecoms, aviation and construction. Between 2003 and 2017 the number of SOEs fell from 189 to 101 as SASAC sought to cut costs and remove duplication and excess capacity. This is not just about cutting state spending – international competition with Western firms is also part of SASAC's calculations and most SOEs have been converted into profit-oriented corporations. These are legally separate from the state and increasingly subject to global market forces while remaining firmly connected to state power in what Chris Harman called a relation of "structural interdependence".[12] The involvement of SOEs in the Belt and Road Initiative illustrates the geopolitical aspect of this interdependence (see chapter six).

The continuing strategic importance of SOEs was emphasised in 2017 by the SASAC chair Xiao Yaqing, who argued that "we must resolutely resist [further] 'privatisation', 'de-state-ification', 'de-main-guidance-ication'".[13] SOEs provide the CCP with a power base for local leaders and generate outputs for infrastructure development. Their structural interdependence with the state, and state-owned banks, ensures that although they operate along market principles they are relatively insulated from the vice-like imperative of profit maximisation that operates on private firms. SOE profit-rates hover between 2 and 5 percent, roughly half that in the US non-financial corporate sector and of private capitals in China.[14] They are also saddled with debt and account for 75 percent of China's corporate debt. Relatively shielded by their relations with the state from the direct pressures of market competition, the SOEs have been central to a vast over-accumulation of capital in the last forty years.

Migrant labour

FDI and domestic capital accumulation represent what Marx called dead labour, which depends on living labour-power to set it in motion. But as accumulation raced ahead, the share of wages in GDP collapsed from 56.5 to 36.7 percent between 1983 and 2005.[15] Even the usually quiescent state-run All-China Federation of Trade Unions (ACFTU) complained about the decline in the share of wages in national income for twenty-two consecutive years.[16] Although millions of Chinese people have been lifted out of the most extreme forms of poverty since 1978, the reform era saw a huge increase in relative poverty and inequality (see chapter five). By 2010, the richest 1 percent of households owned 41.4 percent of the total wealth (slightly more than the US figure of 40 percent), and 50 percent of China's population remained in rural areas with an average disposable income of only $898 compared with $2,900 for urban residents.[17] Even the official social administration reported that the Gini coefficient (a measure of inequality) had deteriorated from less than 0.2 in 1978 to close to 0.5 in 2008.[18] Low wages and inequality were vital parts of China's post-1978 economic growth.

Chinese and transnational capital have reaped huge benefits from the surplus-value produced by 250-300 million migrant workers, mainly rural in origin. The pull factor was the increasing number of jobs in the SEZs, but the flow of migrants would have been far lower without the push factor of the dismantling of the rural communes and the loss of the commune-based public health system and the imposition of new health expenses on the rural poor. The initial beneficiaries of de-collectivisation were the TVEs but by the early-1990s these had proven unable to mop up surplus labour on an adequate scale. In this scenario these migrants are merely objects, pushed and pulled by powerful dynamics unleashed by those in power. This was reinforced by the limits placed on their rights by the *hukou* system.

Rural to urban migration was strictly controlled under Mao by attaching residency rights to place of birth, as the cities were unable to provide jobs yet depended on agricultural production to feed urban workers. Today, migrant workers still have limited rights in the urban areas where they now live and cannot, for example, access local health services or schools for their children without payment. There has been relaxation of these restrictions in some areas facing labour shortages (in some cities nearly a quarter of *hukou* holders have reached retirement age) but this generally involves concessions to migrants, allowing them to buy surplus accommodation for example, rather than granting full local *hukou* rights.

Rightless workers are more easily and more heavily exploited than those who enjoy some measure of security (of job, accommodation, education places for children, etc). Nevertheless, migrants do not face such extreme exploitation that they are unable to remit money to home villages for the upkeep of their children, and even poorly-paid migrants regularly save a quarter of their wages.[19] But the high savings rate is related not only to wage levels but also reflects the under-resourcing of China's welfare and health systems.

With the dismantling of the communes China's rudimentary health care system became even more restrictive, contributing to an increase in infant mortality rates and to the devastating impact of the 2003 SARS epidemic. The severity of the epidemic forced the state to cut agricultural taxes and reintroduce basic health insurance covering 95 percent of rural citizens. Private payments fell from 60 percent of medical treatments in 2003 to around a quarter today. Nevertheless, these measures only alleviated the worst forms of rural poverty while profit-making remains a key driver in the health sphere and hospitals continue to benefit from the sale of drugs. Overall, Chinese state health spending is a secondary concern compared with spending on more direct supports for capital, such as infrastructure. Health spending in China is only 5.5 percent of GDP compared to 10 percent in Britain and 11 percent in France.

In the 2000s three-quarters of migrants continued to work seven days a week, often in dangerous and underpaid jobs with limited safety regulation. The infamous suicides at the Foxconn plant in Shenzhen in 2010 were linked to the overwork and lowly status of migrant workers. But while oppressive workplace regimes of labour control persist to this day (see chapter four), by the mid-1990s migrant-worker strikes began to be more numerous as migrants became more established and confident. This dovetailed with strikes against job losses in the SOEs and figures for "mass protests", an official euphemism for strikes, protests and riots, increased from 10,000 incidents involving 730,000 protesters to 60,000 incidents involving over three million protesters between 1993 and 2003.[20] From 2007 a wave of strikes that lasted nearly a decade started. The CCP response was to combine the rhetoric of a "harmonious" society with limited concessions to workers, such as the 2008 Labour Contract Law.[21] This gave workers increased rights and security at work and sought to control the spontaneous bottom-up riots and disputes by channelling discontent into formal mechanisms. But this served to embolden workers: one Beijing academic estimated the number of incidents to be 180,000 in 2010, averaging 483 a day. These included a strike wave in transnational corporations in southern China where workers managed to win large wage increases. By 2011 protests increasingly addressed issues facing migrants beyond the workplace, and often took the form of major riots. In June 2011 Guangdong, the heart of the southern exporting economy, was rocked by three days of riots and street battles involving 10,000 people after a twenty-year-old pregnant street vendor was forcibly stopped from selling by government security guards. In the same month armoured troop carriers suppressed violent demonstrations in Hubei province after the death in police custody of a popular anti-corruption official.

Strikes and protests were part of the context for prime minister Wen Jiabao's comment about China's "unstable" and "unbalanced" economy in 2007. These leadership concerns had already produced measures to rebalance the economy by boosting the disposable income of peasants and urban workers. In the countryside, the tax cuts were reinforced by increases in government procurement prices for foodstuffs. But this boost to domestic spending also exacerbated problems for big capital: increased rural incomes slowed the flow of migration to the cities, leading to labour shortages and wage increases in the coastal SEZs. Some sections of the coastal ruling class immediately complained about the threat to profitability and demanded compensating policies while attempting to subvert the provisions of the 2008 law (see chapter four).

Capital's concerns about potential cost rises were magnified by the start of the global financial crisis in 2008. In the short term the party-state came to the rescue. Attempting to restore confidence to financial markets and ensure the continued economic vitality, including of export markets, that China's development depended on, the party-state announced a huge stimulus package. Its headline figure of $570 billion represented around 8 percent of GDP in 2008, but this substantially under-stated the real stimulus: Beijing instructed banks to increase their loans to local government, which "accumulated debt more than three times the fiscal stimulus – that is close to US$2 trillion".[22] As Ho-fung Hung pointed out, only 20 percent of the rescue package went on social spending, most of it going to accumulation in sectors already plagued by over-capacity – such as steel and concrete – and infrastructure spending.[23] For Wang Hui, the stimulus caused even more over-production, "understood as production aimed at preserving reproduction".[24]

Growth was maintained, and the stimulus helped global capitalism to recover, albeit weakly and slowly. But since then, the consequences of this stimulus have interlaced with wider problems and produced growing signs of crisis, linked particularly to over-accumulation and the difficulties that debt poses for the financial system.

The over-accumulation of capital

In their drive to catch up with rivals, China's rulers have maintained an average annual investment rate of approximately 40 percent for nearly four decades. The Western average is 20 percent. This increases what Marx called the organic composition of capital (the ratio between dead labour embodied in plant and machinery and value-producing living labour-power) and entails diminishing returns on investment. The average profit rate of China's SOEs is well below 5 percent.

In Huang's "one country, thirty-two economies" over-accumulation is exacerbated by competition between provincial and lower-level governments. As in earlier Asian postwar developmental states – Japan, South Korea and Taiwan – China's central government coordinated the mobilisation of resources and support for strategic industries. But this did not mean that Maoist China had a planned economy, and decentralisation in the reform era has accentuated what Marx identified as the anarchic nature of accumulation.[25] A key feature of this is the uncoordinated construction of redundant productive capacity, which the response to the 2008 crisis intensified. Superficially impressive, the new motorway and high-speed rail networks are under-used, with many miles of almost empty motorways and half-empty trains shuttling back and forth across the country.

Infrastructure spending and credit expansion insulated China from the collapse of exports in the wake of the crisis but deepened the debt problems that had surfaced before 2008. This is explored more fully below, and for now we need only mention the fears that by the time Xi became CCP leader in 2012 China's property sector was heading for its own version of the US sub-prime crisis. Fuelled by debt-financing and speculation, residential prices in major cities increased dramatically in 2009 and 2010 and by 2011 a property bubble had developed as average house prices rose to ten times average household income (three times average annual incomes is normal, rising to five to seven times in other Asian countries). The absence of a rational national planning system in the property sector was laid bare by the mass of empty, half-built complexes across the country and the emergence of "ghost cities" – grandiose new developments that failed to attract firms and people for many years after completion.[26] Today, miles of unfinished and empty apartments blight many cities.

Despite a steady decline in growth rates from 10 percent in 2010 to 6 percent by the end of the decade, investment continued at similar levels as previously after 2008, exacerbating over-accumulation and surplus production capacity. Over-accumulation also leads to surplus production capacity. According to Michel Aglietta's figures, by 2015 capacity utilisation in steel, aluminium, cement, glass, and automobiles averaged just over 70 percent, below accepted profitability levels of 78-80 percent.[27] Figures for 2022 from the National Bureau of Statistics show some improvement, but the overall industrial capacity utilisation of 75.6 percent demonstrates that over-accumulation remains a problem.

Capacity utilisation problems in SOEs are compounded by the long-term damage that infrastructure projects cause to the wider economy. Oxford University researchers have analysed a large number of infrastructure megaprojects in China and their conclusions challenge the widespread belief that such projects create economic value and that China has a particular strength in infrastructure building.[28] Megaprojects in road and rail generate spending while they are being built but this is "followed by a bust, when forecasted benefits fail to materialize and projects therefore become a drag on the economy". Some two-thirds of the projects the Oxford researchers studied lead to traffic volumes well below forecasts, on average by 41 percent. In those where volumes exceeded forecasts congestion problems emerged. Thus, two-thirds of the projects represented waste production, while the other third represented a delayed waste as they would require future expansion that is more expensive than building the appropriate capacity at the outset. It also requires further debt financing, spelling future trouble since infrastructure spending has generated "an accumulation of a destabilizing pile of debt in the economy…and subsequent economic fragility to financial crises".[29]

China's investment boom over recent decades has fuelled a rapid increase in debt, from \$2.1 trillion to \$28.2 trillion between 2000 and 2014. The latter figure is "greater than the GDP of the US, Japan, and Germany combined" and almost exactly matches China's total capital investment in the same period.[30] Sections of the Chinese ruling class and many financial analysts are increasingly concerned that debt and the associated fragility of the financial system pose significant problems for both the Chinese and global economies.

Debt

Since the deep economic crises of the 1970s, global capitalism has not returned to the levels of profitability achieved in the long postwar boom but has experienced periodic crises of over-production and weak growth.[31] It remains superficially healthy thanks to a huge expansion of debt, effectively mortgaging current health against hoped-for future growth and profits. But debt has itself generated crises, as in 2008. Since then world debt has increased further, from 200 percent of global output to over 250 percent in 2022.[32] China's recent growth has also been heavily dependent on debt.

Table 2: Sector debt as percentage of China's GDP		
	2008	Latest
State debt	27	77
Local authority debt	17	76 (2022)
Corporate debt	94	165
Shadow banking sector debt	0	42
Household debt	20	60
Total non-financial sector debt	141	306 (Q1 2023)
Various sources including Bank for International Settlements.[33] Note, the total is not the sum of the rows above.		

Accounting methods of the world's business press and financial institutions like the World Bank differ, but all show large increases in the various forms of China's debt since 2008 (Table 2). State debt has trebled but a default is unlikely as relative to competitors China's central state is not heavily indebted: in 2021 Japan's debt to GDP ratio was 260 percent, the US 128 percent, and the UK 95 percent. Beyond the central state, however, the situation is more serious.

In response to party-state exhortations to stimulate regional economies, local governments accumulated unprecedented debts after 2008. When the 2020-22 Covid lockdowns reduced private capital's confidence to invest and encouraged households to restrict spending, the significance of local government spending was further underlined and by 2022 local government direct debt was 120 percent of revenue.[34] IMF figures show that local authority direct debt doubled to over $5 trillion between 2017 and 2022, but the real situation is more serious still.

Unlike private capital Chinese local authorities cannot raise funds directly in financial markets, but under the decentralised economic system they are key agents of public spending. As their revenues cover only 60 percent of spending they have traditionally found various ways to plug the gap, including the sale of land (or land-use rights) to private developers. But building land in urban areas is finite and over the last decade or so local government party bosses have set up Local Government Financing Vehicles (LGFVs) to raise funds. LGFVs are investment companies that raise bank loans or sell bonds to finance infrastructure and property development. By the second half of the 2010s some financial analysts in the capitalist business press, as well as members of the central bank's monetary policy committee, were warning that LGFVs posed a serious risk to China's financial stability. The concerns are partly about their scale (total LGVF debt is $9.5 trillion, roughly half the size of the economy) but also about the structure of the wealth management products they sell. LGFV bonds are sliced and repackaged into complex financial products that avoid capital adequacy regulations and offer higher yields than bank deposits but contain loans of varying quality and risk, including non-performing loans, and so resemble the complex Collateralised Debt Obligations (CDOs) that generated the 2008 financial crisis. These concerns multiplied in the Covid pandemic, and by 2022 many LGFVs were struggling to repay debt and requesting extended repayment times and reduced interest rates. Today, there are fears that when they begin to default on repayments, as is widely predicted, the entire financial system is at risk of experiencing a contagion effect.[35]

Corporate debt also increased rapidly after 2008, from 94 percent of GDP to 160 percent in 2016. New regulations introduced in 2015 – including limits on new loans to highly indebted companies – helped reduce corporate debt a little, but the economic slowdown under Covid saw a rapid rebound. This makes China's corporate sector one of the most indebted in the world (comparative figures are 77 percent for the US and 67 percent for the UK).[36] Official figures on under-performing loans, or bad debt, suggest that 5 percent of loans may never be repaid, but respected financial analyst Charlene Chu has estimated that the real figure is closer to 25 percent. The zombie firms that have taken on this debt, including many SOEs, are kept afloat by the state-owned banks that, Chu argues, conceal huge debts in complex off-balance sheet vehicles.[37]

A major potential threat to the financial system is the weakly regulated shadow banking sector that developed when the 2008 stimulus threatened to over-heat the economy and, after 2011, the state-owned banks began to restrict credit expansion.[38] The firms operating in this sector do not hold banking licenses and, according to the People's Bank of China, operate "outside the regular banking system" and "could potentially cause systemic risks".[39] Shadow lending grew from almost zero in 2008 to around $9 trillion in 2016 (equivalent to over 60 percent of GDP), but since 2017 state concerns about the risks associated with the complex wealth management products and risky loans in the sector lead to greater restrictions and in 2023 the sector had contracted to $7 billion (42 percent of GDP).[40] Yet, the shadow banking sector remains deeply intertwined with the formal economy: state-owned banks act as retail agents for the sale of wealth management products and corporate borrowers with high debts are still willing to pay a rate premium to the shadow sector for loans. Shadow banking remains an important source of finance but at the cost of increasing corporate debt.

The threat to the financial system from shadow banking was temporarily reduced after 2017, but the property sector it helped stimulate poses major problems for China's rulers. The 2008 injection led to a huge growth in what Marx called fictitious capital, largely unrelated to the strength of the real economy, which, allied to competition between local authorities to develop infrastructure and attract investment, fed vast speculative ventures, particularly in the property sector. Prices rose by up to 25 percent in 2009-10 before state spending restrictions cooled the market. But, partly supported by shadow lending, prices surged again in 2013 and 2016 (rising by 20-30 percent in major cities in 2016), when across China as a whole the equivalent of Rome's residential square meterage was built every six weeks. But speculative spending has over-extended many developers and generated a serious crisis in today's housing market, with prices falling consistently during the pandemic (before recovering a little in the early part of 2023).

Thanks to the peculiarities of "socialism with Chinese characteristics", almost everybody in China is exposed to the oscillations of property prices. As part of the post-1978 reforms, the State Council announced the end of welfare housing in 1998 and in subsequent years there was wholesale privatisation of public housing. Two decades later 96 percent of Chinese families in urban areas are homeowners, compared with 65 percent in the US.[41]

Housing mirrors the inequalities elsewhere in the system. Millions of workers, usually migrants, are denied access to what remains of public housing and live in sub-standard slum-like accommodation, including in basements beneath modern apartment blocks – these people being referred to as "ant tribe" (*yizu*) and "mouse tribe" (*shuzu*).[42] But migrants are not the only victims of the workings of the property market.

Although it has risen from 20 percent of GDP in 2008 to 60 percent today, total household debt is not particularly high by international standards (it is 66 percent in the US, 90 percent in Britain and 68 percent in Japan). But its growth reflects the rise in owner occupation and the increase in mortgage lending, even if China's high savings ratio (up to 40 percent of income) means that average deposits on new homes are much higher and mortgages smaller than in other countries. But, with the decline in welfare and pension spending in the reform era, people's immediate expenses (eg for medical care and children's education) and long-term pension planning are dependent on their savings and wealth, the latter generally measured by the value of their property. In an unplanned and chaotic property economy, where developers build on the basis of speculation of price gains rather than because buyers are in the market, that wealth is subject to huge oscillations.

State measures oscillate in reverse. When the economy looks sluggish the state eases restrictions on credit, as in 2008, and when it threatens to over-heat the state takes steps to cool the economy. In the property market this means measures like increased mortgage deposit requirements and restrictions on developers' access to state bank loans, demanding higher deposits for second homes, etc. Policy zig-zags are common across capitalism, but are more pronounced in China because in the decentralised economic system the private interests of capitalists and local bureaucrats frequently combine to thwart the central state.[43]

In any case, the Chinese state cannot constrain the debt bubble too vigorously for fear of producing a crash that would weaken the whole economy as well as damage regime legitimacy as the guarantor of rising affluence.

Although a clear-out of under-performing loans and debt looks unlikely, the state has instructed banks to remove bad loans from their balance sheets, including by passing them off to state-owned asset management companies like Cinda, established in 1999 for this purpose. Online auctions of bad loans reached $1 trillion in 2019 having increased dramatically in 2017 to 2018 as banks off-loaded debt at knock-down prices (and speculators took a punt on asset-grabbing).[44] But without a more fundamental reduction of debt analysts fear that a severe shock is possible. The property sector is the likely trigger of crisis and has come under pressure from periods of falling prices in recent years, in part due to the clamp-down on shadow banking since 2017. Fearing the inflation of a giant asset price bubble, further measures were taken in 2020 when the state forced property firms to cut their debt and increase their cash reserves. The Covid pandemic accentuated the fall in prices and in December 2021 the giant Evergrande company, China's larg-est property developer, defaulted on debts of $300 billion, wiping out the life savings of many who had bought Evergrande bonds as an investment for their pension.[45] Evergrande summed up the under-regulation of China's financial system. Rising property prices provided collateral against new loans used to finance further housing developments, but when regulators imposed restrictions on loans/debt falling property prices quickly exposed Evergrande's fragility, forcing it to borrow simply to cover monthly loan repayments. Since 2021 China's entire property sector has buckled under the mountains of debt, highlighting the absurdity of capitalism on a colossal scale: Evergrande's empty properties could house 90 million people.

Mitigating factors

Debt is a normal part of capitalism and plays an important role in lubricating the system. For consumers it allows homes and expensive household items to be paid for over an extended period. In commerce it allows firms to buy in the expectation of sales without having to fund purchases up front. In the productive economy it provides start-up funds for new businesses and allows established businesses to expand, acquire new machinery and finance the next wave of production. For states it helps in the building of social and productive infrastructure (schools, hospitals, roads etc).

For China in particular there are mitigating factors that make the threat that debt poses less apocalyptic than some claim. Firstly, China's debt is largely owed to domestic creditors who can be more easily coerced than overseas creditors to, for instance, accept (partial) debt defaults or stakes in the indebted company in lieu of payment. The threat of a currency collapse is greatly reduced. The room for manoeuvre is expanded by the weight of state involvement in the economy since, secondly, most of China's debt is owed by the state sector (the central state, local government and SOEs) and nearly all is owed to state-owned (or state-controlled) financial institutions and less subject to the short-term pressures operating in more market-driven financial systems. State and party power, which we will see in the next chapter has been reasserted under Xi, mediates the competitive pressures on banks. Thirdly, China's high savings rate provides the banking system with liquidity and helps it to continue to provide loans and investment and maintain solvency.

But each mitigation has its limits. As a consequence of China's limited welfare and pension provision millions of ordinary citizens provide for their own welfare needs via savings, property ownership and small-scale investments. When these are threatened protests can erupt, as in July 2022 when hundreds of people demonstrated outside a People's Bank of China branch in Henan province because their life savings had been frozen in rural banks facing financial fraud investigations. The following day tens of thousands of mortgage holders threatened to stop paying for unfinished properties they had paid for. As reported in *The Guardian*, "the faith of ordinary Chinese people in the property market and wider banking industry is beginning to dissolve".[46] As China's growth slows it is likely that many heavily indebted firms (particularly in the property sector, where Evergrande's difficulties have been followed by similar problems for the second largest firm, Country Garden) will default on at least part of their loans. A serious debt-related crisis in the financial system, irrespective of foreign holders of debt, would bring millions onto the streets.

Some of those who defend what they see as China's socialism highlight the state ownership of the overwhelming majority of financial capitals, but even state-owned banks and state-managed financial systems are not immune to crisis. Numerous mainstream commentators have echoed the financial commentator George Magnus of the Oxford University China Centre who has argued that the seriousness of China's debt problems make it "a classic risk case for a fall".[47] Meanwhile, savings are so vast that China is unable to profitably invest the funds in the domestic economy. Savings then feed over-accumulation, but also limit the growth of the domestic consumer market which Xi and others regard as an essential contributor to China's future economic strength.

Policy dilemmas

Mitigation of China's debt problems does not eliminate them. Evergrande's collapse highlights the strategic and policy dilemmas facing China's rulers as the debt-based infrastructure building and accumulation development model runs out of steam. According to Chinese National Bureau of Statistics data, in 1994 it required 1.3 units of credit to increase GDP by a single unit, but this had risen to 3.5 units of credit by 2005. In 2011 it took close to 10 units of credit![48] Yet, after 2008 whenever stabilising measures like restrictions on debt or shadow banking led to a slow-down in the growth rate or falling property or stock market prices, the state relaxed policy, turned on the credit taps and thereby increased the likelihood of future instability.

The dilemma China's rulers face is reflected in the contrasting views of two key figures. Central bank governor, Zhou Xiaochuan, warned of the danger of a "Minsky moment" at the nineteenth CCP Congress in 2017. Writing in the 1970s and 1980s (but largely ignored until the financial crisis of 2008) the economist Hyman Minsky recognised the destabilising impact of banking and finance for capitalism. Periods of stability encourage over-confidence and speculation, which increases the danger of a financial crash. Meanwhile, Zhao Yanqing, ex-state official and Xiamen University economist, argues that reducing debt is a serious danger for China as it reduces demand for firms' output in both consumption and investment goods sectors. Prudence may be sensible for private citizens, but it poses demand problems for the economy as a whole.

For Zhao this is a matter of great urgency, for without increased spending "the achievements of China's reform and opening up will be wiped out overnight".[49] Both Zhou and Zhao are correct – the Minsky moment in the financial sector is accompanied by a deflation moment in the real economy.

These strategic tensions are reflected in the policy dilemmas facing the party-state. Any reduction of debt-fuelled over-accumulation would simultaneously slow the rate of growth of labour productivity, thereby reducing China's competitive advantage over its rivals in global markets. It could, theoretically, compensate for this by an attack on wages, but this would compound the contraction of demand resulting from cuts in accumulation. China's growth rate would be threatened along with the party-state's efforts to rebalance the economy away from external dependencies and towards "internal circulation" (see below). In any case, maintaining growth and rebalancing the economy while reducing the rate of accumulation implies a greater share of GDP for wages and household consumption in GDP. The ruling class has shown few signs over forty years of encouraging wage growth except under pressure from a combination of labour shortages and strikes (see chapter four) and it is unlikely that this will change, particularly as wage growth will face resistance from capitals seeking to maintain profit rates. So, while the ruling class would like to moderate debt and the risks associated with it, the pattern of modest restrictions followed by bursts of fiscal injections and lending when the economy slows too quickly is likely to persist.[50] Other measures to stimulate growth are not available. Tax cuts, for instance, would be insufficient as total tax revenue amounts to less than 20 percent of GDP. Cuts in business taxes in 2017-18 had limited impact.

Yet, the external pressures on China are mounting and the inter-imperialist rivalry with the US in particular increases the urgency to intensify modernisation, deepen the technology base and make China less vulnerable to external pressure. State capitalism exists in a world of rival states, and the international dimension of China's economic transformation has become more significant still in the last decade.

Renminbi internationalisation and its limits

Having kick-started industrial growth in the reform era by linking China's productive economy with global capital, the state has more recently deepened the ties between the financial sector and global finance capital. In November 2017 vice-minister of finance Zhu Guangyao announced a lowering of the cap on foreign ownership in areas like wealth management and insurance, and other restrictions were eased in the following years. Beneficiaries included JPMorgan Chase, Goldman Sachs, Morgan Stanley, and American Express. In practice, Wall Street's optimism was misplaced and these forays have not generated significant profits or provided a launch-pad for a greater penetration of the Chinese market, where domestic banks enjoy state support and established relations with consumers and local firms. In May 2023 the *Financial Times* reported that the Chinese market's contribution to total revenues in 2022 of seven big Western investment banks was just 0.1 percent.[51] But although the opening of Chinese finance was partly a reaction to Trump's demand for greater access for US capital, China's own strategic interests are also involved.

Financial liberalisation is designed to expose the financial sector to competition from foreign financial institutions and draw on neoliberal practice and business organisation in order to increase the efficiency and global role of Chinese finance. But these technical factors operate within a wider geostrategic context and China's party-state hopes also to foster tensions between Western capitals active in Chinese markets and the security interests of Western states in order to reduce pressure on China. A key component of Chinese financial geostrategy is the internationalisation of the renminbi (RMB) and its transformation into a global reserve currency.

The issuers of global reserve currencies, like the dollar, enjoy what the economic historian Charles Kindleberger called the rights of seigniorage: "the profit that comes to the seigneur, or sovereign power, from the issuance of money".[52] A dollar costs a few cents to produce, but if central banks and world market operators can be persuaded to hold dollars in their foreign currency reserves and use them as means of payment in international trade then important advantages accrue to the US. As Carchedi and Roberts put it, US imperialism appropriates surplus value via seigniorage as "value (imported foreign commodities) is exchanged for a representation of value (dollars)" rather than real value.[53] There are also key geostrategic advantages. The US gains leverage over the monetary institutions and policies of other states, and over global payments and inter-bank messaging systems (like CHIPS and SWIFT), providing it with the means of global surveillance over the financial system and the capacity to impose punishments on those it labels as wrong-doers, as it did when it denied access to Russia to the SWIFT system after the invasion of Ukraine. With this sort of extra-territorial power the seigneur can corral allies, impress upon them the potential consequences should they subvert dollar hegemony, and enlist them in its military and geopolitical projects. As Hung argues, even after half a century of relative decline the US is able to finance its "military machine without the risk of debt crisis".[54] Hung remarks that "ironically, the persistence of the dollar standard is now being maintained by the rise of China as the biggest foreign holder of US-dollar-dominated [sic] assets, mainly in the form of US treasury bonds". As recently as 2021, 80 percent of Asian exports were invoiced in dollars while just 20 percent of China's trade was settled in renminbi.[55] Renminbi internationalisation remains a distant goal, but if successful it would present a challenge to US power.

The year 2015 saw a number of small steps towards renminbi internationalisation. China established its own cross-border international payment system (CIPS), although it still depends on the SWIFT messaging system. In the same year the renminbi was included in the basket of currencies underpinning IMF Special Drawing Rights. But while China's rulers may harbour a long-term aim for the renminbi to challenge the dominance of the dollar in the global financial system, their immediate concerns are narrower. Firstly, increased use of the renminbi in international trade would reduce the problem experienced during the 2008 financial crisis when Western banks' severe liquidity problems created difficulties for Chinese producers in accessing trade finance. Secondly, while Western economic power and dominant position within the international financial institutions mean that China can never be fully insured against Western economic warfare, increased international use of the renminbi would help the party-state "to mitigate the impact on China of the United States' ability to wield the US dollar as an instrument of power".[56]

The prospects of full internationalisation are currently slim and would require major financial reforms, including full currency convertibility and removal of capital controls. Only if capital can move freely into and out of Chinese markets can it be confident that its freedom to access its assets and repatriate profits is secure. Such financial liberalisation would risk weakening the state's control over finance that underpins its influence over the economy, enabling it to issue debt without excessive concern about the response of international markets. We are therefore a long way from full internationalisation, yet even the small steps taken along this path exposed China's vulnerability in 2016-2017. In the mid-2010s there was a slow liberalisation of the capital account but between 2014 and early 2017 huge outflows reflected private capital's anxieties over domestic debt, profitability and financial risk, alongside personal concerns over Xi's corruption clamp-down (see chapter three). In 2016 outward FDI surged by 40 percent and $28 billion left China every month – a huge figure when set against EU firms' investment in China of $8 billion in the entire year. Chinese SOEs contributed a significant share of outward FDI, including on acquisitions related to the Belt and Road Initiative, but for sections of private capital Deng's "going out" strategy looked like becoming a "getting out quick" strategy as they disguised capital flight behind overseas investment.

In response, new restrictions were imposed on what were now labelled "irrational" acquisitions at inflated prices in marquee brands like sports clubs and in the property and entertainment sectors. The State Administration of Foreign Exchange had already begun scrutinising investments more carefully and from 2017, with a few exceptions, the State Council required government agencies to approve foreign acquisitions valued above $10bn and SOEs to stop property purchases above $1bn. Acquisitions in high-tech and other strategically important sectors were readily approved, but the clamp-down elsewhere reflected a growing unease that large outflows could lead to a collapse in the renminbi's value and undermine the long-term goal of increasing its use in international trade and payments. It had been under pressure since 2014, and China's foreign reserves had fallen from $4 trillion to $3 trillion between 2014 and the end of 2016.[57] As Martin Wolf argued in the *Financial Times*, without these restrictions on capital exports "capital would pour out, the renminbi would tumble and, in time, a globally unmanageable current account surplus would emerge" that would destabilise the entire global economy and intensify US pressure on China.[58] Thus, the drive for internationalisation, despite its potential long-term benefits, was undermined by the short-term interests of private capital. The renminbi's share of global payments has hovered around 2 percent in recent years (compared with around 40 percent for the US dollar and 35 percent for the Euro). An increasing number of the world's financial centres hold the currency in their foreign exchange reserves, and it is used in trade with Russia and Iran to avoid US sanctions applied to trade in dollars. Yet, central banks and capital markets disproportionately hold and use the dollar – nearly two-thirds of the world's securities and foreign exchange reserves are accounted for in dollars.

The issue of renminbi internationalisation and its consequences points to tensions within the ruling class between more economically orthodox liberalisers in the Bank of China and those favouring continued state-capitalist restrictions on markets. Although ex-governor Zhou Xiaochuan described renminbi internationalisation as premature and supported the reimposition of capital controls in 2017, the Bank of China has been a major driver of internationalisation within the ruling class.[59] It believes that failure to ease capital controls and promote financial deregulation will produce what Zhou called "laziness and weakness" among Chinese financial capitals, including state banks. The statists on the other hand favour continued support for SOEs, including zombies, from state banks and limits on foreign capital's encroachment on domestic markets. The latter are closer to the strategy of Xi Jinping.

Made in China 2025: the domestic economy and dual circulation

The explosive growth of the Chinese economy over four decades is reflected in the growth of individual capitals. SOEs are still the largest firms and dominate in strategic sectors like heavy industry and banking, but they have been joined by privately owned high-tech firms such as Huawei, Tencent and Alibaba, whose success poses problems for the ruling class. Despite private capital's contribution to the party-state's national development project – it generates some 60 percent of GDP and 90 percent of new jobs – large private firms are seen by the CCP leadership as a long-term challenge to the privileged position of SOEs and potentially to the party itself and under Xi the party-state has reasserted its power over private capital. In telecoms for instance, the major high-tech firms have been forced to fund the restructuring of the SOE China Unicom in return for access to its networks and customer base. The government has also placed limits on the payment systems and financial services of the high-tech giants, which had begun to act as quasi-banks. These measures are part of Xi's strategy to develop the domestic economy and to restore national development to the heart of the Chinese system.

When Xi Jinping became CCP leader in 2012, the contradictions of the earlier period were increasingly obvious. Where Deng sought to address Maoist autarky as a limit to China's development and to link China to the global economy to boost economic modernisation, Xi faced the opposite problem of over-dependence on global circuits of trade and capital. His task was to wean China off export markets and inward FDI and to use China's relatively low wages not to enrich foreign firms but to hasten the development of the domestic economy to the benefit of Chinese capitals. At the same time efforts have been intensified to deepen China's technology base and turn dependence on Silicon Valley into the strengthening of a silicon delta in the Pearl River region in Guangdong.

By 2012 debt was an increasing problem, over-accumulation was severe, a wave of protests was sweeping China, migration flows to feed industry were slowing, and China was still heavily dependent on exports to supplement debt as a source of growth and development. And, although the domination of foreign-invested enterprises in China's exports was declining, foreign firms (including joint ventures) still accounted for 50 percent of exports in 2012, more in high-tech sectors.[60] China's relative economic backwardness, even in manufacturing, was underlined five years later when figures showed that there were ten industrial robots per 10,000 workers in China, 100 in the US, 300 in Germany and Japan and over 500 in South Korea. Capital stock per worker was a quarter of South Korea's and only a fifth of America's. As a consequence, productivity was far lower – $20,000 per worker compared to $110,000 in America and nearly $80,000 in the EU. Xi's leadership has been focused on addressing these issues.

In the early years of the Xi era his economic project appeared to revolve around the Made in China (MIC) 2025 strategic industrial plan. This aimed to address the weaknesses noted above by developing China's potential for global technological leadership in ten key industrial sectors (including semiconductors and IT, high-speed rail, renewable energy, communications equipment, medical technologies, and robotics). References to Made in China have since largely disappeared and the official Made in China website has not been updated since 2016.[61] But state-led industrial modernisation remains a priority and the party-state leadership has been promoting what Xi referred to as a "dual circulation" strategy in a series of speeches and pronouncements from 2020.[62]

Under dual circulation, the party-state remains committed to continued linkages with the global economy (the external circulation) while strengthening domestic economic activity (the internal circulation). The external economy remains an enabling factor, particularly where access to key high-tech and raw materials inputs is concerned, but Xi argued that while the domestic and external circulations are mutually reinforcing, the domestic circulation would be the "mainstay". The ultimate aim is to build a domestic consumer society less dependent on exports, and a productive base less at the mercy of foreign multinationals whose quest for profits could lead them to relocate to cheaper production sites. This vast industrial strategy has promoted national champions (frequently SOEs, which can be relied upon to dance more readily to the party-state's tune than private capital) and state-linked private firms, and aims to move China up the value chain and Chinese workers up the skills ladder.

Xi's comment, that competition in science and technology is today's main economic "battleground", highlights the geopolitical dimension of international economic competition. The urgency for faster scientific and technological development stems from the deepening inter-imperialist rivalry with the West (see chapter six), but China's state also faces pressures in the form of vast debt and slower growth rates, which combine to weaken its capacity to address problems by throwing resources at them. Nor can capital rely on fresh supplies of cheap labour in the future. Intensive rather than extensive growth is increasingly urgent.

An illustration of the scope and scale of MIC is micro-processor manufacturing, which has assumed huge significance in the tech-war with the US since the late-2010s (see chapter six). China is closing the technology gap with the West (and may be ahead in some areas), but while it aims to produce 70 percent of the microprocessors it uses by 2025, up from one-third as recently as 2020, its major chip-maker, the partly state-owned Semiconductor Manufacturing International Corporation (SMIC), is five to ten years behind more advanced companies, including Taiwan Semiconductor Manufacturing Company (TSMC), the world's largest producer.[63] Establishing more advanced chip manufacturing and denser domestic supply chains is a priority for China and central to both MIC and the 2021-2025 five-year plan. Factory building is on a huge scale, and numerous state-support measures have been put in place, including the $150 billion China Integrated Circuit Investment Industry Fund (CICIIF). The urgency of domestic chip manufacturing is highlighted by two facts: areas of Chinese focus such as electrical products (50 percent of world output) and car manufacturing require vast numbers of chips (1,400-3,500 in each car); yet China imported $378 billion worth of semiconductors in 2020, 18 percent of its total imports, more than it spent on oil imports.

China's domestic market is less vulnerable to changes in export markets and the activities of foreign firms than it once was – the exports to GDP ratio has fallen from the 36 percent in 2006 to 21 percent in 2022, while the contribution of foreign firms to China's exports by value almost halved to 34 percent in the twenty-five years to 2021.[64] Nevertheless, high-tech companies remain dependent on overseas suppliers for between 50 and 100 percent of high-end inputs in many advanced product categories, including cars, medical devices, computing and semiconductors.[65] Catch-up requires continued access to more advanced technologies.

Conclusion

The structures of Chinese state capitalism have changed over the last four decades, and perhaps it even deserves a new label such as "open state capitalism" or "state-orchestrated capitalism". But whatever the label, the Chinese economy is part of, and shares the general hallmarks of, the global capitalist system.

China's economic ascent has been accomplished by its ability to adapt its economy to the rules of global neoliberalism (using FDI and domestic companies to become the world's industrial workshop and largest exporter) while simultaneously interpreting and bending those rules to protect and develop its own industrial base and wider economy. State influence over borrowers and lenders allows Beijing to delay problems, which would be less possible in more market-driven system, by instructing banks to lend, including to zombie companies. But if reduced dependency on inward FDI and exports provides a degree of insulation from the problems in the wider global economy, China cannot escape the economic laws of motion of capitalism that Marx discovered 150 years ago and its economy is now showing considerable signs of strain.

Annual growth rates have fallen from an average of close to 10 percent a year from 1982 to 2011 to 6-7 percent in the 2010s and 3 percent in 2022. Projections for the next few years are in the 3-5 percent range. These faltering rates have been maintained by mountains of debt but each new injection generates smaller and smaller increases in economic activity. Many economists fear that the conditions for a debt crisis are maturing, but we should exercise a degree of caution here. Firstly, the bulk of Chinese debt is owed to Chinese creditors and we are unlikely to see a debt crisis develop as a result of the off-loading of Chinese assets and the renminbi by international creditors. Secondly, a considerable part of Chinese debt is owed by state-owned bodies (local government and SOEs in particular) to state-owned banks. This gives the Chinese state considerable room for manoeuvre not available to states in more market-driven financial systems. Nevertheless, the financial melt-down in the property sector, including the liquidation of Evergrande and possible liquidation of Country Garden, the two largest property firms in China, indicates that domestic debt problems are beginning to generate a Chinese version of the 2008 credit crunch and cannot be simply regulated away or restructured by the state-dominated financial system. The limitations of state power are further exposed by its inability to maintain company profitability, which has weakened in recent years, or to prevent real wage rises in the last fifteen years. This has forced many capitals to seek new productive locations in inland provinces or abroad. The established pattern of recruiting cheap migrant labour is running out of steam and few working-age people remain in rural areas. Away from coastal China, many cities have reported labour shortages (and Guangdong reported these as early as the mid-2000s). In the longer term the problem will intensify as China's labour force is now declining by up to five million a year.

A crunch point is coming. When it does, the unwritten social contract (which the 99% has never had a say in drawing up) between the national-development state and the hundreds of millions of China's workers – "we will make you richer, develop China and restore it to its rightful position of power in the world, you will not demand democracy, freedom and rights" – will be increasingly difficult to maintain. The problems facing China's ruling class are intensified by the pressures that the world's major power, the US, and its allies are now applying to China to maintain their positions in the pecking order of world capitalist power (see chapter six).

There are no easy solutions for China's rulers but political developments under Xi indicate their determination to maintain their grip on power and pass the costs of economic slowdown and rivalry with the West onto the mass of China's workers. Repression against protesters and potential opponents of state-capitalist rule has been ramped up, the central role of the CCP reinforced, and state influence over the economy deepened. As the next chapter will explore, Xi's mission is to protect the state-capitalist economy, and the interests of its ruling class, from the mounting problems it faces.

Chapter 3
Xi's political project: repression and regime legitimacy

Introduction

All capitalist societies bear the hallmarks of the global capitalist system of which they form part, but each has features that reflect its own history and the social soil in which it develops. Since 1949 Chinese state capitalism has developed particular state-society relations, relations between state and capital, ways of dealing with opposition and protest, and particular sedimentations and institutionalisations of the results of struggles. All characteristics evolve as new challenges emerge, new pressures from external rivals demand responses, and new challenges emerge from internal social movements. Much has changed since 1949, but politics in Xi Jinping's China are still dominated by the party-state's project to preserve the power of the state-capitalist ruling class while trying to resolve (or suppress) deepening problems.

After Mao's death the CCP leadership moved to weaken the regime's identification with a single leader. A convention developed under which the composition of the CCP's key leadership body – the Standing Committee of the Politburo – balanced regional and sectoral interests within the framework of a collective leadership. At the same time administrative powers were decentralised to local governments. Xi has reversed these trends that developed under Deng and power has been re-centralised, including the accumulation of considerable power in Xi's own hands.

At the end of February 2018, the CCP leadership proposed the removal from the constitution of the limit to two consecutive terms in office for the state president and vice-president. The National People's Congress, China's parliament, rubber-stamped the change almost unanimously a few days later. At the twentieth CCP Congress in October 2022, Xi was accepted for a third term as president, adding to his positions as CCP general secretary and chair of the Central Military Commission, effectively head of the armed forces. The seven-man (they are all men) Standing Committee of the CCP Politburo is not completely staffed by his allies, but under Xi it has delegated decision-making to smaller "central leading groups", comprising top party and government bureaucrats. Xi is central to all the key groups responsible for strategy in the various aspects of the system, the most important of which is the Central Commission for Comprehensively Deepening Reform (CCCDR), established in 2013. Other Standing Committee members have been appointed to similar leading groups and therefore owe their political advance to Xi. Reinforcing the centralisation of power around Xi is the establishment of a new body, the National Supervisory Commission: as both a warning to party members and a bid to bolster CCP legitimacy in wider society this body is charged with enforcing stricter discipline in the party. Xi is also head of other key leading groups, the Central National Security Commission (the Chinese equivalent of the USSR's KGB) and the group on Internet Security and Informatization.

Xi draws his power not from his personal qualities but from his position at the centre of a network of "princelings", leaders descended from an earlier generation of leaders. His father, Xi Zhongxun, was a close ally of Mao but was purged on the basis of an accusation of anti-party factionalism in 1962 and later imprisoned during the Cultural Revolution. He was less authoritarian than Mao (favouring some degree of press freedom and leniency towards dissidents for instance) and on good terms with the later despised Dalai Lama. Xi himself was banished to the countryside during the Cultural Revolution and, it is argued, developed a fear of the chaos associated with dissent and the mobilisation of popular forces, even though that mobilisation was initiated by Mao. The fear was personal, for when as a child Xi escaped an episode of bullying at school, his mother reported him to avoid also being accused. Nevertheless, by his late teens Xi enjoyed a privileged life in party schools and Tsinghua university. These experiences shaped Xi's personality but his rise to power was dependent on wider processes. The princeling network was a key factor as he rose from staid provincial governor to the positions he occupies today. In particular, where advisers to previous leaders were largely academics and journalists, as well as liberal economists, the Gang of Princelings around Xi is dominated by major figures in the military.[1]

These political-institutional developments have led mainstream commentators to refer to a new personality cult around Xi, and to Xi as the most powerful man in the world. This simplistic approach reduces vast social tectonics to the machinations and psychology of individuals, minimising the impact of the impersonal social, political and economic pressures within which they operate. Only when they are inserted into these wider social processes can the real significance of individual leaders be properly understood and Xi does indeed play an important role as the figure-head of China's ruling class, the driving force of change, and totemic image of China's global influence. His significance for China's party-state is captured by the elaboration of "Xi Jinping Thought on Socialism with Chinese Characteristics for a New Era". Unanimously approved by the October 2017 CCP Congress, it was incorporated into the party constitution. Of the CCP's previous leaders, only Mao and Deng Xiaoping are named in the constitution.

Before being removed from China's cabinet in March 2023, when he warned Xi that "heaven is watching", then-premier Li Keqiang described Xi Jinping Thought as "the latest achievement in adapting Marxism to the Chinese context". The *China Daily UK*, a party mouthpiece, made even more grandiose claims: Xi Jinping Thought is a development of Marxism, defined as "trans-generational universal truth" that must be "developed so that it can be applied to the reality of modern times".[2] The author, Zhang Yan, a researcher at the CCP central committee's party school, seems unaware of the contradiction between universal, timeless truths and their development. Beyond the ideologues and gate-keepers of official state Marxism, Marxism is not a universal truth but an evolving body of theory, shaped by and developing in relation to a changing social reality. But in the hands of China's leaders it is not a theory of society at all, but a form of state religion from which off-the-shelf slogans can be extracted and used as required. The paeans to Xi's Marxism confirm the joke that Deng Xiaoping had two teams of advisors: the first comprised technocrats who shaped reform; the second produced "theory" that allowed the reforms to be defined as socialist.

Many Chinese universities have launched research centres to promote Xi Jinping thought, and anti-corruption officials are rooting out academic challenges to it. Additionally, the education ministry has published guidelines that children must be taught to love the CCP and cracked down on textbooks that promote Western values. As this chapter will demonstrate, Xi has a particular hostility to universal standards, including freedom of religion, the rule of law, free speech and academic independence. There is a great deal of Western posturing about these standards, whose survival owes more to the activities of trade unions and social movements than the protection of official representatives of the West, but Xi's hostility does not stop China's top political leaders and richest capitalists sending their children to elite Western universities (Xi's daughter studied at Harvard).

The content of "Xi Jinping Thought on Socialism with Chinese Characteristics for a New Era" is as banal as the title is prosaic. Few politicians, in China or elsewhere, disagree with the bulk of its fourteen points, which include national development, scientific innovation, environmental sustainability and national security within a peaceful international environment. But at the heart of Xi's message – widely disseminated by the party-state on the internet, on billboards, in schools and the media – is the party's leadership "over all forms of work" and its "absolute leadership" of the armed forces.

The rest of this chapter will explore why Xi and the central leadership have taken a tighter hold of the party-state, massively intensified the security apparatus of the state, and reasserted the CCP's central role in Chinese society. For, since 2012 an anti-corruption drive has purged perhaps 4 million officials, including many of Xi's rivals, from the top political, military, business and security posts.[3] Beyond the elite, workers' rights activists, feminists, democracy campaigners and environmentalists have faced the heaviest political repression since the aftermath of the Tiananmen Square massacre in 1989. Lawyers have been imprisoned, media criticism has been suppressed, and policing of the internet has been increased. Émigré Uyghur Muslim oppositionists from the western Xinjiang province, like Tibetans before them, have been hunted down and repatriated. China has become more author-itarian, more nationalist, and its citizens more subject to methods of social control than any others in the world.

In 2017 the following phrase was written into the CCP constitu-tion: "government, army, society and education – east and west, south and north - the party leads on everything".[4] Xi is determined that the CCP will not go the way of the Soviet Communist Party (CPSU) and fears that the self-aggrandisement of party members may lead to a replication of the Soviet collapse. A cornerstone of Xi's explanation for that collapse was that CPSU leaders had lost faith in their system, ren-dering it vulnerable to betrayal by "traitors" like Gorbachev and Yeltsin and unable to rely on the army for protection since it had become a depoliticised national army separated from the CPSU.[5] The CCP, Xi insists, should not make the same mistake.

The CCP's 95 million members comprise mega-rich capitalists, state and SOE managers, technicians, teachers and students (who comprise around 40 percent of members), and workers and peasants. In the last two decades it has become increasingly a party of the eco-nomic elite. In 2010 the number of professionals and managers with higher education qualifications was similar to the number of peasants and workers in the CCP; a decade later, they comprise 50 percent of members, while peasants and workers now comprise less than 35 percent.[6] Party training courses cater to the needs of this elite, empha-sising that it is "a neoliberal-inspired managerial structure, aiming at efficient management of the population and the economy".[7]

That management has been highly beneficial to the interests of the ruling class, whose wealth has increased dramatically in recent decades. One 2012 estimate of the family fortune of the out-going prime min-ister Wen Jiabao was $2.7bn.[8] At the same time Bloomberg claimed that Xi's family wealth, one of the highest in China, was approaching $1 billion.[9] As elsewhere under capitalism, as the Asian Development Bank's chief economist put it at the time, "the alliance between the rich and powerful…makes corruption and inequality self-reinforcing and persistent".[10]

Precise figures are not easy to find, not least because of the wide-spread practice of transferring legal ownership to extended family members, obscuring wealth by using numerous holding companies, and because of state restrictions on access to financial documents. But the general thrust is corroborated by Desmond Shum in *Red Roulette: An Insider's Story of Wealth, Power, Corruption, and Vengeance in Today's China*. As a businessman who worked with his wife, Whitney Duan, to take advantage of *guanxi* – personal relations and connections – to gain access to decision-makers and deepen their business contracts, Shum provides a powerful account of the intertwining of the CCP and private capital, and of corruption, in contemporary China. Whether Xi and the rest of the ruling class each have fortunes of millions, tens of millions or hundreds of millions is not the key issue. It is the ruling class as a whole that benefits from China's economic advance.

Given these figures, it is not surprising to find that the majority of CCP members are no longer motivated by collective social projects – national development or even, for those whose blind faith cannot be shaken by empirical observation, "communism". The reason for joining given by one young middle-class woman captures a more general trend: "the party is a kind of club, a network that can be useful for your career – a bit like a professional association". Having joined, her enthusiasm wore off because she has to "toe the party line. I can't say what I think. It weighs heavily on me, because I'm very independent minded".[11] These personal annoyances are outweighed by the consequences of membership: members' children are guaranteed party membership, alongside intellectuals and graduates, and this brings career advancement and other rewards. Although membership growth has slowed under Xi – he is concerned not to stoke popular hostility due to perceptions of a gravy train – it still recruits what it sees as the brightest students and business innovators, binding them into a hierarchically organised and disciplined force that brooks no internal opposition. Eighty percent of students are members of the Communist Youth League, often a stepping-stone to full membership at the age of eighteen. But the woman mentioned above is not alone – many see membership as merely something to add to their CV.

Those with greater wealth and power have other reasons for joining. Reacting to the emergence of private capitalist interests after two decades of reform, CCP General Secretary Jiang Zemin announced the notion of the "three represents" in 2002. Henceforth the party would represent: a) the development trend of China's advanced productive forces; b) the orientation of China's advanced culture; c) the fundamental interests of the overwhelming majority of the Chinese people. Private capitalists would be allowed to join the party, alongside workers, peasants and intellectuals, thanks to their "honest labour". In reality, their social position owed more to class privilege. An internal CCP report in 2006 showed that 90 percent of millionaires were the offspring of senior officials and at the same time over half of capitalists in coastal zones had roots in the CCP or state.[12] As we saw in chapter two, 1 percent of families controlled 41.4 percent of China's wealth in 2010. By 2011, the seventy richest of the almost 3,000 delegates to China's legislative assembly, the National People's Congress, were worth $90 billion, a stratospheric figure even compared to the most neoliberal of Western states.[13] In 2013 the National People's Congress had thirty-one billionaires.[14]

Across China the local state directly engages in capital accumulation and private economic activity in the form of corporate spin-offs of local state agencies, shareholdings in private firms and joint ventures with private capital. It is also involved in other measures to support the private sector, such as the sale of municipal land at knock-down prices. Meanwhile, there is a constant migration of party and state officials into the private sector. Although there is no single model of local state-capital relations, every local authority has responded to national party-state injunctions to engage with private business. As researcher Wing-Chung Ho argues, "local party officials have both the incentive and the responsibility to pursue economic and industrial development, form cadre-entrepreneur alliances, and make profits for private gain".[15] For many this leads ultimately to a move into the private sector, and senior private capitalists can enrich themselves through moving in the other direction by buying official public positions. There is a symbiotic relationship between the party-state and the private sector, an example of Harman's structural interdependence of capital and state.

What had emerged, according to Martin Hart-Landsberg, was "the fusion of party-state and capitalist elites around a shared commitment to continue the advance of China's capitalist restructuring".[16] In similar vein David Goodman argues that the constituent parts of this new hybrid state-private capitalist class "work closely together in both business and politics in the protection of their joint and mutual interests".[17] Indeed, it is not a matter of two easily identifiable parts of the ruling class working together from separate bases in the private and state-owned economies. Rather, "many collective enterprises are owned and run by capitalists, while many private enterprises are spun off of state properties owned and run by cadres or their kin" making it "very hard to distinguish what in the private sector is owned by the state, by collectives, or by capitalists, because the boundaries of their property relations are often blurred".[18]

Despite this blurring Xi has made it clear that this is not an equal relationship. Private capitalists were to join the CCP to be better controlled, not to takeover the party and state. Meanwhile, SOE reform intensified at almost exactly the same time. The State-owned Asset Supervision and Administration Commission (SASAC) (see chapter two) was established in 2003 to restructure SOEs and SASAC retains effective control over the 100 largest in strategically important sectors. The latest reform of SOEs in 2019 had strengthening CCP leadership of SOEs as a key objective. These developments are directly related to the growing power of private capital.

Party-capital relations

The suggestion of an almost total correspondence of party-state and private capitalist interests is mistaken. From Deng's "going out" strategy onwards, Chinese private capital, particularly in coastal regions, has become increasingly associated with foreign capital. The benefits are mutual – foreign capital uses Chinese firms' links to the state while Chinese firms gain access to Western technology, management systems and so on. Nevertheless, the outward orientation of coastal capitalists in particular poses questions over their long-term loyalty to the party-state and the CCP's national development strategy. There is also a tension between what we might call a "globalist" section of Chinese capital, which seeks further integration into the world economy, and a "national developmental" sector, which is more oriented on the development of the internal market. Although there are different factions within the CCP (see below), developments under Xi are best understood as part of the reaction of the party-state as a whole to the increasing significance of the globalist sector in recent decades. The general strategy of integration with the global economy continues, but Xi has tightened controls on China's coastal capitalists as part of a reassertion of CCP power.

In 2012 the CCP's Organisation Department, which manages human resources, called for "exhaustive coverage" of the private sector, to mirror its control over SOEs. Since 2018 companies listed on the Chinese market have been obliged to set up a party cell and today almost all of China's 500 largest companies have one. These operate as parallel power structures within firms and influence HR policies and recruitment. Tencent, a huge digital/high-tech private conglomerate and the fifth largest firm in the world, employs 7,000 party members – a quarter of its staff – over half of which occupy key roles. A key function of these cells is to police workers, but they also monitor the behaviour of private capitalists.

This is part of Xi's securitisation of all forms of behaviour (see chapter five on the draconian securitisation in Xinjiang). In 2015 and 2017 new national security and intelligence laws required that every organisation and citizen must support national security. As the SOEs were rationalised and reduced in number, the state was concerned that its roots in the economy might wither, making it more important to control, monitor and shape the behaviour of capital in general, and foreign capital in particular, via the national security law. Increased control has been especially marked in industries whose potential influence over mass opinion has grown recently and which could harbour long-term opponents and pose a threat to the CCP regime. These include tech, media and entertainment where the clamp-down has been pronounced, illustrated by the treatment of multi-billionaire Jack Ma at the end of 2020. Ma's Alibaba corporation is the world's 132nd largest according to the *Fortune* magazine "Global 500" rankings. The maverick Ma seems to have believed that this, along with having CCP membership since the 1980s, made him untouchable. However, when he criticised the party for over-regulation, particularly in the state-dominated financial sector, Alibaba was soon placed under investigation for monopolistic practices and a major flotation on the New York stock exchange of one of Ma's companies, Ant Financial, in 2020 was subverted by the withdrawal of regulatory approval by the Chinese authorities. Ma then disappeared for three months of re-education. More generally, private firms have had mixed ownership imposed on them, under which SOEs buy stakes in private companies.[19]

Factions and strategic orientations

In the *Communist Manifesto* Marx and Engels wrote that "the executive of the modern state is but a committee for managing the common affairs of the whole bourgeoisie".[20] Common interests were to the fore in the rise of the capitalist class against feudalism, but while the bourgeoisie retains common interests – in suppressing class struggle from below, in measures to increase profit rates, etc – this band of hostile brothers also has uncommon interests. Agricultural, industrial, commercial and financial capital are not uniform in outlook or in the measures they demand from states. The interests of capitals in different regions often clash. Rising industries chafe against state support for declining industries or for nationalised industries. Capitals oriented on the global market do not see eye to eye with more inward-looking capitals. All ruling classes have a relative coherence and unity against rival classes, but their common interests are always in tension with uncommon interests.

In China, these tensions are reflected in distinctions that reflect the geographical and social bases of some members of the ruling class. Export-oriented coastal regions do not share the interests of some inland regions, particularly those in the north-east with outdated industrial structures and heavy industry. While the princelings and populists (who have risen through the CCP's ranks from less exalted backgrounds) share a commitment to economic modernisation and openness to the global economy, the latter are more inclined to express concerns about the unbalanced economy, environmental degradation and inequality as Wen Jiabao did in 2007. Their origins often lie in the Chinese Communist Youth League (*Tuanpai*), whose influence has been greatly reduced under Xi.[21] The elitist princeling coalition is not a monolithic organisation or formal network, but a much looser grouping of high-ranking officials who have used their connections and family influence to derive huge benefits from China's ascent.

In the last few years Xi has consolidated his power while clipping the wings of some leading princelings. Ex-CCP General Secretary Hu Jintao, a *Tuanpai* member, was removed from the October 2022 party Congress against his will, while Li Keqiang (prime minister from 2013-2023), a supporter of increased liberalisation and marketisation, was marginalised by Xi in economic strategy formation, hitherto an area in which prime ministers had considerable input. But the relationship between princelings, populists and regional interests is not straightforward.

The case of Bo Xilai indicates the complexities. Bo was party secretary of Chongqing from 2007 to 2012, widely seen as a rival to Xi for the party leadership position in 2012 and expected to join the politburo standing committee at that year's Congress. He was one of the first leaders to revive Mao's ghost and used Maoist slogans and propaganda techniques – updated for TV and the digital age – to criticise the growing inequality of the reform era. He cracked down on corruption and on private capital, imprisoning many of those involved, whether officials or business-people. As the populists advocate he pursued reform measures in housing, health, poverty reduction and inequality. But, Bo was also a princeling, the son of the late Bo Yibo, one of China's most senior revolutionary veterans, very wealthy and deeply involved in business. His removal from power in 2012 and subsequent life imprisonment on charges of corruption and for his role in covering up his wife's murder of her British business associate may have been orchestrated by his political rivals, for by highlighting inequality Bo drew attention to a serious weak-spot for the party.

A further complication lies in the decentralised system of economic development established in the post-Mao era, designed to moderate the danger of over-centralisation that embroiled the entire country in lurches between polarised policies at the whim of Mao. Decentralisation has produced wasteful duplication that reflects the interests of regional party bosses in boosting local growth rates. It is unlikely that Xi and his inner circle are responding to regional interests in reasserting central state power, and are instead committed to suppressing the destabilising contradictions that flow from decentralisation in their pursuit of CCP legitimacy.

Xi's political instincts were shaped and reinforced by the collapse of the Communist Party in the Soviet Union, which he believed resulted from political liberalisation and *glasnost*, alongside a focus on self-aggrandisement among party members and loss of commitment to the wider system. When Xi assumed office in 2012, he instructed party leaders to study the Soviet collapse and reinforce party discipline. In a telling remark on the collapse of the Soviet Communist Party, he said that there was "no real man who came out to resist".[22] He does not intend to make the same mistake and his strategy to avoid this involves party re-centralisation, intensified control over civil society, the careful management of economic liberalisation, and the deepening of bonds between the state and economy, including a reassertion of state ownership via purchases of major stakes in private firms by SOEs. The increasing control over Hong Kong and clear preparations to reunify with Taiwan are consistent with this reassertion of central-state power.

The private elements of China's dominant class are not homogeneous in outlook. The outward facing coastal capitalists are linked in various ways with foreign capital and generally favour further opening and liberalisation, including full removal of capital controls, the internationalisation of the renminbi, and reduced state involvement in business decision-making. Further liberalisation will, they believe, weaken the idiosyncratic nature of Chinese business practices and the operation of business law and allow even deeper connections with circuits of global capital. Meanwhile, the more national-developmental group, including some SOEs catering primarily to the national market, favours developing the domestic economy. There are, additionally, in every region many small-scale private capitalists who are closely interwoven with local power structures. These petty capitalists have little interest in opening further to foreign capital, which might threaten their dependence on cosy relationships with local bureaucrats. Balancing the interests of inward-looking and outward-looking capitalists has been a constant pre-occupation of the party-state over the last four decades, but for most of the reform era (except for a few years after Tiananmen) the coastal elite has had the upper hand in shaping state policy and there has been a consistent trend towards economic liberalism. But under Xi, while the general thrust of openness continues, there have been moves to rein in some of the power of the coastal capitalists.[23] Xi's dual circulation strategy (see chapter two) is primarily focused on deepening and perpetuating economic modernisation, but it dovetails with his attempts to rein in the power of the coastal capitalists.

Controlling private moneyed interests means also controlling potential funds for rivals who have become increasingly accustomed to living within an environment dominated by global capital and have developed a relatively consistent globalist perspective. Private actors have complained that the reining in of excessive overseas acquisitions has been arbitrary, but this betrays their misunderstanding. Its very arbitrariness was a warning to the private sector that it should be wary of challenging or even appearing to challenge CCP power. The danger for the regime, however, is that in the long-term investment decisions will be based less on market-capitalist rationality than on political calculation. This is unlikely to provide a solid basis for challenging Western economic efficiency.

There are intra-elite tensions, and mutterings of discontent about the gradual reversal of years of reform under Xi, within the top ranks of the CCP. Regional CCP and SOE bosses have built up power networks based on patronage and corruption. There are also gradations of opinion between those who want rapid economic liberalisation (including privatisation of remaining state-owned giants) and those who see state regulation, including moderately enhanced welfare, health and pension spending, as a necessary insurance against social protest and instability and a contribution to economic development. China's ruling class is not homogeneous, but it does share a broadly common outlook – all the key leaders since Deng have been committed to a combination of economic liberalisation and political regulation of firms and markets under single-party authoritarianism. But the negative consequences of the reform of Chinese state capitalism have become clearer in recent years and Xi's solution – notably an attack on corruption and a deepening of authoritarianism – is fraught with danger.

Corruption

Corruption has been rampant in China since the early years of Deng's reforms. By the late-1990s ex-president Jiang Zemin was warning that failure to stamp it out could inflict serious damage on the party, and possibly endanger the regime. Hu Jintao echoed this but like Jiang did almost nothing to address the problem, not least because of the involvement of so many senior leaders, and family members, in corrupt practices. Xi's anti-corruption drive has been more consistent and severe. Corruption is endemic to capitalism in all its forms but had become a serious problem in China when Xi came to office in 2012. Corruption with Chinese characteristics is rooted in state capitalism and the party-state's long-term hold on state power, but had been amplified by competition between local authorities to attract investment and by the temptations offered by thirty years of economic growth.

Paying bribes to party bureaucrats – to get children into good schools or gain promotion, for example – has been part of local every-day life for decades but grew from the petty and everyday to the colossal and strategic as the opportunities for enrichment expanded. Decentralisation of administrative and political power after Mao's death allowed local CCP bureaucrats to enjoy effective managerial influence over state property as part of a wider decentralisation of economic management and decision-making. In the early days of reform local officials used their new-found power to grab money (in the form of local taxes) and land from peasants and enriched themselves as small-scale agrarian capitalists. Later, SOE privatisation often took the form of "insider privatisation", enabling part of the old state-capitalist ruling class to reinvent itself as a private capitalist class.[24] They also built new networks of collusion between local authorities and existing or nascent private capital. The arms-length companies mentioned in chapter two – the local government financing vehicles – became key conduits for corruption and the centre of local state-business clientelistic power structures. Favoured methods by which local party chiefs help their wealthy friends is to appropriate public land to sell cheaply to developers, the non-enforcement of environmental regulations on firms, and the awarding of contracts for local development. The 2008 stimulus made things worse as much of the increased spending was administered by local authorities already deeply interrelated with economic operators.[25]

The more far-sighted leaders recognise the potential threat to the state's legitimacy and under Xi an anti-corruption drive has ensnared approximately 2 million officials, some through the legal system, others via internal party disciplinary measures. Those punished include over 10 percent of central committee members, SOE executives, senior military figures, and financial regulators (including in insurance and banking). Tens of thousands of business executives – the partners of these state officials – have also been arrested.[26] These arrests and punishments have been facilitated by institutional changes and the strengthening of internal party discipline, designed to guarantee the morality and loyalty of both leaders and members. Anti-corruption and CCP disciplinary agencies were brought together after 2012 into the Central Commission for Discipline Inspection (CCDI) under the leadership of Xi's ally Wang Qishan.[27]

Acting as a state-within-the-state, subject to party rules as much as to national legal norms, the CCDI handed out extrajudicial punishments to members ensnared in the anti-corruption crack-down. A common charge is that those under investigation, or charged, "lack the four awarenesses": of their loyalty to the party, to Xi, to the party line, and of their responsibility to carry out orders. Mobilising these party rules in the anti-corruption drive increased leadership control over officials and members. The centre's powers were increased further at the nineteenth CCP Congress in October 2017 when a new Supervisory Commission was created to replace the CCDI. It became a superagency, with oversight not just of the CCP but of all government departments and state institutions and SOEs. The anti-corruption drive was now so serious that Xi's CCP was taking back powers carved out by the civil administration during the decades of economic reform and asserting greater party control over Chinese society. Why?

The temptations of personal power are no doubt a factor for Xi, brought up as he was in an organisation in which the whims of others can pose a threat and where decentralisation provided power bases for potential rivals. Potential opponents have been removed, most notably

Zhou Yongkang, politburo standing committee member and head of state security and law enforcement. In 2015 Zhou was sentenced to life imprisonment on charges of corruption (investigators found some $15 billion of assets held by Zhou, his family members, and associates) and leaking state secrets. For good measure "political plotting" was also later added to the charge sheet (Zhou opposed the removal of Bo Xilai in 2012 and supported Bo's promotion to the highest ranks of the national leadership). As head of domestic security Zhou was regarded as untouchable, not least as he held information on so many people. This move against one of the highest profile leaders to be toppled since 1949 sent a warning to others of high rank – if even Zhou can be brought down anyone can – and by revealing the scale of the problem it provided a public justification of the anti-corruption campaign and increased Xi's popularity.[28] But Zhou's removal was also a threat. If even the most powerful are corrupt, and if one-third of party, state and military officials have been involved in corruption, according to an internal CCP survey in 2013, how can the regime claim legitimacy?[29] And, in a society of vast and widening inequality, why focus on public officials and ignore the private capitalists with whom they collude?

The removal of Zhou demonstrated Xi's power and increased the likelihood of even greater central party-state control over others, who might be expected to exercise greater discipline (and pledge increased loyalty) to avoid being purged themselves. This was particularly enticing to Xi whose own patronage network is regarded as limited compared to many others, ie he enjoys fewer beneficial connections (*guanxi*) which have been a feature of the inner life of the top echelons of the CCP for decades. Zhou himself had been a key player in the oil industry where he built a dense network of patron-client relations to enhance his power. But if the power bases of potential rivals offer some explanation for Xi's anti-corruption drive, it is only a partial explanation. For the risks are great. So great that six years after Zhou's fall anti-corruption investigations began into the security forces – the police, the secret police, the judiciary and the prison service – in February 2021. Was Xi worried that he had created enemies at the heart of security and the state? Was he worried that by increasing the powers of the security forces he himself might be arrested by agents linked to rivals, or that the instability caused in ruling circles might create rivals? These are valid questions about Xi and his personal insecurities or vulnerabilities. But if these were paramount he may well not have moved so forcefully against the state's security apparatus. A better explanation is provided by minimising the personal aspect of Xi's motives, including his desire to remove rivals, and looking instead at his strategy in the context of emerging challenges to the state and economy.

Fearing that the everyday routinisation of corruption, its normalisation and acceptance, poses long-term threat to the regime, Xi has used the charge of corruption to try to restore party-state legitimacy. A comment from the regime's newspaper, *The People's Daily*, captures the wider significance of the anti-corruption drive: commenting on measures against officials in Hunan province who were accused of involvement in schemes to trade bribes for votes the paper said that the measures where designed to "win the hearts of the people and maintain confidence in the country's fundamental political system".[30] Many of those caught in Hunan were linked to Zhou Yongkang. The *Financial Times* journalist Ben Bland echoes this view, quoting a student leader from the Tiananmen protests of 1989, Wang Dan, who argued that the anti-corruption drive is about legitimacy and is designed to protect the power of the Communist Party and Xi in particular as its figurehead and key public face. As Dan puts it, "if Xi attacks the corrupt and rich, it boosts his popularity. But it's very dangerous for him, because the basis of the Chinese Communist party's power is partly based on its alliance with the rich class".[31] So, Xi is treading a tightrope – he is attacking the powerful because their excesses risk provoking a deeper questioning of the entire apparatus of social power – both political and economic – in China.

Xi faces three simultaneous pressures. Firstly, to restore regime legitimacy he must address widespread resentment at corruption and abuses of power. Secondly, to avoid creating such anger or insecurity among potential elite rivals facing anti-corruption investigations that they move against him. Thus, facing a party backlash in 2017 he halted the practice of *shuanggui* (double designation) under which the accused must report at a designated time and designated place for investigation, under which they were held, sometimes for months, without access to lawyers or family until they confessed to wrongdoing. That this had already delivered 60,000 officials to the legal system by the time it was halted may have had something to do with the suspension. There are no signs of party rebellion currently but it cannot be permanently ruled out. Thirdly, to reduce the debt associated with corruption (awarding inflated contracts, selling off public land to developers linked to local authorities etc) while not exacerbating the slowdown in economic growth, which in turn is further threatened by tighter financial regulation to deal with dangerously high levels of debt.

So far Xi has negotiated these various pressures successfully. He has increased discipline in the CCP and demonstrated the severe consequences that officials might expect if they step out of line. He has also successfully eliminated potential rivals in the party leadership, including by weakening the influence of central bodies like the Communist Youth League, the power base of Prime Minister Li Keqiang and ex-president Hu Jintao. He has reined in local corruption, such as perks and free cars for local bureaucrats, and clawed back billions in illegal payments to accused officials. Also, in moving against the local governments at the centre of much corruption, Xi has recentralised state power. This is not an unalloyed success as the scale and complexity of China's economy today poses problems for centralised political control. But the alternative of making state policy more responsive to local popular pressures is unimaginable for China's rulers, for that would weaken the CCP's claim to represent all parts of society and potentially embolden opponents.

But if Xi has shored up party legitimacy and increased economic rationality at the local level, his problems have not been resolved. After a decade in power, corruption cases continue to mount up and the scale of the problem seems undiminished. This poses problems for policy-makers as the climate of fear in the party may produce, as in the USSR, a reluctance to elaborate new ideas and critical perspectives on new problems and so undermine the sort of policy renewal that all systems need in a changing world. The question of regime legitimacy also remains open, because while popular voices welcome the exposure of corrupt officials and so support Xi's clamp-down, the scale of the problem and the continued reporting of tens of thousands of new cases risks ultimately posing more questions than it answers.[32] But if the anti-corruption weapon may be beginning to outlive its usefulness, Xi has pursued other measures to strengthen the power of the party-state and perpetuate its rule.

Authoritarianism

There has been a sharp authoritarian turn under Xi. After the Tiananmen protests in 1989 the state continued to repress dissent for a decade but in the early years of the twenty-first century a gradual political liberalisation coincided with the opening to the global economy and the state's need to attract Western business elites and access new ideas in policy renewal. But, as the next chapter shows more fully, the growth of China's industry produced a wave of worker militancy from 2007, reinforced by the growth of new social movements. While for millions of members the CCP is a vehicle for personal advance, under Xi its prime function is to defend the regime and act as an agent of social control.

Under Mao, party committees and neighbourhood residents' committees, in which party members also played a major role, operated as top-down mechanisms of social surveillance and control but also sent minor complaints upwards to foster the illusion of popular voice and participation. Housing has largely been privatised under the post-Mao reforms and neighbourhood committees are less concerned with housing, rents, estate maintenance etc. But local members see a genuine social support purpose to their work: they register new residents in a locality, organise leisure activities (in arts and crafts, yoga, calligraphy, etc) and distribute welfare payments. These are increasingly important under the atomising conditions of high-rise living, alienated industrial labour, and the departure of family to work in distant cities.[33] But for the national CCP the thousands of new "party-masses service centres" or "community service centres" that have been built in recent years are not only concerned with social integration but also act as arenas for the dissemination of Xi's latest thoughts and discussion of the latest top-down instructions.

These include social credit scoring schemes promoting good citizenship that have developed in many regions and municipalities. Local authorities use data from social networks and smartphone apps, alongside CCTV surveillance and facial recognition cameras, to award points on social credit cards, or remove them for minor misdemeanours such as littering. The results can have devastating consequences, such as the removal of access to mortgages and the humiliation of miscreants via posting of their names and photos in public places.[34] These schemes were established following a comment by Xi in October 2017: "a feeling of security is the best gift a country can give its people". But they are less about security than control – nearly half the world's video surveillance cameras are in China. More generally, the surveillance state has developed an online strategy that atomises citizens and makes them mistrustful of others. As James Griffiths put it in his *The Great Firewall of China*, online censorship (using, it should be added, technology supplied initially by US firms and a model supplied by Facebook) is a means to an end: "China's censors do not care about blocking content… They care about blocking solidarity".[35]

Xi's frequently expresses hostility to "Western values".[36] Two fears lie behind this: that the promotion of human rights risks creating uncontrolled chaos in society and, secondly, creates a space in which challenges to his regime can develop. Attempts to head off such challenges sometimes produce accommodation to popular grievances, but this is always combined with repressive measures. For example, while the state has for many years been complicit with private capital over the non-payment of wages, which reinforces workers' dependency on employers by raising the costs of leaving a job, it has used non-payment to its advantage by paying wage arrears when factory owners flee. It has also provided some welfare increases although welfare remains very uneven and under-funded.

But these are tactical accommodations in the face of popular anger within an otherwise deepening authoritarianism. In education, the slow tendency towards a degree of openness and academic freedom has been reversed under Xi. In 2013 an unpublished party document instructed university lecturers to avoid "seven unmentionable topics", including universal values, press freedom, the CCP's earlier aberrations, and the privileged capitalist class.[37] A directive from the education ministry in 2017 insisted that party secretaries on the Chinese campuses of foreign universities should be granted vice-chancellor status and a place on the trustee board, which is central to a university's development, planning and decision-making. On many such boards decisions can only be reached if members are unanimous, giving the CCP appointee an effective veto power. Foreign universities meanwhile have had to accept the establishment of party cells that monitor their activities. University law departments have the texts used for legal and constitutional studies vetted by the ministry. Some fear that in the coming years the growth of "Xi Jinping Thought on Socialism with Chinese Characteristics for a New Era" institutes in universities will force a wider revision of textbooks to weed out Western ideas about the rule of law, which pose a threat to the CCP, whose internal rules run parallel to the state's judicial system. The clamp-down in the universities has also seen the closure of Marxist study groups, particularly after they began to connect with workers and labour rights NGOs in the first half of the 2010s. These NGOs, and others working on gender violence and harassment and environmentalism, for example, have faced particularly severe repression.

The Chinese state has in fact provided support to NGOs where they are able to fill gaps in service provision or can be useful in remoulding civil society towards the goals of the state. But if the state's approach to NGOs is not one-sidedly repressive, a sharp turn towards repression came with the 2016 charity law. This promoted domestic NGOs, whose numbers rose rapidly, but also required larger NGOs to establish CCP cells and smaller NGOs to regularly report on their activities to the local party branch. Restrictions on NGOs became tighter still in 2017 when a new law against foreign NGOs came into effect. It gave the police increased powers to oversee and close NGO operations. Charities and NGOs were henceforth required to locate an official sponsor for their activities and provide plans of their activities to the police. A list of acceptable official sponsors was published the week before the legislation took effect. NGOs working in the fields of human rights and provision of legal training, for instance, were thus forced to work more closely with the state, thereby risking exposing their activities and members.

The foreign NGO law states that "foreign NGOs carrying out activities within mainland China shall abide by Chinese laws, must not endanger China's national unity, security or ethnic unity; and must not harm China's national interests". These catch-all categories leave the law open to draconian interpretation, particularly where support for LGBT rights, Uyghur Muslims, etc is concerned. The NGO law reinforced the effects of the 2015 National Security Law and rights issues are increasingly framed in official discourse as threats to national security. The restrictive impact of these laws, combined with the monitoring and censorship of social media, have so far achieved their aim of minimising the opportunities for the emergence of potential protest movements. Both are part of, and reinforce, one further feature of politics under Xi Jinping: the intensification of nationalism.

Nationalism

As the Chinese economy has faced mounting difficulties, and in the face of protests and strikes, Xi's conservative regime has mobilised an intensified nationalism to distract people from their real concerns and promote a mythical national unity with the CCP at its head. For Xi, the core of the "spirit of the Chinese people" is patriotism, "a spiritual force that can resolutely unify all Chinese".[38] Core ideas of classical Marxism – workers of the world unite, workers have no country, national chauvinism weakens working-class unity and binds workers to the ruling class – are turned on their head.

Nationalism has been a component of official discourse and ideology since the 1949 national-developmental revolution. Under Mao, nationalism sometimes had an internationalist veneer, but the purpose of sending troops to aid North Korea during the Korean War was Mao's determination that "New China should absolutely not be cowed by foreign military threats".[39] This reaction to humiliation finds an echo in Xi's "China dream for the great rejuvenation of the Chinese nation". Announced when Xi became CCP leader in 2012, the China dream is "the greatest dream of the Chinese people in modern times". Since then, as China has become more exposed to pressures from the wider world and internal problems have multiplied, nationalist propaganda, usually assertive, frequently aggressive, has become more pronounced in official state media and in every area of life. In 2017 China made insulting the national anthem illegal, punishable by up to three years imprisonment.

In higher education the defeat of the GMD and enmity with Taiwan meant that the nationalists' role in the war against Japan was largely ignored, but in recent years there has been a rehabilitation of the nationalist role and the loss of life nationalist forces suffered. A change in tone in academic work on the Korean War that started before Xi took office has continued: Wang Hui notes that there was a shift in scholarship from the late twentieth century away from discussions of "capitalism and socialism, imperialism and internationalism, towards discussions of the historical significance of this war from the standpoint of relations between nations and national interests", a new "overtone of nationalism" in historical research.[40]

Elite nationalism has permeated throughout society, where the phrase "drinking wolf's milk" – referring to the adoption of the extreme nationalist rhetoric of party-state leaders – has become commonplace. When the Covid pandemic started in Wuhan in early 2020, millions read the online quarantine diaries of Fang Fang (the pen-name of prize-winning fiction writer Wang Fang). But when it was announced that her diaries would be translated and published in the West, she faced a furious nationalist backlash and accusations of national betrayal. More generally, widespread anger at the CCP's secrecy and handling of the pandemic was quickly re-focused on Western governments and criticism.

Xi's mobilisation of nationalism emphasises continuity with the heroic phase of post-1949 society and with those elements of the Mao myth that present Xi as the leader of the Chinese nation and of national renewal. He regularly invokes a sanitised version of Mao as the "great helmsman", carefully avoiding the disasters of the Great Leap Forward and the famine, and the insanities of the Cultural Revolution. In China, Mao is associated with national power and dignity, integrity, socioeconomic and gender equality, and industrial progress. A 2013 survey for the *Global Times* (a paper with close links to the CCP) found that 85 percent of Chinese people felt Mao's successes outweighed his failures. A further attraction for Xi in mobilising the ghost of Mao and making ritualised references to Marxism (unrecognisable as such to most Marxists and in direct contradiction to the neoliberal thrust of much party-state policy and party education) is that it monopolises the intellectual space available to would-be Marxist critics of the regime.

Xi's nationalism has also been evident in his self-positioning at the head of a society with a 2,500-year Confucian cultural history. Although Confucian ideas should be thought of as universalist, they are today presented as specifically Chinese: it is an invented national tradition. The revival of Confucianism is more associated with Xi's predecessor Hu Jintao, but Xi himself has called Confucianism "the cultural soil that nourishes the Chinese people".[41] In the early years of the People's Republic, Confucian thinking was frowned upon as conservative, a protector of traditional social hierarchies and cause of China's lack of development.[42] But more recently the party-state regime has mobilised Confucius's emphasis on harmony and unity, order, and respect for elders within hierarchical structures to bolster party-state legitimacy and promote a mythical national unity under its own leadership as the elders of the nation.[43]

Xi's nationalism, like all nationalisms, is Janus-faced and directed at both internal and external targets. Internally, the assertion of an undivided national identity provides ideological support for hostility towards any form of identity (Uyghur Muslim, private capitalist, worker, feminist, etc) that does not involve unquestioning allegiance to the CCP and the party-state (see chapters four and five). Externally, nationalism requires a series of "others", rival nationalisms with separate and hostile interests which are the foil for the elaboration of ideologies of national superiority (see chapter six). The internal and external aspects are interlocking parts of a whole: Xi's "China dream for the great rejuvenation of the Chinese nation" is designed to deflect real and potential popular anger at the regime towards internal challengers and external enemies that state media present as obstacles to that rejuvenation. But the tensions inside the ruling class discussed above pose a problem for Xi, particularly where China's international relations are concerned. His grandiose rhetoric about China's global power – riding "the mighty east wind of the new era" so that China would "cleave through the waves and sail to victory" – has been criticised for provoking US hostility and so intensifying the Western pressure on China's economic modernisation.

Conclusion

The last few years have revealed the enormity of the machinery of coercion that the CCP party-state wields and its impact in every area of social life. Lawyers, environmentalists, feminists, workers, students, Muslims, Hong Kongers, and Marxists, among others, have been arrested in a crackdown on civil society that operates, according to the group Chinese Human Rights Defenders, on "a scale unseen since 1989".[44] The National Security Law has turned civil society into an extension of the surveillance state. NGOs have been forced to disband and activists driven underground. The entire society is subject to CCTV, internet censorship, curriculum redesign, phone tapping, contact tracing, and other forms of state coercion and repression designed to prevent the emergence of networks of opposition and preserve party-state power.

Compared with Deng's collective leadership the repression appears to be built around the personality of Xi, but while authoritarian centralisation and increased party power may appeal to Xi personally, and to the sense of entitlement of the privileged children of an earlier generation of party leaders, the issues cannot be reduced to Xi's personality. Politics in the Xi era are a response to ruling-class fears not a product of Xi's authoritarian personality. Under Mao, legitimacy rested primarily on fulfilling the promise to end the century of humiliation at the hands of imperialism, and to achieve independent national development. After the Tiananmen massacre, 30 years of economic expansion and rising living standards helped cement the CCP's legitimacy. The newly affluent middle class has advanced in that time and the state can claim with some justification that hopes for a better life in an independent China are safe in its hands. Regime legitimacy is further buttressed by increasing pressure from the West. Against this hostile other, the regime mobilises the ideological cements of nationalism and Confucianism, designed not just to elevate Xi and the CCP as defenders of China's interests, but to present an image of national unity and marginalise those who might have a different view of those interests and, in particular, those who might organise to defend that alternative view.

But capitalism has its own automatic destabilisers and China's capitalism faces both the immediate problems of slowing growth, bankruptcies and unemployment, and longer-term concerns that threaten regime legitimacy. Western leaders have long harboured a belief that China's expanding corporate elite will ultimately challenge CCP rule and usher in political liberalisation. In reality, the economic and political elites overlap and both derive enormous benefits from their relationship of structural interdependence. The pressure on private firms to allow party cells is partly to forestall the possible emergence of a politically organised private capitalist class as well as a means to monitor foreign-owned firms, but the party-capital nexus makes an elite challenge to CCP rule a very remote possibility. The real concerns for China's rulers lie elsewhere.

The constant references to Xi Jinping Thought in the media, and the ubiquitous photos of him in routine activities, such as eating in restaurants, are designed to show that he is just like "one of us". Authoritarian populism includes Xi's views on anything that might disturb stability, including new ideas and ways of thinking. Very early in his rule Xi pronounced on modern art, mobilising a crude anti-intellectualism reminiscent of Mao in the cultural revolution. He criticised the vulgarity of modern art and proposed that artists and filmmakers be sent to the countryside to "live among the masses [for at least 30 days] each year", so that they can "form a correct view on art".[45] That correct view means extolling the virtues of the party-state and of China and not exploring beneath the surface of reality to expose underlying tensions and sources of contradiction.

But the contradictions are there. We saw in chapter two that China is today facing the last days of a model of growth in which migration played a central role. Amid labour shortages in the SEZs and rising wages during the 2007-16 strike wave, the party-state tried to sustain growth by issuing debt, but this is now failing. That failure weakens the state's capacity to address problems by throwing resources at them. We noted above Xi's comment about CCP power in every direction and over all things – but a few years into his rule the CCP faced challenges from every point of the compass and in all areas of life. For now, repression has quietened activists and destroyed embryonic opposition. But we will see in the next two chapters that it has not removed the root causes.

Chapter 4
Workers, organisation and activism

Introduction

China's 800 million-strong working class is by far the largest in the world, augmented in the post-Mao reform period by nearly 300 million new migrant workers, and is highly concentrated in many of the world's largest factories and cities. Its potential power was demonstrated in the increased number of strikes in the early 2000s, culminating in the strike wave of 2007-16. Faced with this potential, the party-state and both Chinese and overseas capitalist firms have pursued oppressive strategies to keep workers divided, underpaid and dependent on employers and on the state-led trade union federation, the ACFTU. There is no single model of capital-worker relations in China, but labour scholars have used terms such as "bloody Taylorism" and the "dormitory labour regime" to capture how workers' interests have been subordinated to capital accumulation and profit making.[1]

Under Mao SOE workers in heavy industry were protected under the "iron rice bowl" system that comprised job security, above average wages, employer-provided housing, welfare, medical and pension benefits. These benefits were never enjoyed by most workers but were superior to the employment experiences of rural workers, whose second-class status was reinforced by their almost total exclusion from the SOEs by the *hukou* system. This controlled rural-urban migration and allowed industrial workers to maintain wage levels and other advantages. But the reform period involved massive redundancies, tens of millions of them, and the dismantling of the iron rice bowl.

Flexible working was imposed on a huge scale and the organised dependence of SOE workers was rapidly replaced by disorganised despotism as SOE managers responded to market reform directives and private and overseas capital became increasingly dominant in the

SEZs in the 1990s.[2] This involved the absence of work-based social insurance benefits, a more coercive regime of labour discipline and surveillance, longer working hours, the draconian intensification of work, increases in output quotas and, for many workers, dormitory living. Disorganised despotism impacted most harshly on the waves of rural-urban migrant workers released from the countryside by de-collectivisation in agriculture.

This chapter explores workplace relations, the nature of work and the labour process in SOEs and the private economy, the legal and institutional framework facing workers, including authoritarian management practices, and workers' response in the form of strikes. It also explores the structure of the working class, including the scale and role of migrant labour and other aspects of flexible labour that impact negatively on the formation of a unified movement that can overcome distinctions, fostered by bosses, between formal and informal workers.

Migrant workers

In the 1980s the break-up of the people's communes and the new land transfer policy that allowed for private land ownership combined to restructure the rural economy along market lines. But the mass of small-holdings and TVEs that emerged was only a stepping-stone between the release of millions from the land and the creation of millions of potential rural-urban migrant workers. Over the next two decades a vast multitude migrated to the developing urban industrial centres, swelling the urban population to 850 million today compared to less than 200 million forty years ago.

Although they had limited or no experience of agricultural work, millions of migrants retained attachments to the countryside via small plots of privately-owned land to which they would return once or twice a year. Almost all migrant workers sent money home and while today's urban migrants (ie those without urban household registration (*hukou*)) are generally the children of earlier migrants and have weaker connections to the countryside, millions return home each year as their parents age and their own children can no longer depend on grandparents' labour. Some use their savings to improve village life, for instance by building private primary schools to compensate for the under-funding of state schools.

The party-state has ruthlessly exploited the *hukou* system to divide workers. Welfare rights and access to state services are attached to birth place. Consequently, although the lives of rural-born migrants are overwhelmingly lived in the cities, they do not enjoy equal status with urban workers. They are forced to pay for their children's education, which can cost up to a third of their wages, and have faced the violent demolition of migrant housing areas to make way for property developments by construction companies in cahoots with local government. Of the 850 million city dwellers, approximately 250 million do not have a local *hukou*.

The marginalisation of migrants is slowly changing as the state reacts to demographic and infrastructural pressures on mega-cities and seeks to dissuade further migration. In 2014 it instructed authorities in cities of less than a million to offer a *hukou* to any applicant, extending this to cities below 3 million people in 2019. Additionally, competition between local authorities to attract firms relocating from the higher wage coastal zones has led poorer inland cities to lower the requirements for a local *hukou*. These pull factors are reinforced by push factors in the mega-cities such as slum clearance and migrants' difficulties in accessing education for their children.

Hukou reform would also help corporations to retain workers in the context of an ageing population and current annual 5-million decline in the number of people of working age. But the benefits of a divided working class for the party-state and big capital have so far meant that there has been no systematic reform of the system. For Dexter Roberts, the retention of the *hukou* is designed to guarantee that "there would be no end to China's pliable, low-cost labour force", with few rights, long working hours and poor working conditions.[3] Even without reform, however, migrant workers have become more settled, more confident to organise in the workplace, and more likely to engage in strikes and protests in the under-resourced neighbourhoods in which they live.[4] As Hsiao-Hung Pai has shown, in the 2000s migrant anger produced a growing militancy and a growing level of class consciousness.[5]

The despotism of workplace regimes

Jobs in SOEs remain popular because workers there retain residual social benefits, but the decline in importance of SOEs means that disorganised despotism has displaced organised dependence in academic scholarship on the workplace regimes facing Chinese workers today. This broad category does not capture every workplace, and recent developments hint at the gradual emergence of workplace regimes with some of the characteristics found in Western capitalism, but millions still experience forms of workplace despotism.[6]

An extreme form of despotism is subjugation, which has been the experience of migrants in the export manufacturing sector. Here "workers are spatially separated from families; they live apart from hometown, local cultures, and sources of socialisation and solidarity within family and community. Labour control is tight and labour contracts are used to segment workers".[7] The *hukou* system is an important enabler of subjugation, one symptom of which is late payment of wages, a regular cause of disputes according to the Hong Kong-based *China Labour Bulletin* strike map. This may sometimes reflect a firm's financial difficulties, but routine and systematic late payment is a means to intensify subjugation and dependency – workers are less likely to change jobs if they risk losing the substantial arrears they are owed.

The dormitory system is another aspect of despotism, used in many of the large factories owned by multinationals such as Foxconn (which manufactures Apple products) that often demand that workers are available for extended overtime working. Careful design, from the perspective of capital, of factories and dormitories minimises interaction between workers and maximises management control of their movements.[8] Interaction in dormitories is of course possible, but heavy surveillance combined with workers' exhaustion and fear of the consequences of infringing oppressive factory regulations limit the opportunities for the organisation of resistance. Dormitory living is rarely permanent and in recent years many workers have moved to their own accommodation and reduced their dependency on their employer. Autonomous living is a source of limited freedom which can strengthen workers' bargaining position and, for the millions of women migrants in particular, offers a route to greater control over their lives, including spaces to organise workplace struggle.[9]

An infamous example of the intensity of despotism was the spate of suicides at Foxconn's Shenzhen plant in 2010, when ten workers committed suicide by throwing themselves from a factory roof.[10] The initial response of the bosses was to install nets to prevent subsequent suicides and maintain production, but marginal changes in the factory regime followed. The practice of humiliating punishments was reduced and shop-floor managers retreated from the more draconian micro-management techniques. A sense of the previous disciplinary regime was given by one worker: "if you didn't meet your production target, you had to stand facing the wall for six hours, reflecting on the error of your ways." But discipline remained strict – workers still had to leave mobile phones at the entrance, toilet breaks were strictly monitored, and talking or taking a drink of water were prohibited during shifts.

Researchers into Chinese labour regimes have referred to workplace or labour-force dualism, which takes a number of forms all of which are used by employers to divide the labour-force. Firstly, segmentation between formal workers (with greater job security, higher wages, etc) and informal, peripheral or temporary workers with fewer employment rights.[11] Secondly, the use of sub-contracted, or dispatch, workers, whose numbers increased rapidly after the economic crisis of 2008. These are sent by outside employers into large plants where they often perform the same tasks as directly employed workers while facing an even greater despotism at the hands of their own direct employer. The directly employed workers may experience an erosion of their status, particularly as sub-contracted workers are often highly specialised, but can also have a sense of privilege due to their greater job security.[12] A third illustration of dualism is the use of students seconded from local colleges and vocational technology schools at the behest of giant multinationals such as Foxconn. Colleges, and local authorities trying to attract investment with the promise of lower wages than in the coastal zone, collude with the multinationals, presenting the students' cheap labour as an internship or work placement. These are especially common in periods of peak demand shortly before Xmas. Unwilling students receive various "incentives" from college management, including non-graduation!

Labour shortages at peak times accentuate another problem, labour turnover, which huge numbers of workplaces face due to the harsh working conditions, long hours, and boring routine work. It is especially marked in the early days of a new plant as new workers discover the reality behind the glossy recruitment posters and offers of higher wages than those available elsewhere. In 2012, labour turnover was 24,000 a month (around 7 percent of total staff) in one Foxconn plant, Longhua, while in Pixian, when a group of friends tried to leave, "the human resources director asked them to wait as he already had 40,000 letters of resignation to process".[13]

Segmentation, sub-contracting, student interns and other forms of dualism are designed and imposed by managements in their own interests, but the divisions between workers that they carefully foster can have unintended consequences. They create resentment and anger while also providing a yardstick for informal workers to measure their pay, conditions and experiences against. For the non-core workers (disproportionately migrants) they "become a continuing source of irritation and an impetus for the temporary workers to demand equal treatment".[14] Dualism is not fixed but is unstable and subject to pressure from below.

For Marx, capitalists see factory workers as appendages to a machine, mere human resources employed to work in tandem with the factory's physical resources. This is as true in China today as it was in nineteenth-century Britain. The inevitable consequences include workplace deaths and injuries. Official figures show that the number of people killed in workplace incidents was 100,000 a year in the mid-2000s and although it fell to less than half that a decade later Chinese workers are still ten times more likely to die at work than workers in Britain, for instance.[15] Workplace injuries and long-term disabilities as a result of under-regulated industrial processes and weak health and safety legislation are on a similar scale.

Workplace regimes are not cast in stone, and a combination of pressures from below and wider economic change have produced signs of labour regimes more familiar to workers in the West, albeit unevenly distributed between sectors and regions. A developing labour shortage in coastal areas has forced firms to invest in new technologies, reducing dependence on labour and lowering overall wage costs. Against this, a strategy of labour upskilling has been pursued by many firms, particularly Huawei and others in the high-tech sector, which are then under pressure to retain workers by improving working conditions and pay to reduce the risk of losing them to rivals. The retention of the oppressive factory regime and its relocation to the hinterland and to the west of the country where labour is cheaper is another option.[16]

Overall, by the standards of richer countries most Chinese workers continue to experience oppressive labour regimes, involving long hours, enforced overtime, limited social benefits, draconian micro-management, etc. But these regimes are not fixed and do not close off all opportunities for struggle. The same is true over the issue of wages.

Wages

A key factor in China's take-off was the existence of a vast pool of rural-urban migrant workers whose wage-rates were less than one-tenth of those in advanced countries in 1990. This is reflected in the labour share of national income. The official trade union federation, the All-China Federation of Trade Unions (ACFTU) was complicit in maintaining low wages. But after over two decades of economic expansion, even it was forced to complain in 2010 about the dramatic fall in the share of wages in national income to 37 percent by 2005, against an average of close to 60 percent for the OECD group of richer countries (see chapter two). Different methodologies produce different labour-share figures – the International Labour Organisation (ILO) for instance suggests a consistent figure for China of just over 50 percent for 2004-20, below the world average and the average for middle-income countries and for the Asia-Pacific region.[17]

The ILO data also shows that despite CCP leaders' rhetoric about boosting domestic consumption, the labour share has been declining since 2014 and was lower in 2020 than in every other year since 2004 except 2007. But in an expanding economy, in which a huge proportion of national output is dedicated to accumulation and the fabulous enrichment of the ruling class, the labour share may be static or falling even as wages rise. Wages have risen over the last two decades, but the persistent need for Chinese state capitalism to retain competitiveness against economic competitors imposes limits on the increases that can be tolerated. Chinese workers remain lower paid than workers in more advanced countries, but the gap has closed.

There is no standard measure of wages that provides a completely accurate picture of Chinese workers' wages relative to workers elsewhere. The US Bureau of Labor Statistics stopped producing comparative data a decade ago, but its data showed that China's hourly wage costs in manufacturing were just 2.2 percent of those in the US in 2002, rising to 11.3 percent in 2013.[18] The *Forbes* business website has more recent data and shows that wages in China have risen consistently since China joined the World Trade Organisation (WTO) in 2001. Average annual wages were 27 times higher in the US in 2001 but by 2021 only 3.5 times higher.[19]

The oppressive labour regimes discussed above aim to maximise productivity and profits and maintain the wage-cost advantage that has contributed to China's economic growth. China's minimum wage legislation appears to contradict this, but across the capitalist world national or sectoral minimum wage levels reflect the impact of workers' struggles within the context of wider political factors and the rhythm of growth and crisis in the global economy. Minimum wage legislation was introduced in the US in 1938 under Roosevelt's New Deal and in the 1960s in Latin America in response to ruling-class fears of increased Soviet influence during the Cold War. In 1995, forty-six years after the so-called socialist revolution, an amendment to China's labour law required local governments to set minimum wages, framed by the state as "protecting workers rights".

The protection is minimal in law and worse in practice. The law stipulated that local authorities were to adjust the minimum rate every two years (three from 2015), effectively demanding that the real value of minimum wages should fall for two (later three) years before a brief catch-up is followed by a further fall. Even then local authorities have been late with their upward revisions, and in 2019 only half of provinces increased them, calculating that labour market conditions allowed them to evade the law. Although Shanghai has faced labour shortages and generally increases its minimum wage annually, the poorer province of Hebei still bases its attractiveness to capital on cheap labour.

Pressure from local authorities' friends in business also weakens the impact of the law as minimum wages are set at low levels, ensuring that they have a depressive effect on wider wage levels. Jing Wang has calculated a notional national minimum wage by averaging provincial minima and shows that the ratio of minimum to average wages has fallen from 40 percent in 1995 to 26 percent in 2018. The decline was interrupted during the strike wave between 2007 and 2016 when local authorities came under pressure to approve occasionally significant increases, but since Xi's crackdown on workers' struggles and labour NGOs there has been a further consistent decline. Meanwhile, in the OECD the minimum wage was 35 percent of the average in 2000 but rose to 42 percent in 2018.[20]

The relative decline in China's minimum wage and the lax enforcement of minimum wage increases are closely related to the CCP party-state regime's wider project of maintaining China's competitive position in the global economy. Under pressure from the strike wave after 2007, the 2011 five-year plan set a target to increase minimum wages by 13 percent a year. Many firms complained, and in the 2016 plan no minimum wage targets were set. By 2019 the state-controlled *Economic Daily* reminded readers of where the party-state's priorities lay, arguing that minimum wage levels should reflect not just the interests of wage-earners but the burdens that companies faced. China's workers increasingly placed themselves at the centre of those burdens in the two decades from the mid-1990s.

Strikes, organisation and consciousness

Individual acts of desperation, like the Foxconn suicides, expose the depth of alienation and hopelessness of many Chinese workers. Small group acts, including physical attacks on managers in the streets outside factories that were common in the 1990s, underline this. But they offered as little chance of collective progress for the working class as a whole as another common feature in China, labour turnover, ie escaping one terrible boss in the hope of finding a slightly less terrible one, despite the use of wage arrears to limit turnover and maintain dependency. But while individual actions persist, as China's industrial expansion developed so too did the collective action of industrial workers.

The Chinese state does not publish strike figures, rolling strikes into the category of mass incidents, but official figures show an increase in mass protests from 10,000 to 60,000 between 1993 and 2003.[21] In this period strikes by SOE workers facing mass redundancies and factory closures dominated the statistics. Their scale was such that the state responded with police violence and mass detention while in Beijing the party-state leadership adopted the rhetoric of a "harmonious" society along with conceding some limited rights to workers (see below). It did not work. In 2007 there were 360,000 strikes, but the following year this doubled to around 700,000 and there was a further increase after the 2008 crisis, in part because minimum wages were not raised in 2009 and many factories laid off considerable numbers of workers (over 50 percent in Shenzhen for instance).[22] The number dropped back to 450,000 by 2011, but over the next three years there was a steady increase before an explosion of strikes in 2015 and 2016.[23]

One of the earliest strikes in the 2007-16 wave involved crane drivers in Shenzhen's ports. Its impact was considerable, winning a significant pay rise along with back-pay for unpaid overtime and housing subsidies. As Minqi Li put it, "this was a significant victory for Chinese workers in their struggle against sweatshop exploitation in the export-oriented capitalist sectors".[24] By 2010 millions of workers were involved in strikes in the automobile, textile, and electronics industries, including important strikes at Honda and Foxconn in Guangdong, and Toyota in Tianjin in the north-east. At the end of 2010, 70,000 workers joined a strike in the Dalian industrial zone. Many of the strikes were relatively brief and won their demands in one or two days, but some lasted for three or four weeks. The strike wave was focused primarily in the private export sector but also involved public service workers such as hospital staff and teachers, most of whom were relatively low paid. Protests and strikes by teachers became commonplace in the 2010s, not least because as in the West schools recruited under-qualified staff on insecure contracts and lower pay. One such strike, in Heilongjiang province in 2014, involved 20,000 teachers.

The strikes forced increases in minimum wage rates set by local authorities, some of which doubled them between 2010 and 2014, and also won significant wage increases and other improvements from private capital. But the greatest impact was on workers themselves, who demonstrated not only determination but also a growing, although still limited, capacity to act independently of the official trade unions affiliated to ACFTU, which have never called official strikes. This suggests that embryonic plant-level rank-and-file organisation was developing, a suggestion reinforced by the Honda workers' demand that the official union be restructured.

The party-state responded to the increase in strikes in the 2000s and the beginnings of the 2007-16 strike wave with a new Labour Contract Law in 2008. The law increased workers' rights and security in the workplace, covering issues such as working conditions, health and safety protection and length of the working day. It also placed limits on the use of fixed term contracts, which can only be issued twice before a worker is offered a permanent contract. Although corporations complained about the law, the state was acting as the ideal collective capitalist to "sustain the stability of the exploitative order".[25]

But the consequences of the 2008 law were contradictory. It sought to channel workers' action into formal state structures (the ACFTU and the legal system, both of which handle cases on an individual basis), but because the 2008 law and other measures such as the 2008 Labour-Dispute Mediation and Arbitration Law and 2010 Social Insurance Law (providing insurance covering injury, unemployment, ill-health and maternity) increased awareness of workplace rights, the attempt to restrain action became instead "a significant stimulus to protest and strike".[26] Anger reinforced this awareness when evasions of the law at the local level were discovered. As in other areas, such as the environment, laws are passed to promote state legitimacy but implementation is neglected. When breaches occur the state deflects criticism onto local authorities or individual bureaucrats, and sometimes the businesses they collude with.[27]

In collusion with local authorities bent on attracting and keeping investment, capital also developed various means to evade the requirements of the law. Huawei and others, for example, undertook internal restructurings that changed the status of millions of workers from formal employees covered by the law to informal staff beyond its reach. So re-designated, workers then had to compete for re-employment on the same sort of the fixed-term contracts that were now outlawed for existing workers.[28] Other firms moved production inland to provinces with labour surpluses and even harsher workplace regimes and/or clawed back the costs incurred by compliance with the law by taking larger deductions from workers' pay (for accommodation etc) or by reducing overtime payments where increased basic pay was required. Thus, while the 2008 law appeared to modernise China's labour regime, the reality is more complex. Capital's efforts to escape the restrictions of the law led to increased flexible work and the growth of informal labour markets. According to the International Labour Organisation, informal workers, with limited social protection and insurance, "accounted for more than half of the total urban labour force in recent years".[29]

A similar contrast between appearance and reality exists in the role of the official trade unions. The All-China Federation of Trade Unions has a total membership of about 300 million workers, but its potential influence has long been negated by its position as an arm of the state. Its officials are not elected by the membership but civil servants who are required to implement state policy and promote national development and maintain social peace and stability. Much of their day-to-day work is not focused on workplace issues but on state programmes for poverty relief, training, job seeking, and "even marriage introductions, and celebrating great craftsmen and model workers etc., tasks that should never be part of a trade union's core work".[30] At a local level many ACFTU officials genuinely support workers, albeit within the narrow limits of the state's growth agenda, but the leadership remains a conservative force and deeply hostile to independent labour organisations.

The company unions affiliated to ACFTU share this approach and see their primary function as maintaining production and encouraging productivity.[31] Their officers are generally company managers or imposed by management, adding an extra constraint on their defence of worker interests. They are so committed to the internal regime of the company that when a collective issue is raised the union immediately de-collectivises it and divides it into individual cases. In sum, "if you are a worker in China, you cannot count on your union to protect your rights and interests".[32] Indeed, the very opposite is often the case – in 2010, for example, the union sent gangs of thugs to try to break the Honda strike. By definition, the 2007-16 strike wave represented an upsurge in unofficial strikes as worker-activists bypassed the official unions.

Strikes by women workers, a key feature of the early twenty-first century, illustrate this point. Many of these strikes were "unorganised and spontaneous" and used "methods such as roadblocks, demonstrations, blocking government officers, and collective petitions".[33] In what were becoming increasingly routine confrontations with the police, mobilised to physically and psychologically scare workers back to work, women would move to the front to face arrest in order that they could then make accusations of sexual harassment against the police.[34] This developing political consciousness about state-power strengthened the tendency to bypass the official unions. In her analysis of self-organised informal women workers in the garment sector, Lulu Fan argues that one positive consequence of the official unions' role as agents of the central and/or local states, or of company owners and managers, is that "workers have no choice but to rely on their own pre-existing localistic networks to build cultures of solidarity, but once the workers' solidarity is built, they can articulate their aggregate interests along the line of class".[35]

Hao Ren's *China on Strike* uses the voices of participants to bring the strikes in the first dozen years of the twenty-first century to life.[36] She explores the experience of worker militancy, the dynamics of strikes, forms of organisation and the emergence of a deeper class consciousness and confidence. Most of the strikes were defensive – many concerned wage cuts, while others were against wage arrears, unpaid employer social insurance contributions, protection of jobs, and the prevention of factory closures – but there were examples of more offensive strikes for higher wages. It adds human form to the concept of exploitation, concretises it in particular workplaces, and shows workers' creativity in organising solidaristic action and trying to overcome the hurdles of despotic workplace regimes and ACFTU's obstruction and opposition to collective action.

One important strike, which highlighted workers' relationship with both ACFTU and wider support networks, was at the Yue Yuen shoe factory in Dongguan, Guangdong, in 2014. When a worker retired in March after eighteen years at Yue Yuen, she discovered that her pension was far lower than expected. She posted her anger on social media and by early April workers began to walk out in what became one of the largest strikes in China for two decades. Most of Yue Yuen's 40,000 workers, who produce for giant global sportswear companies such as Nike and Adidas, went on strike for over two weeks. The individual's pension deficit resulted from under-payment to the local authority social insurance scheme by Yue Yuen's Taiwanese parent company, which calculated its contributions based on average wages, which are only around 60 percent of actual wages including overtime and bonuses. As one worker put it, "the factory has been tricking us for 10 years", while another said that "the [local] government, labour bureau, social security bureau and the company were all tricking us together".[37] The police arrested strikers and used riot police and dogs to try to break the strike.

ACFTU's provincial body promised to help the workers as the dispute began but was useless in practice. Instead, the Shenzhen Chunfeng Labour Dispute Service Centre advised on collective bargaining, organised workplace delegate elections, and helped to draw up the workers' demands.[38] The police again intervened on the employer's side, arresting the Chunfeng advisors and charging them with "picking quarrels and stirring up trouble".[39] Social media were again used to push back – various posters including Professor Wang Jiangsong of the China Labor Relations Institute, publicised the arrests and the two Chunfeng organisers were released. The local authorities eventually pressured Yue Yuen to pay the social insurance arrears and some compensation, but the workers were excluded from the negotiations and rejected the deal. Pay was their biggest issue and many groups of workers in the factory now pushed for a 30 percent rise. The issue of pay also revealed what *China on Strike* said about the 1995 Labour Law – it was "a mere scrap of paper, with virtually no enforcement at all".[40] For, although increases in minimum wages have often been won by workers' pressure, higher wages are a challenge to both corporate profits and local authority attempts to attract investment. To evade the consequences of increases in the minimum, Yue Yuen, like many other companies, simply reduced its bonus payments.

Collusion between the local state and capital, who assumed that they could count on the docility of the official unions, was also apparent in another important dispute in 2014. In Changde in Hunan province the American Walmart corporation, on some measures the world's largest company, announced the closure of its local store. It sacked many workers believing that the ACFTU-backed unions in Walmart would "not defend workers' rights, but would be instruments of management".[41] This was true until this strike, when the local ACFTU leader Huang Xingguo rejected Walmart's offer of a new job and sizeable relocation payment and stood with the workers. He organised a committee, which voted to strike against the closure, while Huang himself demanded effective collective bargaining. The strike lost – the local government ruled that the Walmart closure was legal and the strike and pickets were illegal, the police evicted the strikers, and the workers received almost no compensation. But it demonstrated that the wave of strikes had moved some local officials into a more pro-worker trade unionism.

Han Dongfang, co-founder of the Beijing Workers' Autonomous Federation (BWAF) at the time of the Tiananmen demonstrations in 1989 and of *China Labour Bulletin*, overstates the significance of the Changde dispute when he argues that it "proved that employees and unions can act together, even if the union is part of ACFTU". But he is right that the Yue Yuen and Walmart strikes, at the end of nearly a decade of major struggles, showed that "workers are no longer passive victims of political repression: they are becoming powerful agents of change".[42]

By the early 2010s worker militancy was causing concern in Beijing. In response to strikes in the Pearl River Delta, notably the 2010 auto workers' strikes, ACFTU had begun to accede to strikers' demands for the election of workplace union officers and new collective bargaining arrangements. But Chan and Hui's analysis shows that democracy only operated at the lowest levels of the workplace, above which "only the branch committee and the election preparatory committee, dominated by the managerial staff, had the right to nominate candidates for the union executive committee".[43] The purpose of this strategic turn on the part of local authorities, ACFTU officials and company managers was to maintain control over workers under a thin veneer of democratisation. But Yunxue Deng reminds us that all such reforms can have unintended consequences when workers take advantage of new political spaces, however limited, to build pressure on their employers and unions. She argues that workplace elections and collective bargaining constitute "a contested terrain" and are "not merely a means for the state to control worker activism, but also a mechanism manufacturing new workplace militancy".[44]

Demands for workplace elections and meaningful collective bargaining marked a significant step forward for Chinese workers. They had previously seldom by-passed the unions and avoided electing workplace representatives because of their fear of retaliation by companies or their hired thugs, including members of local criminal gangs employed as on-site security firms.[45] By the 2010s, there was an increasingly strong belief among workers and activists, "bordering on a sense of inevitability", that a militant labour movement with durable and deep-rooted organisations was being developed.[46] These developments brought home to Beijing the danger to the regime's legitimacy of too great a gap between ACFTU's contradictory roles as one of the agents of national capitalist development and as a representative or workers in the workplace. The state's two-pronged response, combining national ACFTU reform with the repression of strikers and labour activists, came in 2015.

The proximity of company unions to local management can make ACFTU local committees appear attractive alternative sources of support for strikers. In the same way that the 2008 Labour Contract Law was designed to channel workers' grievances into official structures and processes, so in November 2015, the high-point of the strike wave, Xi launched a reform of the ACFTU, ostensibly to encourage it to build on recent moves to more substantive collective bargaining and play a more proactive and prominent role in addressing workers' concerns. Behind these concerns lay the real fear of the ruling class – state media claimed that its aim was to counter instability.

Xi's reforms had two objectives: "eliminating four impediments" (regimentation, bureaucratisation, elitism and frivolousness) and "increasing three positive attributes" of ACFTU – political consciousness, progressiveness, and popular legitimacy.[47] The language of reform was grandiose but the practical outcomes were limited. ACFTU has clawed back some of the functions it lost to more active and consistently pro-worker NGOs in the previous decade (see below) by establishing workers' rights centres that provide legal and other forms of assistance and have occasionally pressured bosses to implement laws and regulations more fully and enforce the workers' rights enshrined in law.

The move to address workers' immediate workplace concerns – sometimes only symbolically, always moderately, rarely on pay – coincided with a recognition on the part of some large employers that minor concessions under local collective bargaining (or collective consultation as the CCP prefers) may create greater stability in the workforce. As Chan and Hui put it, the goal of promoting collective bargaining was moving from "collective bargaining by riot" to "party-state led collective bargaining".[48] As a consequence many local authorities have promoted collective bargaining with ACFTU and its affiliated unions in order to reinforce the channelling of discontent into official channels. These moves also dovetailed with the perspectives of many moderate workers who favoured working within the ACFTU's district committees and member unions to push them towards greater engagement with workers' immediate concerns. As elsewhere, more moderate workers favour an "incremental modernisation of the labour law" in line with collective bargaining arrangements promoted by the International Labour Organization (ILO).[49]

ACFTU cannot, however, fundamentally overcome the constraints placed on it by its role in policing workers and incorporating workers' activity into the safe spaces offered by state structures. A report by *China Labour Bulletin* in 2019 based on 250 telephone interviews with ACFTU local officials underlined the limited results of the changes initiated in 2015.[50] Beyond legal support and advice "ACFTU's efforts have been little more than window dressing", it continues to act as "an adjunct of government" and its officials remain "agents of CCP propaganda" who "serve the Party" and have "largely failed to implement programs that improve workers' pay and conditions". The results of new collective bargaining arrangements have been extremely modest as most unions think of it as "an administrative exercise that involves nothing more than establishing minimum wage guidelines". Wage negotiations themselves, where they exist, "specifically exclude the workers". Regarding the content of collective agreements, they "bear little or no relation to the most pressing concerns or grievances of the workers". In the construction industry, for example, "the issues most important to the workers – safety and wage arrears – were not covered by collective bargaining arrangements". Worse still, in Wuhan a union official thought that the daily wage of construction workers, less than $50, was sufficient to mean that "pay levels were not the problem". Despite workers' suspicions of enterprise unions, ACFTU officials continued to promote them. They "remained far removed from the workers they were supposed to represent and trade union officials had little understanding of what genuine collective bargaining entailed". Enterprise union officials remain largely unelected and "the workforce and unions remain controlled by the employer and management". One ACFTU official, in Qinqdao, was completely relaxed about enterprise unions, informing the interviewer that "unions could only be established by enterprise managers, not by the workers".

The *China Labour Bulletin* and *Made in China* journal contributor Geoffrey Crothall concluded that despite its repeated claims about responding to workers' concerns, ACFTU reform had achieved little. Working conditions had not improved, and while the number of large strikes declined rapidly after 2015, "workers continued to stage thousands of strikes and collective protests each year over wage arrears, lay-offs, and unpaid social insurance contributions".[51] But if ACFTU reform was designed to provide the carrot, the party-state also wielded a stick. Alongside ACFTU's legal support, service centres and minor changes to what remained weak collective bargaining arrangements, the party-state moved aggressively against labour activists and labour NGOs that had provided support to strikers over the previous decade.

Labour NGOs and student-worker activism[52]

Labour NGOs did not initiate, but responded to, the collective workplace activism of Chinese workers. The increasing number of such NGOs did not develop into "anything comparable to mass organizations, such as historic trade unions or political parties", but for a decade or more played an important supporting role in the strike wave and contributed to the growth of factory-based workers' organisation and the development of class consciousness.[53] The work of NGOs ran parallel to the efforts of labour lawyers to train workers as local labour representatives and negotiators and of the many radical students who took factory jobs and worked with established workers to draw up demands, build factory organisation, and establish meaningful collective bargaining in workplaces.[54] The work of NGOs and students complemented each other as both worked with grass-roots activists to forge wider networks to link factory groups and organise solidarity with strikers. Some involved in NGO-student activist networks joined ACFTU district committees as an organising base and to apply pressure from below, while others worked to establish independent unions. The NGOs provided important support services to workers, including legal advice and guidance on what to do if arrested or if picket-lines were attacked by the police. In the absence of independent trade unions this support was invaluable and grew rapidly. For instance, by 2010 Shenzhen alone had around twenty-five labour support groups or worker centres. Labour NGOs had some success in forcing managements to pay wage arrears and make back payment of social security contributions.

The rise in NGO activity in the 2000s and 2010s was encouraged by a relaxation of authoritarianism, particularly in Guangdong where there was a brief period of liberalisation in universities and civil society under provincial party secretary Wang Yang. NGO activity was accompanied by the emergence of independent Marxist student groups on university campuses, initially mainly in Beijing. These groups involved a few revolutionaries in the tradition of classical Marxism, but those influenced by Maoism were more numerous.

These had a nostalgic view of Mao's apparently pro-worker policies, particularly where they had links to ex-SOE workers who had enjoyed the advantages of the "iron rice bowl". But the members of these groups shared an orientation on workers struggles, and all sought to learn from workers on campus or in nearby factories in small but potentially significant student-worker alliances. In the Pearl River Delta the student Marxists forged important connections to the emerging networks of labour activists as the strike wave developed.

In 2015, with economic growth slowing as the initial impact of the 2008 stimulus package waned, the state's toleration of independent journalists, labour lawyers, NGOs and radical students went into reverse. A fierce repression of all forms of opposition that might cohere into serious challenges to the party-state's legitimacy began. Feminists planning a campaign over sexual harassment on International Women's Day were arrested in March 2015.[55] Hundreds of human rights activists and lawyers were arrested in the summer. In December the state's attention turned to labour activists and NGOs as the party-state unleashed a wave of repression to break the links between workers across industries and factories, head-off the challenges this posed to ACFTU control over workers, and limit the spread of the strike wave from its core in the southern SEZs.

The crackdown seriously limited the capacity of worker centres – many of them supported by NGOs – to support workers' collective actions. Almost all of Shenzhen's twenty-five centres closed and those surviving have both limited and moderated their activity.[56] The crackdown was given a legal veneer with the Foreign NGO Management Law, designed to end international support for NGOs, that came into effect on 1 January 2017. The anxiety among activists deepened a few months later when students who had built links with workers in Guangzhou, were arrested in November 2017.[57] The following year the crackdown intensified.

The two-week struggle at Jasic Technology in Shenzhen in July 2018 marked a serious escalation of repression. Workers were sacked after forming their own union, despite the intention to register it with ACFTU, and demanding the reinstatement of a colleague and improved conditions – including payment of salaries on time and stricter safety measures. The significance of the Jasic struggle was captured by Kevin Lin: it forged "a student-worker alliance, even if on a small scale, turning a labour struggle into a political struggle and generated a leftist and class discourse which challenges the state monopoly of Marxism".[58]

For this reason the repression, of both those involved and others, was particularly severe. The Dagonzhe Workers Centre was falsely accused of organising the Jasic struggle by the state's Xinhua news agency in August 2018, leading to a purge of local labour NGOs as well as the mass arrest of Jasic worker-organisers. Student solidarity protests were organised in over twenty universities, but the state extended its repression over the next year with the arrest of activists in unrelated disputes. In January 2019 the director of Chunfeng Centre, a key support in the Yue Yuen strike, was arrested for "disturbing social order" and three of the centre's five workers left in fear for their safety. Over 100 workers, activists and student supporters were arrested, labour groups across the south closed, and university Marxist groups were closed down, or "reorganised" as university authorities put it. University research in labour studies has faced increasing restrictions.

Many of those detained since 2015 faced months of detention without trial and many recent detainees have been charged with the serious crime of "subversion of state power". The arrests have reduced markedly since 2020 and most of those arrested were ultimately released, but this is not a sign of a new party-state leniency. The intention of repression is to intimidate current activists and deter potential future activists. The combination of arrests, detention, and intense surveillance leads to a decline in activist numbers, and therefore of arrest, while the release of activists is on the condition that they refrain from further activism.

After 2015 "the decade of hope and excitement quickly gave way to disappointment, then despair, reinforced by repression" that dismantled networks of resistance and curtailed worker, student and NGO activism.[59] The political space for opposition to the party-state regime that had opened up over the previous decade rapidly closed as both activists and their possible replacements faced criminalisation.

Weaknesses and strengths in the 2020s

State repression slowed the development of workers' struggle and the emergence of embryonic rank-and-file organisation and independent workers' organisations that threatened to breach the limits on workers' activity imposed by ACFTU. In the "unbelievably repressive and hyper-nationalist political environment" fostered by Xi Jinping the possibility of a nationally organised labour movement independent of the state unions remains a hope for the future.[60]

There are other obstacles, some more significant than others, to the transformation of the working class from a class in itself to a class for itself. Some have noted a slow deindustrialisation in the SEZs as the service sector grows (it now accounts for 53 percent of GDP) and capitals begin to relocate to inland provinces.[61] They are pushed by rising wage costs and pulled by lower wages and inducements and subsidies offered by inland local authorities.[62] Others highlight the differences in class consciousness between migrants and established urban workers. Writing in 2014 the Marxist Au Loong-yu argued that the millions of migrant workers of the previous quarter-century had "no collective memory as a class prior to coming to the cities",[63] while many retain their rural household registration and their claims to land as a means of subsistence livelihood. Deindustrialisation, relocation and differences between migrants and established workers hinder the development of working-class consciousness and the building of long-term organisation and solidarity networks. But none are insurmountable.

The Italian Marxist Antonio Gramsci argued that in periods of working-class retreat the Left and labour movement should adopt "pessimism of the intellect, optimism of the will" (ie a realistic assessment of the current balance of class forces and the problems confronting the movement, combined with hope that these difficulties will be overcome and that socialist revolution will develop).[64] This motto remains helpful, but while negative conclusions can be drawn from the obstacles above about the prospects for a deeper working-class consciousness, there are grounds for optimism.

The structure of working classes everywhere has never been monolithic and based only in factories, and has always undergone long-term change. Service workers (47 percent of China's total workforce in 2022) are also part of the working class and there is no fundamental difference between their experiences and those of factory workers.[65] Those migrants working in factories have, in any case, put down deeper roots in the cities over time and, while still denied the rights attached to an urban *hukou*, are a key part of the Chinese working class. They were centrally involved in the 2007-16 strike wave and revealed through their "intermittent discontent and protest the beginnings of an increasingly active collective consciousness".[66]

The relocation of production, which in the short term weakens the bargaining power of coastal SEZ workers, is also not a straightforward positive for capital. The wages paid to inland workers by relocated capitals are lower than those in the coastal SEZs, but are generally higher than the previous wages of inland workers. This allows these workers to work closer to where they live and retain *hukou* rights. In the long term this is likely to give a greater sense of security and confidence to resist employer demands and fight for higher wages. When thousands of workers escaped from Foxconn's Zhengzhou plant in 2022, many were able to return to their home villages and towns on foot because they are also in Henan province. The fact that capital is beginning to relocate to where workers live, rather than demanding that they come to it, is a reflection that the wage dynamic of 30+ years of mass migration is running out of steam. Lower wages in inland areas may only be temporary.

Increased security does not remove workers' anger and alienation. Where migrants work part in industry and part on the land (so-called "peasant workers" *Nongmingong*), this can create great anger since most of these dual-workers are not protected by labour laws because their industrial work is defined as provision of intermittent or temporary labour services rather than full employment with attached rights.[67] Meanwhile, the state's promotion of agribusiness threatens the viability of their farm work to the extent that a process of proletarianisation is unfolding in the countryside.[68]

Even if the obstacles prove harder to clear than these arguments suggest, "industrial workers still comprise a significant fraction of China's proletariat...and their collective power should not be underestimated. We have been surprised time and again, just as we turn pessimistic, when a new wave of factory workers' strikes has suddenly erupted"[69] As the Covid pandemic unfolded, and particularly in the immediate aftermath of the easing of zero-Covid lockdowns at the end of 2022, there were signs that China may have been on the cusp of such a wave, involving both factory and service workers.

A new wave of struggle?

Even under repression new struggles and strikes developed. White collar and service sector strikes involving teachers, sanitation workers, retail workers, and others were already well established by 2020. In 2019 the 996:ICU online campaign highlighted the toxic culture and overwork in the IT sector (by no means the most oppressive).[70] In 2020 workers and social activists responded to the Covid pandemic by organising solidarity with key workers (in health and sanitation, for instance) who lacked protective equipment. Labour rights activism, now focused on Covid-related issues, also revived. Feminist activism, focused during the pandemic on domestic violence, also increased, as did that of LGBT+ activists. The state responded with further repression, but although the revival was on a modest scale during the pandemic it demonstrated that the party-state had been unable to destroy solidaristic impulses and forms of organisation in the post-2015 crackdown. The roots of solidarity and organisation are nourished by anger, one site of which is among delivery workers in the gig economy.

In 2020 there was an explosion of organising and strikes among delivery drivers. Western trade union leaders often insist that informal sector workers are difficult to organise, but Chinese workers have shown greater imagination in organising people who face identical conditions but do not share a workplace for eight hours (or more) each day. Food delivery worker Chen Guojiang (known as Mengzhu, "head of the association"), angry about delivery workers' low pay and the pressures bosses put them under to work in dangerous conditions, especially in the rain, organised mutual aid, online chat groups and posted online videos. Although Mengzhu was arrested in Beijing in 2021 and imprisoned for a year, his message was not lost on other gig workers – their collective actions fell dramatically from the highs of 2018 and 2019, but China Labour Bulletin reported a pick-up in strikes and protests among gig workers in the first few months of 2023.[71]

That increase was repeated in manufacturing, where there were 100-plus protests in the first third of the year, twice the number for the whole of 2022.[72] Despite the repressive environment that Chinese workers face, struggle has picked up after the end of the Covid lockdowns and there are signs that a new generation of workers and activists is emerging both inside workplaces and amongst supporters.

Conclusion

Capitalists are caught in a profound contradiction. They have an interest in destroying working class organisation but must also bring workers together and thereby create the basis of that organisation. Writing at a time when factories were the main workplaces of urban workers, Gramsci wrote that "the factory, which they created… naturally organises the workers, groups them, puts them into contact with one another… The worker is thus naturally strong…concentrated and organised inside the factory." Outside the factory workers are "isolated, dispersed, weak".[73] An elementary class consciousness, a sense of "us and them", and intense anger flow from the experience of exploitation in the workplace, frequently generating apparently spontaneous protest.

But Gramsci also argued that "mass ideological factors always lag behind mass economic phenomena, and that therefore, at certain moments, the automatic thrust due to the economic factor is slowed down, obstructed or even momentarily broken by traditional ideological elements".[74] For long periods, therefore, workers have a contradictory consciousness, comprising oppositional "good sense" and conformist "common sense".[75] Good sense derives from workers' workplace experience and forms of collective activity that contain the embryo of the "practical transformation" of society, while common sense reflects an uncritical acceptance of prevailing social practices. For workplace-based class consciousness to develop into a political class consciousness focused on the organisation of society as a whole, factors beyond the experience of immediate workplace conditions come into play.

Writing in 2016 Minqi Li believed that "under the current trend, in a few years, a militant Chinese working class movement will emerge. The 'specter' of a working-class revolution...is resurfacing in China in the twenty-first century."[76] Reminding the Left, and the workers themselves, that the working class is what Marx called the gravedigger of capitalism serves a general ideological purpose, but gravediggers need tools, and the harder the ground the sharper the tools need to be. These include access to critical ideas, including a socialist press, time and spaces within which ideas and different strategies can be debated, freedom to organise on a society-wide scale, etc. Party-state surveillance and repression impose serious constraints in all these areas.

Socialists must recognise that the concentration of Chinese workers in giant workplaces and mega-cities, their anger, courage and creativity do not automatically supply the tools needed to build the sort of organisation required to mount a successful assault on the party-state. That state is presiding over deepening problems: the rate of economic growth has fallen from an average of 10 percent a year for four decades to less than half that today; growth is maintained by a huge growth in state debt; the population is ageing, the birth-rate slowing and migration flows drying up; there is huge industrial overcapacity; and lower-cost production locations compete with China to host foreign investment. The party-state and its billionaires will redouble their efforts to pass the costs of these pressures on to workers. But, as the Arab Spring and other protest movements around the world have repeatedly shown, resistance can erupt from the most unpromising of circumstance. The partial recovery of activism in 2023 marks a small step towards recreating the solidarity and networks that enabled the passing of lessons and ideas between strikes and factories in the 2007-16 strike wave. The history of the world's labour movements shows that if these lessons are not embodied in a revolutionary organisation, and kept alive in revolutionary publications, then the raw material for change provided by the strikes and resilience of workers will be lost.

Ching Kwan Lee's 1999 book *Against the Law* is one of the founding documents in the sociology of labour in China. She argued that "workers' insurgent consciousness exceeds their insurgent capacity" and that struggle is mostly "localised and fragmented".[77] Building that capacity and beginning the process of forging independent regional and national workers' organisations are urgent tasks for China's workers.

Chapter 5
Oppressions and resistance

Introduction

Were the capitalist system of social production organised to satisfy human needs, the stupendous economic expansion of China could have been used to address pressing social problems. Instead, a system built on the interests of the state-capitalist ruling class, driven by a powerful global logic of competitive capital accumulation, has exacerbated the problems inherited from the Maoist era. Relative poverty and inequality have ballooned, while national oppressions, in Tibet and Xinjiang in particular, have generated huge anger and protest. The position of women has improved in material terms but women continue to face intense oppression, and feminists and other women are regularly engaged in protests. Environmental concerns are also severe and routinely generate local protests. The official solution to these problems is not democratic engagement in evidence-based discussion and negotiation but a combination of repression and further debt-financed expenditure, somewhat randomly thrown at the problem. But national, gender and other oppressions are not reducible to levels of material well-being, and four decades of growth have left untouched their underlying causal mechanisms, rooted in core structures of capitalist society, including competitive accumulation, exploitation, the family, and the metabolic rift with nature. The mass of Chinese people are objects of the modernisation process not its creators or controllers. But they also have subjectivity and agency, which have been mobilised in waves of resistance to the party-state. This chapter looks at the resistance that has developed across a range of issues outside the workplace. For, despite the repressive crackdown of recent years "proletarian unrest has continued" as the party-state shares "capital's global push to cut the costs of social reproduction as the population ages and economic growth continues to stagnate."[1]

Poverty, inequality and welfare

Four decades of growth have produced a dramatic fall in absolute poverty. It is widely reported that using the World Bank international poverty line figure of $1.90 per day (at the 2011 purchasing power parity rate) China's poverty rate fell from over 80 percent in 1980 to less than 5 percent by 2014 as 800 million people were removed from extreme poverty. These figures are contested. Chen Shaohua and Martin Ravallion use China's official poverty line figures set by the National Bureau of Statistics to argue that only about 400 million have been removed from extreme poverty since 1980. That falls to 140 million if we take 1985 as the base year – this was when China established a rural poverty line, by which time many had already been lifted out of extreme poverty by the impact of the early agricultural reforms under Deng.[2]

How does the party-state explain the persistence of poverty? In a speech in April 2020 Xi revived Mao's concept of "common prosperity", suggesting that the party-state recognised that there were systemic causes of poverty and that it was considering policies to address inequality.[3] Yet, Xi emphasised that this increasing prosperity would not involve significant improvements to China's minimal welfare state – China should not "go overboard with social security" and should avoid "the idleness-breeding trap of welfarism".[4] The focus should instead be on hard work, particularly for those whose response to intense workplace regimes has been "lying flat", ie turning their backs on long working hours. Much of Xi's speech could have been penned by a neoliberal speech-writer in the West. But poverty reduction should not just fall on individuals – entire minority communities can do their bit. A quote from the CCP secretary in Sichuan province, home to 2.5 million people from the Yi minority, provides a clue to official thinking. He says that "conservative and outdated thinking is the root cause", including the Yi people's "undesirable habits" that include "not caring for their elderly parents while they are still alive".[5] Yi poverty is explained, in part at least, by their inadequate embrace of privatised elderly care! In any case, as economic growth has slowed, references to common prosperity have decreased.

In March 2020, having identified poverty reduction as a critical battle for the party-state in 2017 (alongside reducing pollution and financial risk), Xi Jinping claimed that the number of rural poor had fallen to 5.5 million in 2019, just 0.4 percent of the population.[6] Yet in May, prime minister Li Keqiang claimed that there were 600 million people (over 40 percent of the population) living on a monthly income of 1,000 yuan or less ($145). The discrepancy is explained by a number of factors: where the poverty line is set relative to the World Bank's global poverty line figure; whether purchasing power parity calculations are used (which doubles the value of rural incomes relative to US figures for instance); and problems of averaging. But all this is splitting hairs! China is a country of fabulous wealth for its billionaires, many of whom are CCP members, and alienation and impoverished life experiences for hundreds of millions. It is not only more unequal than most other countries in the Global South but its increase in inequality far outstrips that of other countries since 1990.[7] As Barry Naughton noted, "there may be no other case where a society's income distribution has deteriorated so much, so fast".[8]

In 2016 the BBC News reported that there were nearly 600 dollar billionaires in China, more than in the US. The monthly minimum wage, averaged across the various regions, was only about £200.[9] The physical experience of inequality is degrading, but what Chinese economists have referred to as a subjective poverty line is also important and can fuel discontent. Echoing the work of sociologist WG Runciman on relative deprivation, these economists argue that in rural areas the subjective poverty line is twice the level of the poverty line and that on this basis perhaps a third or more of rural workers regard themselves as poor, despite the party-state's quest for legitimacy leading to increased spending on poverty reduction from under CN¥10 billion a year in 2000 to over CN¥120 billion per year in 2019.[10] Shaohua and Ravallion conclude that based on figures for relative poverty there has been "no progress in reducing poverty, and even a rise in the poverty rate over time until quite recently".[11]

Income inequality is compounded by underfunded and uneven

welfare support. In healthcare, there is a huge gap in quality between cities and rural areas, forcing millions to travel for treatment to the cities, where they may queue for a few days to get a cursory consultation with a doctor (the standard consultation lasts 90 seconds). In the rural areas themselves, in 2016 just 0.2 percent of doctors had the minimum qualification required, a BSc in medicine, while fewer than half the doctors in township level clinics have a degree.[12]

These illustrations of poverty contrast with ultramodern transport infrastructures and business districts in China's cities, and expose the pro-capital priorities of China's party-state. Public healthcare spending is about 2 percent of GDP, far below advanced country levels and only around half the figure for countries at a similar level of development. Social spending suffers more generally – welfare spending is only 12 percent of state spending, compared to 37 percent in the US.[13] Worse still, the state remains "reluctant or unable to force employers to comply with existing social insurance obligations. Rather, the government is trying to reduce the social insurance burden faced by employers and shift the burden of pension and other social insurance contributions onto individual workers".[14] In rural areas, domestic plots provide people with additions to their incomes, and with them a safety valve for the state, allowing it to keep payments low and encourage self-sufficiency and self-provision, but overall Chinese workers face lives of considerable hardship with minimal state support.

Pensioners suffer particular hardship and pensioner protests against health benefit cuts and proposals to raise the retirement age have become a regular occurrence in recent years.[15] These protests are a minor irritant compared to those on other issues, but are likely to increase as the party-state searches for ways to tackle the problem of a rapidly ageing population and decline in the working-age population while maintaining its competitive advantage in the global economy. The percentage of over-60s in the Chinese population rose from 13.3 to 18.7 percent between 2010 and 2020.[16] Inequality and relative deprivation provide the backdrop to the rise of protest in recent decades, revealing the depth of the contradictions facing China's state capitalism.

National minorities

In a letter of 1870 Marx wrote:

> The ordinary English worker hates the Irish worker as a competitor who lowers his standard of life...feels himself a member of the *ruling* nation and so turns himself into a tool of the aristocrats and capitalists against Ireland, thus strengthening their domination *over himself...* This antagonism is artificially kept alive and intensified by the press, the pulpit, the comic papers, in short by all the means at the disposal of the ruling classes. *It* is the secret of the *impotence of the English working class,* despite their organisation. It is the secret by which the capitalist class maintains its power. And of this that class is quite aware.[17]

Racism and nationalism divide the working class and hinder the development of class consciousness and unity in action. But state-driven forced assimilation of national minorities, far from eroding racism and nationalism, serves to intensify ideologies of supremacy. Unity cannot be imposed from above, but can be achieved when workers, whatever their ethnic or national identities, engage in common action in pursuit of their shared class interests. This in turn demands, as Lenin insisted, that the workers of the oppressor nation, the national majority, consistently oppose all forms of racism and national oppression and support the right of national minorities to self-determination. These arguments are not of purely historical interest but point to vital issues in China today.

Mao's national-developmental revolution united most in China against foreign control and humiliation, forging a nationalism of the oppressed that transcended ethnicity in the struggle against external intervention and imperialism. Here Mao put into practice the ideas of the 1890s' reformer and state official Liang Qichao: "if we want now to oppose the national imperialism of the powers, rescue China from disaster and save our people, we have no choice but to adopt the policy of pushing our own nationalism".[18] Indeed, in the struggle for power the CCP acknowledged the right to self-determination for national minorities who they hoped to enlist in the struggle against the nationalists and Japan, whose brutal occupation was a key factor in creating a popular sense of a Chinese nation.

Once in power, however, the CCP mobilised nationalism not to unify but to divide, converted nationalism from an expression of the oppressed into a tool of the oppressor majority and of the unitary state to which it was firmly committed. That unitary state makes verbal reference to ethnic pluralism but has in practice promoted the dominance of the Han Chinese, who comprise 92 percent of the population, and used them to impose Beijing's rule against the wishes of local populations.

The new regime grouped China's communities into fifty-six ethnic groups. This was often done somewhat arbitrarily – the Zhuang, China's largest minority, lived primarily in Guangxi but were also scattered across the southern provinces and previously identified themselves as members of various more localised groups. Minority ethnic groups include Uyghurs, Mongols, Tibetans, Koreans, Manchus, Yi, and Hui (albeit that the Muslim Hui are otherwise indistinguishable from Han Chinese). All suffer various forms of cultural, religious and linguistic oppression, alongside economic marginalisation, but the two best-known cases are Tibet and the Uyghur Muslims of Xinjiang.

Tibet

Until recently Western support for the Dalai Lama and Tibetan rights made Tibet the most high-profile case of national-minority oppression in China. The core of feudal and decentralised Tibet had been brought under Chinese control in the early eighteenth century by the Qing dynasty (1644-1912), which restructured Tibet under the central authority of the Dalai Lama. But after 1949 local allegiance to the figurehead of the Tibetan nation posed a threat to the unitary state and although Mao's China initially worked with the Dalai Lama and attempted to govern Tibet via the established Tibetan ruling class, it also moved Han Chinese into Tibet, particularly into leading positions. To avoid direct confrontation in the core of Tibet Beijing did not initially impose the full policy programme of the

New China or fundamentally uproot existing practices. But the CCP did start imposing the new order outside core Tibet, where some Tibetans also lived, eg in parts of Qinghai, Yunnan and Sichuan. This provoked resistance and sporadic guerrilla war in the east of Tibet and many Tibetans fled into the core of the Tibetan area, spreading the conflict there. In 1959 the People's Liberation Army occupied Tibet and partitioned it, joining the east to Sichuan province. The Dalai Lama fled to India.[19]

The attitude of Beijing to Tibet had been expressed in the early 1950s by leading military figures who referred to efforts to "tame" minorities and suppress "barbarians".[20] The Cultural Revolution reinforced both the Han-centric hierarchy and Mao's opposition to the "four olds" – old ideas, culture, customs, and habits – which was mobilised against traditional Tibetan society, Buddhism and monasteries, many of which were destroyed. The economic growth of the last forty years has scarcely reached ordinary Tibetans, most of whom remain impoverished and tied to the land, while the development of Tibet, through infrastructure spending for instance, benefits Chinese firms from elsewhere, who often import Han labour. Many Tibetans have followed the Dalai Lama to India, but those remaining have periodically resisted Han dominance, as they did in major riots between 1987 and 1989.

Protests and riots did not end in 1989, despite the fierce crackdown, reinforced by post-Tiananmen repression. There was an uprising in 2008, after which some 150 monks set fire to themselves over the next seven years to protest at continued occupation.[21] Beijing's response to such acts of desperation is to label them as religious terrorism and to maintain the 200,000 troops stationed in Tibet, closely policing Tibetans' cultural and religious practices. Many monasteries remain closed to reduce regime fears that they become organising centres for opposition. Public prayer is tolerated as an expression of Tibetan culture but must not become the basis for demands for independence.[22] Beijing fears allegiance to symbols, ideas and institutions, other than the CCP and party-state, that all oppressed national minorities possess. This is nowhere truer than amongst Muslim communities in Xinjiang in the far west, among whom the Uyghurs are best known.

Xinjiang's Muslim Uyghurs

In the mid-eighteenth century the Qing dynasty incorporated large parts of what is now western China, many of whose Turkic communities had converted to Islam between the tenth and seventeenth centuries as they encountered Muslims travelling along the ancient Silk Road trade route. The Qing named the province Xinjiang ("new frontier"), inadvertently weakening the contemporary party-state's claim that Xinjiang has always been part of China.

Resentment at Beijing's over-lordship is deep and abiding. In 1933 Uyghur and other Turkic forces declared independent East Turkestan republics after five years of increasing authoritarianism and a sinicisation drive that promoted inward Han migration and the banning of the Hajj pilgrimage to Mecca.[23] The southern republic was largely controlled by Uyghurs while the northern republic was predominantly Kazakh, and the rebel forces were internally divided and sometimes fought each other. These divisions were further complicated by the role of the USSR, which supported the official state out of fear that the rebellion might inspire opposition forces in Soviet Central Asia. The republics lasted only six months, before the GMD's Nanjing government restored control in 1934. Nevertheless, the forces that had driven Uyghurs and others to a declaration of independence that proclaimed an end to China's dictatorial rule and the equality of all nationalities in East Turkestan did not disappear. GMD and CCP focus on the east during the civil war created an opportunity for a second declaration of independence in 1944. Stalin supported this declaration to strengthen the USSR's hand in Central Asia, but in 1949 he accommodated Mao, who incorporated Xinjiang into a greater China.

In 1949 Uyghur Muslims comprised three-quarters of Xinjiang's population and Han just 6 percent.[24] Fearing a revival of opposition, Mao sent 200,000 troops into Xinjiang while also using state investment to promote its economic integration with the rest of China. Since then Han migration to the region has been consistently promoted, and over seventy years the population balance has been transformed – by the time of the 2020 census the nearly 26 million population was 45 percent Uyghur and 42 percent Han.[25]

Mao considered Xinjiang's minorities to be backward, but there was an initial relative tolerance of cultural difference after the revolution. But during the Great Leap Forward (1958-1962) the demonisation of backwardness as a barrier to progress intensified and CCP rule became increasingly repressive. The failures of the Great Leap Forward led to a relaxation of repression, but the Cultural Revolution again increased pressure on Xinjiang's minorities to assimilate amid attacks on their religion and culture.[26]

This was again relaxed under the post-Mao reforms and minorities were employed in state positions to encourage their allegiance to the CCP regime. But continued Han immigration and occupation of top positions in Xinjiang's social and political bureaucracies, alongside cultural discrimination and economic inequalities, reinforced a sense that Xinjiang's minorities were living in a Han-centric settler-colonial regime. There were protests in Urumqi, Xinjiang's capital, and elsewhere between 1985 and 1989, by which time some Uyghurs had elevated religion as the prime focus for their resistance. In the south of Xinjiang *madrasas*, centres for groups of *talibs* (students of religion), were established and small numbers of Uyghurs advocated the adoption of Muslim social values and the creation of an independent Islamic state. In 1990 the Turkestan Islamic party, a recently created network, staged an insurrection in Baren.

The March 1989 riots in Tibet, which were followed by the Tiananmen protests in June, produced fear in the party-state that events could spiral out of control. This was reinforced by the collapse of the Stalinist states in Eastern Europe (and the USSR in 1991) and its reaction to the 1990 uprising was ferocious. Since then Uyghur-Beijing relations have gone through recurrent cycles of resistance and repression, which reignites the very resistance that it was designed to stop.[27] Meanwhile, in response to the repression some Uyghur expatriate activists made contact with the Taliban in Afghanistan and Pakistan and established what Beijing refers to as the East Turkestan Islamic Movement (ETIM). Its influence inside Xinjiang was minimal, particularly after the 9/11 attacks, when China collaborated with the American CIA and joined the war on terror in exchange for a free-hand in Xinjiang.[28] Within weeks the label Beijing applied to Uyghur activity changed from "separatist" to "terrorist".[29]

Under Xi, Xinjiang has been subjected to what Darren Byler refers to as "terror capitalism".[30] Proclaiming that "three evil forces" (*sange shili*) are at work – terrorism, ethnic separatism and religious extremism – the central state has pursued a strategy of sinicisation of Uyghurs, and Muslims more generally, involving an elaborate system of repressive institutions and practices.[31] The CCP declared a "people's war on terror" in 2014, when Xinjiang's regional government imposed increased restrictions on the accreditation of imams and on the operation of mosques and remaining religious schools. In subsequent years a wide range of repressive Islamophobic measures have been implemented. Restrictions on mosque building and religious education have increased, party-state loyalists have been imposed on religious organisations, minority languages have been replaced by Mandarin in education and police powers and surveillance have been greatly increased. These include checks on "suspicious" behaviour such as using banned social media apps like WhatsApp, not drinking alcohol, eating halal meat and not eating pork, observing Ramadan, and giving children first names like Muhammad or Fatima.[32] "Abnormal" beards and wearing the veil in public have also been banned. School children are regularly interrogated about the behaviour of family members, including whether they speak about Muhammad or use Islamic greetings.[33]

Mosques have been a particular target and subjected to a "four-enter campaign" that requires them to incorporate the Chinese flag, support China's religious laws and state-approved "socialist" values, and promote China's own culture. Arab-style minarets have been replaced by new ones built according to Chinese traditions, chosen from a list of designs approved by *Kansu,* the official Islamic association. Control is accompanied by destruction: in 2020 the Australian Strategic Policy Institute estimated that 16,000 mosques in Xinjiang (65 percent of the total) had been destroyed or damaged on state orders since 2017. This has also occurred, along with closure of Arab language schools, in Gansu and Yunnan and Ningxia, where Hui communities live.[34]

These measures against mosques and Islamic cultural practices only partly explain why life for Uyghurs has been described by Amnesty International as a "dystopian hellscape".[35] They have also been subject to a regime of mass surveillance, particularly after 2016 when Xi appointed Chen Quanguo, who had previously imposed similar measures in Tibet, as Xinjiang CCP secretary.[36] The surveillance regime comprises extensive CCTV, facial recognition cameras, iris detection devices, DNA sampling and 3D identification imagery.[37] People's data and mobile phones are constantly monitored and intrusive apps loaded by police onto mobile phones, which are subject to random police checks. Most Uyghurs have had to surrender their passports, destroying the hopes of those who want to emigrate.

Surveillance is a mild form of social control compared to more draconian measures against Uyghurs. Many Uyghur women have been forcibly sterilised or had forced abortions, to slow the birthrate and, in the long-term, reduce the Uyghur population. And at the centre of CCP attempts to erase Uyghur culture and language and silence opposition is a system of re-education and internment camps.[38] These are consistent with Xi's words in a secret speech: the virus of extremism requires Xinjiang Muslims to experience a "period of painful, interventionary treatment". Although the figure of 1-2 million detainees, originally from the US alt-right, may be an exaggeration, few dispute that Beijing has built a network of what it calls "vocational education centres" in which Uyghurs are re-educated in order, according to official statements, to "wash brains" and "cleanse hearts".[39]

This has taken a particularly sinister form with the Xinjiang government's "unite as one family" programme under which officials live in the homes of Uyghur detainees' families for several days. Their aim is "to identify subversive behaviour, encourage denunciations and carry out patriotic education. More than a million state officials may be involved".[40] The children of those detained are no doubt reassured by the script widely used in these cases – "treasure this chance for free education that the party and government has provided to eradicate erroneous thinking".[41]

The terror aspect of "terror capitalism" is clear, but what about the capitalism? Capitalism is generally characterised by free labour in that workers are not tied to any single capitalist employer. But forms of unfree labour persist and Byler argues that millions experience forms of forced labour in a region that has been increasingly integrated into the wider Chinese economy as a producer of primary products for export and to feed and supply the rest of China. In the countryside, productivity drives have forced farmers off the land and into an even more severe form of the dormitory labour regime noted in chapter three, a modern version of the workhouse regime of Victorian Britain. The intrusive surveillance and intense security at the factory gates are tolerated out of fear of detention in internment camps. Many of those Uyghurs who remain free workers have experienced displacement by Han immigrants, who Beijing regards as more trusted to deliver economic modernisation.[42] Thus, Byler reports how Uyghur bank professionals have been downgraded to the role of cash-tellers, teachers as janitors, and home-care givers as street sweepers.

The current regime in Xinjiang is building on an earlier model of militarised labour. Xinjiang is home to key mineral and energy resources, including 25 percent of China's oil reserves and 40 percent of its coal. It produces c.25 percent of China's natural gas and is also a major agricultural area, producing over 80 percent of China's cotton and vast quantities of tomatoes and other fruits. Believing that economic development will head off separatism and radicalisation, investment in Xinjiang was increased in the early 2000s as part of the Great Western Development Strategy.

Economics is inseparable from security in Xinjiang.[43] One illustration of this is the Xinjiang Production and Construction Corps (XPCC, or *Bingtuan*), a militarised production unit with approximately 3 million members established in 1954 to accommodate demobbed Han soldiers. It is a key component of the Xinjiang economy, involved in oil, construction and agriculture, where it organises 400,000 farmers. 100,000 of its members belong to a militia that monitors Uyghurs. The intertwining of economics and politics is demonstrated in the treatment of Uyghurs outside Xinjiang too. The Australian Strategic Policy Institute claims that between 2017 and 2019 80,000 former detainees in Xinjiang's security system were forced to work in factories in other provinces, many of them producing for global companies such as Apple, Dell, Mercedes-Benz and Nike.[44] These arrangements, part of the state's Xinjiang Aid scheme ostensibly designed to promote Xinjiang's development and stability, bear many of the hallmarks of the terror regime in Xinjiang. These workers are forced to live segregated from the rest of the workforce, eat in separate canteens and receive less than Han workers. The scheme also entails the break-up of Uyghur families, thereby undermining cultural transmission and, in Beijing's view at least, fostering the sinicisation of Uyghur children and the annihilation of Uyghur culture. For added insurance, Xinjiang has also witnessed the removal of up to 1 million children, particularly of detainees, from their families and their placement in newly-built boarding schools.

Hong Kong

The Chinese state's actions in Hong Kong do not involve the same level of repression or entail the effacement of the local culture that we see in Xinjiang but are also highly significant. Hong Kong was returned by Britain to China in 1997, having been ruled by Britain since 1842. Under British rule there were no democratic rights, but Hong Kong's position as an outpost of Western (relatively) free market capitalism ensured that there was a political space for individual rights and other liberal freedoms. Where struggle was collective and from below, however, as in the 1967 riots against British rule, the state's response was brutal. Britain was equally adept at repression in Hong Kong as China is today.

Ultimately, China's rise made Britain's position unsustainable. When Britain handed Hong Kong over, the Chinese accepted that there would be a degree of political autonomy and a separate legal system for the next fifty years. But China's rulers had to balance reintegrating Hong Kong with the mainland, as part of the final removal of imperial outposts, against the recognition that Hong Kong's role as a financial centre and its links to the global economy were useful to China's reform strategy and could be jeopardised by complete incorporation. This balance was captured in the phrase "one country, two systems".

Relative to China's economic might today Hong Kong's significance has declined. In 2004, for instance, Hong Kong's container port was the largest in China, but by 2020 it was only ninth. But its role in international finance remains important – over half of inward FDI is routed via Hong Kong, which is also home to the main stock exchange listings of Chinese firms, including SOEs, and the links between mainland and Hong Kong financial markets have multiplied. Hong Kong's strategic importance stopped Beijing from fully imposing its own system after 1997, and the one country, two systems model meant that the limited space for critical thought, opposition and human rights activism persisted. Activists took advantage of this space in major protests in 2014 and 2019.[45]

In 2014 China's party-state reneged on a 2007 promise that Hong Kong's chief executive (hitherto an appointee of the so-called professional sectors – meaning industrial, financial and commercial leaders) would be elected by universal suffrage after 2017. In June, protesters organised in the Occupy Central movement organised an unofficial referendum on democratic reforms and 20 percent of the population took part. On 1 July half a million demonstrated in support of democratic demands, including universal suffrage in open and transparent elections, election of the chief executive and opposition to the political screening of potential candidates. The regime's rejection of these demands precipitated a student boycott of classes, supported by hundreds of academics, in September. The following week school students joined the boycott and shortly afterwards occupations began in the Admiralty district of the city, the business and state administrative centre.[46] As in Egypt in 2011, protesters quickly moved their attention to the central square. The violent police response paved the way for the naming of the protests as the umbrella movement when protesters used umbrellas thrown over the barricades by supporters to protect themselves against tear-gas attacks.

The forces ranged against the movement were enormous. They not only faced the Hong Kong authorities, themselves backed by the CCP party-state, but the movement was infected by small numbers of Hong Kong nationalist provocateurs. A bigger problem was the opposition of the pro-regime and pro-China Hong Kong Federation of Trade Unions (HKFTU), which tried to derail the political demand for universal suffrage by raising counter-posed economic demands.

Nevertheless, unions representing teachers, transport workers and social workers within the more radical Hong Kong Confederation of Trade Unions (HKCTU) supported the movement in a one-day strike on 24 October. The longevity of the movement stimulated debate – on state power and the nature of the Chinese and Hong Kong systems, for instance – but ultimately the movement reached an impasse and failed to overcome the celebration of spontaneity to develop a strategy for real change against a regime that refused to make concessions. After months of protests the organisers called off the occupations.

The movement had, however, achieved important results. Many young students and workers engaged in direct action for the first time, learned first-hand about police brutality, and felt the potential of mass action. And in demanding the democratic election of the chief executive, the movement challenged the 1997 Basic Law for Hong Kong. These results mean that, as Lam Chi Leung put it, the movement "will have a lasting impact on the democracy movement in China and Hong Kong."[47] Within five years these words were shown to be more than wishful thinking.[48]

In February 2019 a new extradition law between Hong Kong and Taiwan was proposed, with the support of chief executive Carrie Lam. Most people in Hong Kong understood that it would not be limited to Taiwan and that if passed would make extradition to China easier, deepen the trend towards a single judicial system, and allow China's National People's Congress a larger say in Hong Kong politics. Most people also knew that the real target of the law was not the individual businessman accused of killing his girlfriend but the mass of pro-democracy protesters.

Protests against the extradition law were initially peaceful and avoided confrontation with the state. But opposition slowly grew and in June 2 million people, out of a population 7.4 million, demonstrated against the government. Students were again to the fore, but 2019 also saw a wave of unionisation and the creation of over 400 new unions representing hundreds of thousands of members, many affiliated to the non-official HKCTU. This organisation played an important role in the 2019 movement. Many activists who had participated in the 2014 movement understood that organised working-class power would provide a defence against the expected heavy-handed police response to the 2019 protests. When it materialised, some protesters responded in kind.

Lam subsequently apologised for the police violence but stopped short of promising withdrawal of the law. This led to a hardening of demands, particularly from the Students' Unions of Higher Institutions. They made four demands: complete and permanent withdrawal of the bill; retraction of the government's definition of the violence as a "riot"; dropping of all charges against protesters; and an independent commission to investigate claims of police brutality". A fifth demand was later added – universal suffrage in democratic elections for Hong Kong's legislative council and for the chief executive. Eighty percent of Hong Kong residents supported the demands, but the government's refusal to accept them meant protests continued through the summer.

On 4 September Lam announced withdrawal of the bill, and later made minor concessions on community engagement in social policy and the police complaints machinery – adding two new members, widely regarded as stooges, to the complaints committee. But she again refused the wider demands of the movement. The response from protesters was unequivocal: a headline in *The Guardian* read "Hong Kong protesters vow to stay on the streets despite Carrie Lam concession".[49] Having refused an enquiry into police brutality, Lam now increased the level of violence against demonstrators. The following month, frightened by the size and resilience of the movement, the state activated the Emergency Regulations Ordinance, a colonial-era law last used under British rule in 1967. Wearing face masks was now criminalised. A few days later Apple bowed to state pressure and removed an app widely used by protesters, claiming that it broke the law. *The Guardian* reported that "neither the company nor the Hong Kong police were able to say which law".[50]

As in 2014, the protests eventually subsided as a result of police violence and loss of momentum. The authorities took the opportunity to then speed up the process of legal integration between Hong Kong and the People's Republic by imposing a new national security law that came into effect on 30 June 2020. This made four offences — secession, subversion, terrorism and collusion with foreign powers — punishable by life imprisonment, giving the Chinese government the power to repress all dissidence using its own secret police and courts. China's Office for Safeguarding National Security has now been extended to Hong Kong. Where Chinese laws did not, in the main, apply in Hong Kong before 2020, henceforth the PRC's courts can intervene if they consider national security at risk. Freedom of speech and criticism of the state are now treated as crimes. Censorship and monitoring of social media and vetting of school textbooks have been increased. The ban on pro-democracy candidates in Hong Kong elections remains under what Xi refers to as a patriots-only electoral system.

For the time being, Hong Kong protesters had been silenced. They showed a remarkable tenacity, bravery and imagination over many years, but the analysis of the weaknesses of the 2014 movement by Au Loong-yu and Lam Chi Leung applies equally to the 2019-20 protests.[51] Without time to mature and for the conflicting interests of workers and business leaders to condense out, the protests remained at the level of a broad cross-class alliance that subsumed workers' interests within a wider and ultimately fatally divided whole. The students frequently idealised spontaneity and therefore the absence of centralised organisation and coordination. There were divisions between pro- and anti-China perspectives, with parts of big business and the HKFTU siding with Beijing. There was also provocation from right-wing nativist and Hong Kong nationalist opinion that fostered illusions in US democracy, sometimes put their hopes in US intervention, and hindered the spreading of the protests to China and the search for solidarity there (albeit that some protesters sang *The Internationale* to mainland tourists). These weaknesses were multiplied by state repression and the criminalisation of activists and civil society organisations, including labour NGOs that organised solidarity with Chinese strikers in the previous decade.

Under intense pressure from Beijing and the threat of action under the national security law, the Hong Kong Professional Teachers Union, the HKCTU's largest affiliated union, dissolved itself in August 2021.[52] By then the HKCTU's former chair, Carol Ng, and general secretary Lee Cheuk-yan were in prison for their pro-democracy activism, and in September Lee was charged with the more serious offence of inciting subversion of state power. Fearing arrest, HKCTU chief executive

Mung Siu Tat fled abroad, and on 3 October the executive committee of the HKCTU disbanded the organisation. At its height the HKCTU represented 160,000 members in over 90 affiliated unions, but in the following months some of these also disbanded themselves.

Shortly after the decision to disband the HKCTU, former vice-chair Leo Tang wrote that "the relationships forged among workers will not be dissipated by today's decision… The struggles in every industry and workplace have proved that 'where there is oppression, there is resistance'. We believe that this will continue to be the case in the future."[53] For now, the Hong Kong labour movement remains cowed, but the conditions that provoked the protests have not changed. The majority still suffer from low wages and long working hours. Gross inequalities persist, notably in housing, where the state derives income by leasing land to private developers but tries to maximise that income by limiting supply. As a result housing costs have increased dramatically – by 250 percent in the decade to 2019 – with severe consequences for living space, domestic stress and mental health.

The anger at economic inequality is reinforced by the erosion of Hong Kong's special status and the closure of the political space available for progress and protest. But the closure has not completely extinguished the increased interest in Marxism among small groups of young people that has developed in the last decade. Meanwhile, the identification of Hong Kongers as Chinese has fallen rapidly: according to a University of Hong Kong survey it was 20 percent in 1997, at the height of the hand-over celebrations, rising to a third by 2006, but by 2019 it had fallen to 12 percent (and close to zero among young adults).[54] The Left should note this without celebration, for identification as Hong Konger rather than Chinese can strengthen the pro-US right, but should celebrate the failure of China and its Hong Kong puppets to bend popular opinion to its will. The on-going crack-down on pro-democracy campaigners has forced many into exile, while many more have faced trials for sedition and collusion with foreign powers under the national security law. Repression has shored up state power for now, but its scale emphasises the enormity of the crisis of legitimacy facing the regime.

Women and feminist activism

Protests and opposition to Beijing in Tibet, Xinjiang and Hong Kong expose the myth of national unity. The anger of many women reinforces this. In his *Economic and Philosophical Manuscripts* of 1844 Marx argued that women's position in society could be used as a measure of the development of society as a whole. China provides ample evidence to support this argument. The picture is contradictory – there has been some progress and some regression since 1949 – but the overall conclusion is damning.

In traditional, pre-1949 China women's position was one of profound oppression and servitude. Under Mao, although very few women achieved leadership positions women's social position improved in numerous areas as the whole society was mobilised behind the national development project. This challenged a number of traditional practices and for the first time women were legally entitled to work outside the home, gained the right to divorce and to own land. Maternity care improved and as a consequence the number of women and children who died in childbirth decreased. The demand for women's labour increased, including on collective farms and in state industry, albeit that women were concentrated in the lowest paid jobs. But in the post-Mao period women were severely impacted by the mass lay-offs that accompanied the closure of SOEs in the 1990s – women made up 63 percent of those made redundant.[55] The pressure on women in the early period of reforms has persisted, producing a contradictory picture of improvement and regression.

The second-class citizen status of women was reflected in the outcomes of the one-child policy, which was imposed in 1979 at a time of economic weakness and fear that China would be unable to feed a growing population. This policy promised to end the long cycle of pregnancies experienced by many women, but also increased the policing of women's bodies by the state – local officials forced millions of women to terminate their pregnancies and millions of others faced forced sterilisation. Additionally, female infanticide reached about a third of a million per year in the early 1980s. It was traditional for women to move into the husband's family after marriage as weak pension provision created material reasons to value women's unpaid domestic care for the husband's parents in their later years. The resultant preference for male children was reinforced by the one-child policy.

More recently, massive rural-urban migration, and the *hukou* system initially designed to control it, have had contradictory impacts on women. Tens of millions of women, who make up over a third of migrant workers and 43.5 percent of the total Chinese workforce, have been lifted out of rural poverty, but the limited welfare rights for migrants and their children force many to leave their children behind when they migrate.[56] Up to 40 percent of rural children are cared for by either one parent or their grandparents. The attraction of women workers for employers is captured by Lulu Fan: "labour-intensive industries…have a strong preference for female migrant workers since they are believed to be patient, meticulous, docile, and able to handle repetitive and boring work".[57] Nevertheless, the experience of collective factory work has increased their confidence to challenge sexist practices and women have been heavily involved in recent struggles, including the protests in solidarity with Uyghurs in 2022.

Social media have also had a contradictory impact on women. Challenging the sexualisation and demeaning images that reinforce prevailing sexist attitudes, women have used social media to publicise gender inequalities, domestic violence and other oppressive practices and to build support networks when they face official and police indifference or hostility. Women's online activism has met with increased censorship in recent years: feminist and activist social media accounts have been removed from both the WeChat and Weibo cyber messaging services, while phrases such as "anti-sexual harassment" have been censored.

There have been some victories, although they are again contradictory. In 2016 a new law on domestic violence was passed after two decades of campaigning. Even the All-China Women's Federation (ACWF), a state body, has claimed that a quarter of wives have suffered domestic abuse (the official status of this claim suggesting that it is an under-estimate). The law is limited however. Domestic violence, including marital rape, is not a criminal offence and, in line with the official view that the family is the essential bedrock of a "harmonious society", one of the intentions of the law was to "promote family harmony and social stability". The responsibility for this falls heavily on women who, the official *China Daily* has argued, should head-off the temptations their husbands may face by being "soft, understanding and caring", and although the courts have become more willing to grant women restraining orders in recent years divorce is harder to win.[58] Domestic violence has been grounds for divorce since 2001, but threats of violence from husbands should divorce be granted have led courts to force wives to stay in the marriage. As a study by Ethan Michelson of Indiana University argues, "for women seeking relief from abusive husbands, courts are not the solution but rather part of the problem".[59] Xi's own words have reinforced the social prejudice women activists face when he said during a 2018 visit to the ACWF that it should not become an organisation "like they have in other countries for feminists or posh women".[60]

Women in other countries do of course experience not only routine gender oppression but also the gross abuses perpetrated by men like Harvey Weinstein, Jeffrey Epstein and Prince Andrew. When the latter behaviour is exposed China's state media contrast the oppression faced by women in the West with the supposedly better experience of Chinese women. When activists focus attention on China, however, they face censorship and harassment. Shortly after the #MeToo movement gained prominence in the West, "MeToo" and "sexual assault" were listed as sensitive words on social media platforms and many posts relating to them were censored. Weibo then removed the #MeTooinChina hashtag when it began trending. Despite this censorship #MeToo has a Chinese parallel – the #MiTu movement (a phonetic translation of "me too", meaning "rice bunny"). A 2017 survey by the Guangzhou Gender and Sexuality Education Centre found that 70 percent of university students had experienced sexual harassment. The following year #MiTu was launched when Luo Xixi posted on social media an allegation of sexual harassment against her PhD supervisor. The post was viewed millions of times and the supervisor sacked. Within weeks women from over fifty universities made similar claims and public figures in the media and other areas were also outed. Many university professors reacted in solidarity, signing a petition calling for measures against harassment. Under pressure, and fearing that #MiTu activism might become the touchstone for wider protests, the Ministry of Education and state media condemned the harassment of students by lecturers.

Under Covid lockdowns women's position deteriorated and there were widespread reports of increased domestic abuse, mirroring similar experiences in other countries. But the combativity of women did not disappear. In early 2020 new animated cartoon characters were launched on Weibo to promote the Communist Youth League. The campaign focused on a young couple named after extracts from Mao poems – Jiangshan Jiao (Lovely Land)) and her partner Hongqi Man (Abundant or Free-spirited Red Flags).[61] Within hours they were removed after 100,000 comments were posted ridiculing the characters and highlighting gender inequality. Jiangshan Jiao was asked if she was still a virgin, if she received smaller portions than men in the staff canteen, whether the police respond when her husband hits her, whether her value as a bride goes down after she turns thirty, and whether she will be forced to leave school if a teacher harasses her.

Despite the ubiquity and reach of official discourses on gender, the regime of censorship, and the crack-down faced by feminists over the last decade, women's activism chalked up another success during the Covid pandemic. Since 1 January 2021 employers have been required to prevent sexual harassment in the workplace. The #MiTu movement, like #MeToo, has been criticised for its narrow focus (on PhD students in China, the media industry in the West) and for paying little attention to "commonplace sexual harassment in the workplace or that inflicted upon more marginalized social groups, such as those based in rural China or low-income workers".[62] Yet it represented a step forward and provides grounds for optimism. China's #MiTu campaign demonstrated the persistent capacity of "resilient Chinese women battling socially ingrained harassment as well as resistant social and political forces".[63] The contradiction between official ideologies on gender relations, the family and social harmony on the one hand and the lived experiences of women on the other, suggest that this resilience is likely to be an increasingly important component of struggle from below in the coming years.

LGBT+ repression and activism

The official reassertion of traditional family structures and gender relations reinforces the workplace inequality faced by women by promoting their role as providers of privatised caring labour. The conservative drive for "normal" gender relations has become more urgent as the ruling class grapples with China's deepening demographic problem – a shrinking and ageing population and falling birthrate. Women who do not want to marry have been particularly targeted - official media consistently referring to single women as "leftover women" – but LGBT+ people also face oppression as a threat to established patterns of sexual behaviour and, in conservative eyes, social harmony.[64]

In the face of increased oppression millions of LGBT+ people conceal their real selves out of fear of the potential repercussions of identifying as LGBT+. Accurate numbers are therefore difficult to ascertain, but it is estimated that China's LGBT+ community is, at up to 80 million, the largest in the world.[65] There have been some improvements to their legal status in recent decades - homosexuality was decriminalised in 1997 and in 2001 it was removed from the psychiatric disorders listed by the official Chinese Psychiatric Association. But these legal changes are severely limited. Discrimination on the basis of sexual orientation or gender identity is not illegal, same-sex marriage is not recognised and adoption by same-sex couples not allowed. Forced conversion therapy for LGBT+ people is not uncommon and it is reported that young trans people have been incarcerated in re-education camps.[66]

In recent years the state has sought to legitimise the marginalisation of LGBT+ people by warning of the dangers that expressions of non-traditional sexual orientation and gender identity pose for morality, and even for national survival. Speaking to the ACWF in October 2023 Xi Jinping said it was necessary to "cultivate a new culture of marriage and childbearing and strengthen guidance on young people's view on marriage, childbirth and family". The links between Xi's message to women and intensified attacks on the LGBT+ community are clear. China's television regulator, the National Radio and Television Administration, has demanded that broadcasters must "resolutely put an end to sissy men and other abnormal aesthetics".[67] Same-sex relationships are not allowed to be shown in the media, and even the rather anodyne US sitcom *Friends* has had scenes depicting lesbian characters excised. In schools and other public bodies education and training about sexual orientation and gender identity is almost entirely absent, and in 2021 the education ministry argued that schools should recruit more gym instructors to prevent the "feminization" of boys and improve their "masculinity power". In recent years the slogan "save our boys" has become commonplace in schools.[68]

Many LGBT+ people took advantage of the safe spaces that were created throughout China in the last twenty-five years by *tongzhi* (comrade – a word used to refer to LGBT+ people in China).[69] But since 2020 these safe spaces, and the events that *tongzhi* groups organised, have been under threat from state pressure. In 2017 new censorship rules were passed that limited social media content concerning "abnormal sexual behaviours". China's most important pride event, ShanghaiPRIDE, was suspended without explanation by the organisers in August 2020. In 2021, the founder of LGBT Rights Advocacy China was arrested and only released after being coerced into closing the organisation. Many LGBT+ activist social media accounts were also closed in 2021. In May 2023 China's best-known LGBT+ centre, in Beijing, closed after fifteen years of providing support and advice to LGBT+ people, as well as acting as "an incubator for a young generation of queer activists".[70] Even the distribution of rainbow flags on university campuses has led to disciplinary measures against students.[71]

Stephanie Yingyi Wang's comments on the pressures facing LGBT+ men captures the oppressive atmosphere for the wider LGBT+ movement in Xi's China:

> …with the revival of national heteronormative and paternal discourses about the imperative to build the Chinese Dream and enhance Modernity with Chinese Characteristics, gay male sexualities and homosociality have once again been stigmatised as deviant and responsible for the 'boy crisis' – that is, the corruption of hegemonic masculinity with effeminate gender expressions that threaten the dominant heterosexual nuclear family form – and therefore a national crisis.[72]

Despite systemic repression and surveillance, LGBT+ activism is remarkably resilient, albeit that it is currently localised and on a small scale. Social media sites are routinely used to discuss issues of concern to LGBT+ people, to express solidarity with those facing direct discrimination, and to make demands for sexual and gender rights, particularly the right to same-sex marriage. Thousands of same-sex couples use the *Hunli* (wedding) WeChat app to marry online. Each June Pride month is marked by in-person events.

Popular support for LGBT+ rights has not been destroyed by repression and extends beyond the numbers of *tongzhi* activists. Young people in particular are less conformist and less likely to swallow dominant narratives and can learn from struggles in other countries through the internet. Meanwhile, LGBT+ activists themselves are not simply retreating in the face of repression and marginalisation, but taking stock in order to "re-establish their connection to the movement and recharge to envision alternative strategies for the future".[73]

Environmental protests[74]

In 2017 Xi Jinping spoke of developing China into an "ecological civilisation". Speaking at the UN in September 2020, Xi announced that China would peak carbon emissions before 2030 and reach net-zero emissions before 2060 via a combination of reduced emissions and steps towards carbon capture. Claims are not the same as outcomes and Xi's promise to go from peak to zero in three decades diverges wildly from the plans of other large polluters and will be difficult to meet.[75]

China's economic expansion has accelerated the damage to China's air, land and inland waters that began under Mao's industrialisation programme. This had a peculiar irrationality which belied the claim that the economy was rationally planned. Mao's drive for economic self-reliance meant that every local authority constructed a heavy industrial base, leading to huge inefficiency, duplication and waste. This continues, and the environmentally destructive consequences cannot easily be checked for fear of choking off the growth that legitimacy depends on. Studies have shown that 92 percent of Chinese people breathed air classed as unhealthy under World Health Organisation standards in 2014.[76] Toxic waste has poisoned rivers and lakes and just as Xi was talking about

China becoming an ecological civilisation, a 2017 report by Green-peace East Asia showed that millions of people, living in over half China's provinces, use water that is unsafe and contains high concentrations of harmful chemicals that produce clusters of enormous increases in cancers and other illnesses.[77] Even the most advanced cities suffer - 85 percent of the river water in Shanghai was unsafe for human contact. Agricultural land is also poisoned. In 2013 Beijing admitted that "an area the size of Belgium was 'too toxic to farm' because of the overapplication of fertilizers and pesticides, irrigation with toxic industrial wastewater, and the dumping of toxic waste on fields".[78] In 2014 a national soil survey showed that 19 percent of farmland was polluted by chemicals and toxic heavy metals – cadmium and arsenic were found in 40 percent of the affected land.

The waste and duplication of the Mao era continues in the form of unnecessary infrastructure, ghost cities, and the shoddy construction, and often premature collapse, of bridges and buildings. All this uses vast quantities of often poor-quality cement, the production of which has an immense carbon footprint. As Vaclav Smil has pointed out, China used more cement between 2009 and 2011 than the US did in the entire twentieth century.[79]

Electricity production compounds the environmental problems. China accounts for over half of global coal output and despite a long-term trend away from coal as a percentage of China's total energy production – from an average of over 70 percent between 1960 and 2010 to 55 percent in 2022 – there was a surge in coal-fired power station construction in 2020, when China built well over half the world's new coal-fired power stations.[80] The environmental consequences include respiratory diseases, including cancers, while lax environmental standards more generally entail the blighting, and loss, of lives in industrial deaths and accidents on a colossal scale. China is also the world's largest oil importer and consumer – from 2000 to 2014 it accounted for 47 percent of the total growth of world oil consumption and from 1992-2021 its oil use rose from 2.5 to 15.4 million barrels per day (mbd). Taken together, fossil fuels contributed 82 percent to China's total energy output in 2022.[81]

To the extent that emissions are controlled, part of the explanation lies in the fact that China has around sixty nuclear power stations.

The expansion of renewables also contributes, but these are insecure – when China's carbon emissions rose by 3 percent in 2017, part of the explanation was that as a result of climate change rivers were less able to drive the mass of hydro-electric dams that have been built in recent decades, using huge quantities of environmentally destructive cement and at great human cost to displaced people.[82]

In recent years authoritarian state power has been mobilised to address some of the environmental problems that capitalism, and China's own form of capitalism in particular, generates. After Jiu-Liang Wang's 2016 documentary *Plastic China* revealed the scale of the problem of waste plastic, as well as the extreme poverty and alienation of those working in recycling and incineration, waste plastic imports were banned in 2018. Beijing claimed the ban would "protect China's environmental interests and people's health", but failed to explain why three-quarters of the world's plastic waste imports went to China before 2018. This pollution by proxy should be highlighted whenever the West attacks China on environmental issues, but also applies to China, whose recycling firms responded to the ban by diverting plastic recycling to other Asian countries, notably Malaysia.[83]

Frequent chemical plant explosions, such as that in Jiangsu province in March 2019 that killed seventy-eight and injured 566, have produced an equally inadequate response. Since 2008 these plants have been progressively relocated to chemical industry parks away from residential areas. This merely moves the problem sideways. In 2017 a Greenpeace analysis of one such park found 226 different chemicals, three-quarters of which were not covered by hazardous-chemical regulations and among which were carcinogenic and illegal chemicals.[84] The problem was also moved sideways in another way. The official enquiry into the Jiangsu explosion argued that the problem was not under-regulation or collusion between local authorities and business, but that the local authority had applied national law with "insufficient rigour". Urban air pollution has also been reduced by relocating industry away from urban areas.

Some supporters of Chinese "socialism" are seduced by the speed with which it has adopted green technologies such as solar panel and electric vehicle manufacture.[85] They present China as in the vanguard of action on climate change and an ecologically more sustainable alternative to Western capitalism, arguing that although China's carbon emissions are now twice those of the US, its per capita emissions are far lower as its population is five times larger. This is a selective use of the evidence. The "lakes of toxic effluent…sulphuric acid poisoning and 'cancer villages'" that Chinese state capitalism has produced will take decades to clean.[86] Meanwhile, China's carbon emissions are similar to those of the next five largest emitters combined – the US, India, Russia, Japan and Germany – yet its population is only two-thirds of their combined total and its national income only one-third as large. China's emissions per capita and per unit of output are colossal.

State action on the environment is less to do with Xi's "ecological civilisation" than with the needs of China's employers for healthy workers and the state's drive to dominate in strategically important technology sectors. In any case, even an increase in renewables' proportion of total energy production following the 2005 Renewable Energy Law (and later revisions) has not stopped carbon emissions increasing. Solar and wind farms are often built to attract central funds to strengthen local authorities in their competition with each other and in their inter-dependent dealings with local private capitals. Their output is frequently not connected to the national grid and local party leaders and managers of SOEs prefer the reliability of local coal-fired power production.[87] Even in Xinjiang, China's wind-power capital, most electricity comes from coal-fired power stations, and far from replacing fossil fuels with renewables China is "building more capacity of *both*."[88]

To say that China is not *en route* to becoming an "ecological civilisation" but is an ecological disaster that over seven decades has caused immense environmental damage does not imply favouring the West. Echoing Richard Smith, no form of capitalism "can brake the drive to global environmental and ecological collapse".[89] All capitalisms have their national particularities, but all are trapped in an international system of competition – both economic and geopolitical – that provides the structural framework that shapes the actions of corporations and state managers. A comparative analysis of the features of Chinese and Western capitalisms as isolated systems fails to explain China's environmental destruction as rooted in their mutual relationships within an integrated, but differentiated, whole. China's party-state played a part, and "attracted many of the world's dirtiest and least sustainable industries [which] – facing increasingly tough environmental restrictions at home in the US and Europe – relocated to China after 1980".[90] But if the party-state had its own interests in enabling environmental degradation by Western firms and allowing them to produce emissions from their Chinese bases, ordinary Chinese people have conflicting interests.

Environmental protests and activism have mushroomed in the last two decades. Guillaume Pitron has highlighted the growth in environmental activism since around 2005.[91] Environmental NGOs sometimes received official encouragement before Xi's crackdown as they filled gaps in public provision and engaged in popular activities, such as local clean-up campaigns. The first environmental NGO, Friends of Nature in Beijing, appeared in 1993. The French embassy in Beijing counted nine environmental NGOs in 1994 but 8,000 two decades later. But these NGO activities were heavily constrained and when the party-state began to fear that they might bring regime legitimacy into question and challenge the growth strategy upon which it is based, the control and repression of green activists and groups intensified. Like other NGOs, under the 2017 NGO law environmental groups must be sponsored by an official institution to register as a bona fide NGO, foreign funding has been outlawed, and foreign NGOs must now gain accreditation not from the environment ministry but the ministry of public security. Like Islam, environmentalism has become a matter of national security under Xi.

China's environmental activists have protested before and the memory of those protests has not been eradicated. Continued protest will be needed because the environmental consequences of the party-state's growth strategy remain largely negative. For all the improvements in urban air quality as a result of industrial relocation, a 2019 survey of Chinese workers from the Hong Kong based *Globalization Monitor* revealed that environmental devastation and pollution remain very serious: 20 percent experienced air that was polluted or very polluted where they lived; 34 percent did not have access to clean water; 27 percent reported air pollution at work; many reported negative consequences for their health from these polluted environments.[92] Meanwhile, as growth slows, the resources available to the national and local authorities for environmental programmes are dwindling. In the long-term, Chinese environmentalists, like their counterparts across the globe, will need to develop strategies for linking with powerful workers movements if they are to successfully address the impending environmental catastrophe. As Smith argues, to do this effectively demands that polluting capitalist industry and the political regimes under which it has thrived be replaced by "an ecosocialist world economy based on public ownership of most means of production, democratically planned production for need, and democratic management of the economy and society".[93] China's workers' contribution to this would amount to a new Chinese revolution. The prospects for this are currently remote, but building action today in preparation for radical change tomorrow is a far better place to start than sowing illusions in the Chinese state to build an ecological civilisation.

Conclusion

The inequalities and oppressions of capitalist society generate permanent discontent, but it is frequently internalised as mute acceptance and fatalistic resignation. It occasionally finds expression in individual acts of defiance, especially where people feel isolated and lack confidence in the solidarity of others. Predicting when popular anger will explode in collective protest is an inexact science, usually conducted with hindsight. Nor do we know which of the myriad potential detonators (gender violence, environmental catastrophe, self-immolation, a tower-block fire, a strike, etc) will provide the spark. The Tiananmen Square protests of 1989, like the 2011 Arab Spring, came seemingly from nowhere and rocked the foundations of CCP power. Protester unity began to break down divisions fostered by the state between Han and Uyghur, male and female, young and old. When workers joined the movement the state-capitalist ruling class feared a more fundamental threat to its power. It responded with state savagery.

The state combined that coercion with moves towards winning mass consent. It sought to transform university campuses from sites of opposition into support structures for the regime. The recruitment of students from poorer backgrounds declined, and the student body could look forward to a middle-class life in the developing consumer society. Access to critical ideas was limited by the close monitoring of campus life and repression of discussion.

The repression unleashed on movements and activists since 2015 is not on the scale of the Tiananmen massacre, but demonstrates the regime's fear of a repeat detonation of social anger. The discontent of environmentalists, women and feminists, workers, students, oppressed national minorities, the elderly etc has not been erased by repression. Nor can repression return China to its earlier growth path or relieve the unemployment that millions of young people face. "Graduation equals unemployment" (the two words have a common character in Mandarin) had become a common saying even before the impact of the Covid pandemic, but in May 2023 youth unemployment reached 21 percent.[94]

Declining growth rates will put pressure on the costs of both the state and capital, which will inevitably try to pass them down to workers. Pressure on wages, environment devastation, even weaker welfare, are likely. Repression, harassment and imprisonment of activists will continue. An increase in the retirement age, which unites the entire working population, is likely.

For now, repression has closed down the networks that were built before 2015, with many of those not arrested retreating into hiding. As we saw in the last chapter, working-class activity and confidence have declined and the crackdown has had its desired effect. But, as the events described in this chapter, and the Covid lockdown protests of late 2022 illustrate, protests can emerge apparently out of nowhere. Indeed, despite years of repression and the tightening of national security in the region, the protests in solidarity with the victims of the Urumqi fire in November 2022 spread to Hong Kong.

To maximise their impact these struggles need to be clear that the CCP is the enemy and that divisions along national lines, between men and women etc, only serve the interests of Beijing. Beijing has often successfully deflected criticism onto local authorities, which are made to take the blame for state failings. Nevertheless, as the protests in late 2022 showed, the idea that the Chinese people face a monolithic party-state power, with an all-powerful Xi Jinping at its head, is misplaced.

Chapter 6
China, the US and inter-imperialist rivalry

Introduction

The claim that China is non-capitalist (either socialist or a transitional society) does not stand up to scrutiny. The corollary – that since imperialism is rooted in capitalist social relations China is not imperialist – is also mistaken, for China's state-capitalism is embedded in a global system of inter-imperialist rivalry that imposes its competitive logic on all its parts. Chinese imperialism is not equivalent, or identical, to that of the world's foremost imperialist state, the US, but the hallmark of imperialism is stamped on all of China's external relations, with the Global South, the BRICS economies, with the countries linked to China via the Belt and Road Initiative, and with the advanced Western countries. As China's power has increased so too have the tensions with the US and its Western allies, particularly in Asia, where rivalry over Taiwan and in the South China Sea present dangerous flashpoints. The developing global tensions between China and the West are the focus of this chapter.

A system of inter-imperialist rivalry

The theory of inter-imperialist rivalry developed by Lenin and Nikolai Bukharin during the First World War built upon the classical Marxist understanding of capitalism's economic dynamics in the context of changes to capitalism as it develops.[1] The key changes identified by Lenin included the massive concentration of capital and the rise of monopolies, the growth of finance capital as a result of the merging of bank and industrial capital, and the export of capital alongside that of commodities. Domestic over-accumulation, diminishing opportunities for profitable domestic investment, and demands for new sources of surplus value creation and raw materials were intensifying the pressures on capital to spread across the globe – pressures Marx and Engels had noted in the *Communist Manifesto*. One of the features identified by Lenin, the territorial division of the world between the major capitalist powers, drew attention to the geopolitics of imperialism. This was underlined by Bukharin, who noted that as "national systems" of capitalism became more systematically organised, states assumed a greater economic role. The increasing inter-penetration of politics and economics at the national level was dialectically related to the international sphere – as forms of state capitalism developed, the competition between giant capitals was accompanied by military and political competition between states. Inter-imperialist rivalry is rooted in capitalist competition.

Marxism is not a religion or a set of fossilised slogans to be mechanically applied, but a living, dynamic tradition that is modified as the world it seeks to explain and transform changes. Lenin and Bukharin are not above criticism and later Marxists have noted that not every imperialist state, at every stage of its development, demonstrates each item in Lenin's list.[2] Nor is the relative significance of these items explored by Lenin. Nevertheless, taken as elements of the imperialist system as a whole rather than as illustrations of, say, British imperialism in every historical conjuncture of the last 150 years, "these features are still relevant now", as Carchedi and Roberts put it.[3] But their elaboration of the Marxist theory of imperialism suffers from economism and an under-developed appreciation of the geopolitics of imperialism.

Focusing on "the economy's determining features" and arguing that "military, political and ideological power are determined by superior technology and economic power", Carchedi and Roberts define imperialism as the "long-term net appropriation of surplus value by the high-technology imperialist countries [they later refer more accurately to "capitals in the imperialist countries"] from the low-technology dominated countries".[4] Of the four mechanisms they identify by which value flows from poor to rich countries – currency seigniorage (see chapter two), changes in exchange rates, income flows from capital investments, and unequal exchange (UE) through trade – their main focus is on UE.

Carchedi and Roberts are critical of the best-known approach to UE, that developed in Arghiri Emmanuel's 1972 book *Unequal*

Exchange: a study of the imperialism of trade. Emmanuel argued that the "chief mechanism" of UE was high wages in the rich countries due to the strength and organisation of their labour movements. This led to higher prices for manufactured exports at the expense of producers of raw materials and foodstuffs in the Global South. Many Marxists have pointed out that high wages are the result and not the cause of higher productivity in the advanced countries. They also criticise the conclusions Emmanuel drew from his analysis: exploitation operates between countries, rather than classes, and imperialist country workers and capitalists have a common interest in the exploitation of the workers of the Global South.

Carchedi and Roberts provide a Marxist version of UE focused on the transfer of surplus value between capitals with a lower organic composition of capital (OCC), often in the Global South, to those with higher OCC, largely located in the richer countries. This takes us into the complex areas of Marx's transformation problem, the capture by advanced capitals of part of the surplus value produced by less advanced capitals, and the tendential equalisation of profit rates. This complexity is magnified when international transfers are considered and there is no generally accepted Marxist solution to this complexity. But while we can accept, as far as it is developed, Carchedi and Roberts' argument that UE plays a part in imperialist value transfers, we need to go further.[5] For by excessive focus on this mechanism, and neglect of similar transfers to China at the expense of others in the Global South, Carchedi and Roberts conclude that China is a victim of UE and, as one of the "dominated countries", not imperialist.[6]

Their data also allows them to adopt a relatively benign view of China on the issue of the export of capital. While recognising that "China has been expanding its investments abroad", Carchedi and Roberts argue that "the size of foreign direct investment is still small".[7] This may be true as far as the historical stock of FDI is concerned, but this should not obscure the significance and scale of recent flows: UNCTAD figures place China in the top three sources of outward FDI in every year from 2012 to 2022.[8] But criticism of the arguments of Carchedi and Roberts, and others on the Left, that China is not imperialist do not rest simply on different interpretations of data.

Alex Callinicos has developed the analysis of Lenin and Bukharin in an attempt to locate geopolitical rivalry more centrally in the Marxist theory of imperialism.[9] He argues that the logic of state interests/geostrategy on the one hand intersects with the logic of capitalist competitive accumulation on the other, neither being reducible to the other. A useful way to think about these separate logics is to contrast capitals' shorter-term time-horizons (product cycles, annual dividends and shareholder meetings etc) with state managers' longer-term commitment to systemic reproduction and to enhancing the competitive position of the national economy.[10] These should be seen not as fundamentally separate logics but as differentiated moments in the wider totality of the global capitalist system. Within that system the largest capitals search globally for investment opportunities and sources of specific inputs and markets. This impels them towards various forms of cooperation with overseas capitals, but capitals retain their densest organisation and networks of influence at a national level. It also impels them towards conflicts with other capitals and with the states with which these other capitals have constructed their own dense networks of cooperation and mutual interest. In this scenario, inter-state competition is as much an aspect of imperialism as the specific economic mechanisms of value transfers.

Using such a holistic view of imperialism leads us to broadly agree with the Hong Kong Marxist Au Loong-yu that China is "an emerging imperialist country, a very strong regional power with a global reach. It possesses the intention and potential to dominate lesser countries but has not yet consolidated its position in the world".[11] The key features in Lenin's theory of imperialism are highly developed in China, whose imperial expansion to become the major challenger to the United States' leading position in the global system is driven by the state-capital/party-state nexus that institutionalises the power and interests of the collective (but not monolithic) ruling class. China's new-found capacity to project power in pursuit of its economic and geopolitical interests, in Asia and globally, creates the potential for strategic and military conflict with the US and its allies, with whom it is locked in a relationship of inter-imperialist rivalry, albeit that it remains on most measures substantially less powerful.

US and Chinese strategy: conflict tempered by cooperation

In the early 1970s the US ruling class faced a combination of military challenges (Vietnam), political challenges (anti-war protests, the women's movement, the black liberation and anti-racist movements, and the labour movement) and economic challenges (relative decline and competition from its allies). US President Richard Nixon and his national security advisor Henry Kissinger turned towards Mao, hoping that improved US-China relations would pressure the USSR and North Vietnam and allow the US to extricate itself from Vietnam and focus on other challenges.

Mao's foreign policy, meanwhile, combined occasional rhetorical revolutionism with practical conservatism. Where Lenin had placed the young Soviet state at the service of the international working class after 1917, Mao's fundamental goal was defence of the interests of China's state-capitalist rulers, to achieve which he "endeavoured to win foreign ruling classes as allies", particularly among states in the Global South that were the product of anti-imperialist and anti-colonial struggles.[12] In a world of nation-states ruled over by more or less authoritarian ruling classes, the concept of "peaceful coexistence", formulated by Stalin and elaborated by Mao after the Korean War, signified that working-class struggles were matters for the national ruling class concerned. In practice, non-intervention in the politics of other sovereign states, one of the key principles of peaceful coexistence, meant acceptance of prevailing relations and complicity with them.

As the imperialist system changed, the defence of Chinese state-capitalist interests required occasional geostrategic somersaults. In the 1950s the CCP identified the US as the dominant superpower, but as Sino-Soviet relations soured in the 1960s it claimed that the two superpowers now dominated the world. After Sino-Soviet border clashes in 1969 the position changed again: the world was again increasingly dominated by one superpower, but this was now the USSR.[13] Nixon and Kissinger seized on their opportunity and formal diplomatic relations with China were ultimately established in January

1979. Later that month, Deng Xiaoping said that the two were "duty bound to work together [and unite] to place curbs on the polar bear".[14] For now, US rulers' interests dovetailed with those of the reformers around Deng. Foreign investment flooded into China's coastal regions, initially from the Chinese capitalist diaspora across Asia and later from Taiwan, the US and the EU.

By the second half of the 1990s US President Bill Clinton was pushing for China's World Trade Organisation (WTO) entry despite domestic concerns about human rights abuses and potential job losses. China's still heavily state-regulated economy did not fully meet the membership criteria, but the potential benefits made China's entry a gamble worth taking for US strategists. As the US-China Relations Act was passed in 2000, paving the way for membership, Clinton argued it would "open new doors of trade for the US and new hope for change in China".[15] Meanwhile, Chinese premier Zhu Rongji moved against opponents of further reform, arguing in a report to the National People's Congress that "China's economy has reached the point where it cannot further develop without being restructured".[16] China actively embraced WTO membership, albeit at its own pace and after sometimes bitter negotiations with Clinton's team.[17]

When China joined the WTO in December 2001, US geostrategists congratulated themselves on a further defeat for "communism". This was partly ideological triumphalism, but China's economic transformation also promised access to new profit streams for Western capitals facing the profitability crisis that had gripped them since the 1970s. The geostrategic consensus in 2001 was that China posed no significant threat to the West, when its economy was only one-eighth of the size of the US and widely regarded as little more than a low-skill, low-wage final assembly platform for inputs from more advanced economies. Before long, however, US strategists were revising their views and warning of the dangers that China's emergence as a superpower posed.[18]

WTO accession came after three decades in which US-China rivalries occasionally threatened to spark military conflict – over the US bombing of China's embassy in Serbia in 1999 and when China forced down a US spy-plane over Hainan province in 2001 for instance. The common rivalry with the USSR until its collapse in 1989-91 and common commitment to China's economic reform contained the threat, and the overlap of interests continued through the 2007-8 global financial crisis, when China's stimulus package underpinned the weak and debt-driven recovery of the global economy. But such a stimulus would have been inconceivable in earlier decades and underlined the increasing challenge that China now posed to US economic power. Today, US-China relations have become more acrimonious and for US geostrategists China has moved from being a strategic partner to a global rival.[19]

Reform had seen exports increase from $10 billion in 1978 to $253 billion in 2000 and WTO membership now boosted them further, to $1,500 billion at the start of the financial crisis in 2008 and $3,590 billion in 2021.[20] The trade infrastructure expanded at a similar rate: in 2000 just one of the world's top twenty container ports by volume was Chinese and one more had Chinese investment – by 2015 eleven were Chinese and a further four had Chinese investment.[21] A considerable proportion of China's manufactured exports were made by Western capitals and as late as 2005, 70 percent of profits in electronics and information technology went to foreign transnationals, but the surge in China-based production served both Western and Chinese ruling-class interests.[22] It generated profits for Western capital and cheap imports that cushioned wage repression under neoliberalism. For China it enhanced national development and provided a basis for moves towards more advanced manufacturing and greater competitiveness.

Economic growth also emboldened China's rulers. As reform progressed, Deng had begun to denounce US "hegemonism" and allied this to a "good neighbour" foreign policy intended to extend China's influence among US allies in Asia. Relations were improved with ASEAN, despite its anti-Communist Cold War origins, and at the end of the 1990s China joined Japan and South Korea in the ASEAN+3 talks, contributing to deeper regional economic integration. It also helped the regional recovery from the 1997 Asian financial crisis, supporting the renminbi to moderate competitive pressures between Asian currencies and joining regional arrangements to protect those threatened by financial speculation. Yet, by 2010 a new assertiveness in foreign policy was evident – Foreign Minister Yang Jiechi told his ASEAN counterparts that "China is a big country and other countries are small countries and that is just a fact."[23]

US military failure in Iraq reinforced China's assertiveness while enlarging the geopolitical space for it to operate in, and US geostrategists became increasingly concerned about the limits of Washington's power. They and their allies began to warn of "a global power shift in the making", that US-China military contest "will define the 21st century", and that China was now an "inevitable superpower" that would soon dominate the world.[24] The West's dependence on China's response to the 2008 crisis reinforced their fears, in response to which Barack Obama announced the pivot of 60 percent of US military power to Asia in 2011. His 2015 State of the Union address showed the wider US goal: "China wants to write the rules for the world's fastest-growing region... We should write those rules".[25] Simultaneously, Secretary of State Hillary Clinton launched a drive to reinforce US military alliances in Asia, prompting *Financial Times* journalist Geoff Dyer to argue that the US was trying to bandwagon the rest of Asia against China.[26] The Trans-Pacific Partnership (TPP), proposed under Obama in 2013, was the economic component of this containment strategy, a vehicle to tie non-China Asia more closely to the US economy.

The confidence of China's rulers continued to grow however, illustrated in 2013 by Xi's "dream" that the "great revival of the Chinese nation" would "let it stand more firmly and powerfully among all nations around the world".[27] For Beijing University's Ye Zicheng, this revival requires that China becomes a world power, a core component of which is the military modernisation of recent decades.[28] In particular, according to China's State Oceanic Administration, building naval power is the "historic task for the 21st century", enabling the global projection of China's power consistent with the Chinese navy's 2015 strategy of "far seas protection". Senior defence strategist Liu Mingfu has written of an aim to displace the US as the "number one in the world", while Yuan Peng, president of the official China Institutes of Contemporary International Relations think-tank believes that China should prepare for armed confrontation with the US.[29] China's main focus is on regional hegemony, but the dynamics of inter-imperialist rivalry allied to the resource needs of its economy are generating global military tension with the West.

Tension co-exists with persistent economic interdependence, the two combining in Xi's 2013 announcement of the BRI, a massive infrastructure development programme designed to enhance China's global economic reach. In response, a working group of the cross-party US geostrategic think-tank the Council on Foreign Relations (CFR), comprising US defence and national security big-wigs such as Richard Haass and neoconservative Paul Wolfowitz, produced the 2015 *Revising US Grand Strategy Towards China* report. For Laurence Shoup, the CFR is "the think tank of monopoly finance capital" and its report presents "an aggressively imperialist view" of US interests.[30] It recommended various measures to contain China and preserve US power: excluding China from new Asian trade arrangements; controlling technology exports that might assist China's military modernisation; reinforcing US strategic alliances with its Asia-Pacific allies; and upgrading US armed forces to enhance power projection in Asia. Containment of the USSR, the report insisted, was not a defensive strategy but "an instrument to achieve victory in the Cold War".[31] These measures have underpinned US geostrategy ever since.

Trump's 2017 National Security Strategy announced that the US should rethink policies that "assumed that engagement with rivals and their inclusion in international institutions and global commerce would turn them into benign actors and trustworthy partners. For the most part, this premise has turned out to be false".[32] The 2018 defence bill, co-sponsored by a Republican and Democrat and overwhelmingly supported by both parties, declared that "long-term strategic competition with China is a principal priority for the United States that requires the integration of multiple elements of national power, including diplomatic, economic, intelligence, law enforcement, and military elements".[33] The military contribution to this strategic rethink indicated the urgency of the task: in 2017 General Joseph Dunford, chairman of the Joint Chiefs of Staff, told the Senate Armed Services Committee that "China probably poses the greatest threat to our nation by about 2025." Biden shares these views and there is an almost complete consensus in the US ruling class that China should be contained within the framework of Western rules, that Western firms should retain (or gain) access to Chinese markets, and that China's advance across a range of technologies, and associated military modernisation, should be constrained by a combination of economic and military means.

Trump's trade war with China after 2018 flowed from this long-term strategic perspective, represented by Trade Secretary Peter Navarro, co-author of the book *Death by China*. Although it was suspended in January 2020 – the US reduced tariffs and China promised to increase imports from the US and improve protection of US intellectual property rights – the relationship has deteriorated further and taken a sharp military and geostrategic turn.[34] Western military alliances in Asia are being strengthened and pressure applied in the strategically important high-tech sector. The rhetoric of rivalry, reminiscent of the Cold War, was especially marked under Trump, yet Biden's 2020 campaign insisted that Trump was soft on China and that without US global leadership "either someone else will take the United States' place, but not in a way that advances our interests and values, or no one will, and chaos will ensue".[35] Aggressive protectionism in high-tech sectors, intensified denial of advanced micro-processor technology to China, and moves to rebuild US military alliances characterise Biden's presidency.

US-China high-tech rivalry and economic decoupling

Trump presented his tariffs as a reaction to the huge US trade deficit with China, but when China promised increased US imports his complaints shifted to wider issues, including the state's role in the Chinese economy.[36] The US and EU have resisted China's claims to the status as a market economy, which under WTO rules strengthens access to export markets and makes it more difficult to refer China to the WTO's trade disputes mechanism. The trade imbalance provided a justification for US actions, but the real issues were far deeper. As Singapore's ex-UN ambassador Kishore Mahbubani argued in 2019, the West is trying to "thwart China's long-term, state-led industrial plan, Made in China 2025, designed to make China a global competitor in advanced manufacturing" and strategically important technologies of the future.[37] Chinese success in these areas would enhance its capacity to challenge US leadership and intensify the economic vulnerability that has concerned the US ruling class for decades.[38]

Between 2018 and 2020 the US applied huge pressure on Huawei, the world's largest telecoms equipment provider, justifying its actions by claiming links between Huawei and the Chinese security state.[39] Huawei executive Meng Wanzhou was arrested in Canada charged with breaking anti-Iran sanctions, the US passed legislation prohibiting the supply of components to Huawei, and US allies came under intense US pressure to exclude Huawei from their new 5G networks. Competition within the West delayed the achievement of US goals: Britain resisted for six months while US firms re-routed sales via overseas subsidiaries, allowing Huawei to increase purchases of US-made components from $11 to $19 billion between 2019 and 2020. Nevertheless, Britain capitulated in mid-2020 and the US mobilised its extra-territorial power to extend the sales ban to any firm using US technology.[40]

US pressure on China is partly driven by commercial interests. Western dominance over the production of faster micro-processors provides its capitals with advantages in growth areas such as AI, product design, medical research, and 3D-modelling. Sanctions and tariffs increase China's production costs and encourage multinationals to diversify supply chains and relocate production outside China. The dominant US firms in the data economy (Google, Amazon, Facebook and Apple (GAFA)) are largely excluded from China, the world's largest and fastest growing market, and cannot use the personal data of 800 million web-connected Chinese people to shape their consumer spending.[41] This partly explains why the US and GAFA promote free data circulation (storage need not be in the countries where people live), which weakens foreign states' ability to regulate storage and GAFA activities. They want to sweep up global data, transfer it "wherever they want" and store it "on servers wherever they want, most of which are in the United States".[42]

For its part, the Chinese ruling class's drive to boost the domestic economy reflects its concerns over competitiveness, high-tech vulnerabilities and the long-term danger of an accelerating decoupling of the Western and Chinese economies. But the ferocity and pace of US actions in the tech-war took it by surprise, prompting Xi to use a neoliberal argument in praise of free-trade at the Boao Forum for Asia in 2021: protectionism and decoupling run "counter to the law of economics and market principles".[43] He went further at the 2022 World Economic Forum: to support "economic globalisation" the world "should uphold true multilateralism…remove barriers, not erect walls… open up, not close off…seek integration, not decoupling".[44] Protection of Western firms provides part of the explanation for US pressure and the routine US accusations that China breaks WTO rules, by providing subsidised loans from state banks, for example.[45] But the tech-war is also firmly rooted in inter-imperialist military and geostrategic rivalry.

In April 2023 the *Financial Times* reported on a leaked CIA claim that China is developing the technological capability to disable or take control of Western satellites upon which military strategy and conflict operations depend.[46] Strategic considerations explain US hyperactivity on high-tech matters in recent years, including a raft of new laws giving the national security state greater control over inward FDI, high-tech exports and outward FDI, and to boost state support for high-tech research and manufacturing. The 2022 Creating Helpful Incentives to Produce Semiconductors (CHIPS) and Science Act, for instance, promised $280 billion of state support. The purpose of Biden's revved-up industrial policy was captured by Democrat senator Charles Schumer, co-sponsor of the 2021 Innovation and Competition Act: it "lays the foundation for another century of American leadership". Biden added his support: "we are in a competition to win the 21st century, and the starting gun has gone off". A 2021 executive order criminalised dealings with Chinese firms linked to its military-industrial complex, and in August 2023 Biden signed an executive order tightening restrictions on US high-tech investment in China.[47]

Evidence of the consequences of this pressure on China is multiplying. FDI into China suffered a rapid decline from the second half of 2022, magnifying a longer-term slowdown from the start of the pandemic in 2020.[48] Nicholas Lardy, specialist on China's economy, noted in late-2023 that Western firms are not reinvesting profits and "for the first time ever" are selling-off "existing investments to Chinese companies and repatriating the funds".[49] The figures are complicated by the mixing of long-term real FDI and short-term portfolio investment, but the trend away from China, especially in high-tech, is clear. In August 2023 Bloomberg reported that FDI into China fell 89 percent in the year following the second quarter of 2022 to just $5billion.

US pressure on China also involves its allies. Under a January 2023 joint agreement with Japan and the Netherlands, who are key producers of capital goods for semiconductor manufacture, restrictions on exports of cutting-edge chipmaking equipment to China were imposed. The Taiwan Semiconductor Manufacturing Company (TSMC), which produces 90 percent of the world's highest specification chips, is building two new plants in the US, the $40 billion cost subsidised by up to $15 billion of state aid under the CHIPS act. Both Taiwan and Japan have increased state support for firms looking to disengage from China.[50]

For *Financial Times* journalist Rana Foroohar high-tech decoupling is a "fait accompli", and other business commentators argue that in the long term global production could split into China-centred and Western-centred supply chains.[51] These views are reinforced by the fall in China's US-bound FDI to its lowest level since 2009.[52] But, while there is no doubt that US geostrategists would like to inflict a devastating blow to China's economy, any attempt to force the pace beyond the strategically important high-tech sector risks increasing intra-western economic tensions. In 2021 the US Chamber of Commerce China Centre argued that wider decoupling would have serious economic consequences for the US and encourage companies from other Western countries to replace US firms in China.[53] For Chris Miller, author of the best-seller *Chip Wars*, Biden faces the possibly insurmountable challenge of reassuring its allies that it can "strike a balance between security considerations and economic considerations".[54]

Decoupling is a real, but currently limited, tendency. China's state managers have created dependencies between Chinese and foreign firms, in part to dissuade the latter from applying excessive pressure on China and to encourage their home states to moderate their criticism of China. Those dependencies – including provision of skilled and relatively low-paid workers, infrastructures, and integrated supply networks – cannot easily be replicated in the short term. The difficulties facing Apple's new Indian operations illustrate this: Apple plans to produce 20 percent of its iPhones there, but in 2023 the *Financial Times* reported that the defect rate for phone casings produced by the Indian company Tata was 50 percent, against a company target of zero.[55] Meanwhile, although Samsung has moved production of its mobile phones to cheaper bases in Asia, it is, along with TSMC, expanding semiconductor production in China. The Chinese ruling class remains committed to, in Xi's words, increasing "international production chains' dependence on China".[56]

To that end China has attracted many scientists from Silicon Valley and elsewhere in recent years, including via its *Qianren Jihua* (Thousand Talents) scheme and provides cutting-edge research facilities in micro-processing, artificial intelligence, biopharmacy, robotics, electric cars, gene sequencing and green technology. The West is also dependent on China for strategically important rare earth minerals, vital inputs for the electronics, electric vehicles, wind turbines, and defence industries.[57] The US aims to reduce this dependency and has restarted production in the Mountain Pass mine in California that closed in 2002 under cost pressures from China. The US Department of Defense has funded new refining capacity, and the US has pressured Australia and Canada to develop rare earth mining (at huge ecological cost). But Western dependency is unlikely to decline rapidly: the West still imports about 90 percent of its rare earths from China.

The financial sector reinforces the view that decoupling will not be straightforward. Even under Trump the US and China became more financially coupled: inflows into China totalled $620 billion and many share issues by Chinese firms were launched on US exchanges. By the end of 2019, US investors owned over $800 billion of Chinese assets, double the 2016 figure.[58] In 2020 alone foreign firms moved $200 billion into China's capital markets, while foreign ownership of stocks and bonds jumped by 50 and 28 percent respectively.[59]

The impact of US moves to decouple the Chinese and Western economies is also likely to be limited by intra-western rivalries. One hundred thousand foreign companies operated in China in 2020, when China was still the top destination for global FDI, much of it geared to production for export. FDI into China also set new records in 2021 and 2022 as Western capitals remained committed to their Chinese operations. The European Chamber of Commerce reports that its members derive healthy profits from their business in China; a 2021 report on European firms found that five times as many were moving into China as moving out, and in 2022 overwhelming majorities of German firms planned increased investment in China. US firms can no more easily stand aside from competitive capital accumulation than China can exit the system of inter-imperialist rivalry: despite pressures for decoupling from the US, Craig Allen, president of the US-China Business Council, said in 2022 that the overwhelming majority of members had not moved any production or any part of their supply chain out of China or slowed investment in China in the previous twelve months.[60]

These countervailing tendencies suggest that a fundamental decoupling is not taking place and that the emergence of China-centric and West-centric economic blocs is in its infancy.[61] Nevertheless, the geostrategic context in which China operates has become more difficult in the last decade, including in Xi's flagship project, the Belt and Road Initiative.

The Belt and Road Initiative and the Global South

Departing from Deng's 1990 advice, drawn from Sun Tzu's *Art of War,* that China's rulers should "bide your time and hide your capabilities", Xi argued that "it is time for us to take centre stage in the world". The BRI is at the heart of this drive for global influence. Originally called the "Silk Road Economic Belt" and "21st Century Maritime Silk Road" and sometimes romanticised as the "New Silk Road", the BRI was launched in Kazakhstan in 2013. Its intention, Xi claimed, was to deepen economic ties and cooperation and enhance development in the Eurasian region. Now global in its scope, the BRI is not a single coherent project but a portfolio of projects in trade and transport infrastructures, energy and power, and digital and fibre-optic telecommunications. Estimates vary but nearly $1 trillion was spent under the BRI in 147 countries by 2022.[62] If successful, it would challenge US power and influence in regions that have been central to US global strategy since 1945.

As China has become the major trading partner of over one hundred countries and an increasingly important foreign investor, its rulers have made grandiose claims for the BRI and promoted a "win-win" narrative on China's relations with the countries of the Global South. They present the bilateral deals between China and partner countries under the BRI as a benign counterweight to the US-led rules-based global economic order and a contribution to a new developmentalist agenda for the Global South. As Xi declared at the CCP's 19th National Congress in 2017, China offers an alternative for countries seeking "to speed up their development while preserving their independence".[63]

Against those on the Left who accept the CCP's "win-win" rhetoric, Sean Ledwith argues that China is bound by the logic of capitalism and imperialism and that, whatever Xi's intentions, "the laws of motion of world capitalism, as Lenin and Bukharin argued many decades ago, ultimately operate outside the remit of politicians".[64] While not subscribing to "win-win" arguments, Carchedi and Roberts reject the view that China is imperialist. They write that China does not invest abroad "because of 'excess capital' or even because the rate of profit in state and capitalist enterprises has been falling". They then write that:

> many authors claim that these investments and loans to poorer countries are exploitative and designed to put weaker countries into a 'debt trap'. Yet the evidence of the most detailed studies shows no such thing and that the terms of China's loan and investment deals are not iniquitous and are not draconian as they often are with loans from the imperialist bloc.[65]

To support this they refer, without comment, to a major September 2021 study on the AidData website.[66] Yet this contradicts Carchedi and Roberts' claims. On the "excess capital" argument the report's executive summary says that China's international lending reflects "domestic challenges – specifically, an oversupply of foreign currency, high levels of industrial overproduction…".[67] On their claims for non-exploitative etc loans, the report says "Chinese state-owned lenders act as yield-maximizing surrogates of the state. Consequently, most of Beijing's overseas lending is provided on less generous terms than loans from OECD-DAC [OECD's "Development Assistance Committee"] and multilateral creditors". The report also refers to China's use of debt "to establish a dominant position in the international development finance market" and to the conditions attached to many Chinse loans, such that China is "contractually obligating its overseas borrowers to source project inputs (like steel and cement) from China". Finally, the report refers to Beijing's preference for the collateralisation of loans, thereby ensuring that the energy, natural resources, etc whose exploitation the lending facilitates pass into China's hands in the event of non-payment.

Like earlier European imperialism's claims about the "white man's burden" and its "civilising mission", official claims for the BRI invert reality. A key component of the BRI is the export of capital. In China SOEs in particular face low profit rates and, as He Yafei, vice-minister of the Overseas Chinese Affairs Office of the State Council, let slip in January 2014 the BRI's purpose "is to export overcapacity".[68] This also improves access to overseas markets and sources of raw materials and energy while fostering relationships that might enhance China's global geopolitical position. Specific projects may generate "win-win" outcomes, but Au Loong-yu argues that the Left should recognise that the BRI "is driven by the logic of profit and the geopolitical interests of the CCP's monolithic regime".[69] The evidence supports his argument.

China's FDI and loans to the Global South expanded dramatically after 2000. The total value of China's loans to Latin America between 2005 and 2020 was $137 billion, more than the World Bank, US-dominated Inter-American Development Bank and the CAF-Development Bank of Latin America combined.[70] In 2011 the total stock of China's FDI in Africa was $16 billion, compared to $57 billion for the US, but by 2018 had risen to $46 billion against the US's $48 billion.[71] Loans to Africa tell a similar story: between 2000 and 2015 China's Eximbank lent $63 billion (spread across all African countries) while the US Eximbank loaned $1.7 billion (to just 5 countries). BRI loans are distributed by two state-owned banks and, like Western loans to the Global South, come with conditions, notably that Chinese firms should deliver the funded projects. Figures from the Center for Strategic and International Studies on transport infrastructure projects show that in Chinese-funded projects 89 percent use Chinese firms and that the 7.6 percent of local content compares poorly with the 41 percent in multilateral development bank projects.[72]

There's a great deal of hypocrisy in Western criticism of China's "debt diplomacy" and the conditions attached to its lending. The West's historical loans to Africa, and its current lending, are far greater than China's and for over half of African countries facing debt distress China accounts for less than 15 percent of public debt. Nevertheless, China is an increasingly important factor in Africa's debt problems. Zambia offers a good illustration.

Zambia increased its mineral exports by 500 percent early in the twenty-first century, but under IMF pressure the transnationals that quarried the minerals were exempt from tax, thereby depriving Zambia of billions in tax revenue. The Zambian state turned to China, now its major bilateral lender: official data shows that one-third of Zambia's external debt is held by China but the unofficial figure may be closer to two-thirds.[73] The interest rate on World Bank loans to countries that do not qualify for the preferential rates offered to the poorest countries is generally 2 percent above market rates, but the China Development Bank charged a 4.5 percent premium on its loan for Zambia's Mansa-Luwingu Road Project.[74] A significant proportion of Chinese investment is in Zambia's main export earner, the copper industry, where unions complain that Chinese firms breach International Labour Organisation standards.

The fate of Hambantota port in Sri Lanka provides another example of debt diplomacy. Its failure to meet the loan repayment schedule led ultimately to the partially state-owned China Merchants Port Holdings Company Limited acquiring the port on a 99-year lease, reminiscent of the concessions that European imperialism once demanded of China. Chinese loans were not the prime cause of Sri Lanka's debt problems – only 10 percent of its external debt is owed to China – but Bukharin's comment on London's loans to Russia applies equally to China's relations with Zambia and Sri Lanka:

part of the surplus value expressing the relation that exists between the English worker and the English capitalist is transferred to the municipal government of the Russian city; the latter, in paying interest, gives away part of the surplus value received by the bourgeoisie of that city and expressing the production relations existing between the Russian worker and the Russian capitalist.[75]

Criticism that the BRI overwhelmingly prioritises Chinese interests is widespread. In Africa, although there have been recent increases in the use of African content in Chinese firms' supply chains and some technology transfer, there have been many complaints that Chinese FDI uses imported Chinese labour, even for unskilled work, feeds Chinese workers with imported Chinese food, and fails to create local jobs.[76] Kenya's Mombasa-Nairobi railway, built with great fanfare by China, cost three times more per kilometre than the global average and four times the original estimate. Its earnings cover barely half the repayment costs as Chinese imports regularly make up 90 percent of its cargo and empty trains return to Mombasa. In Laos and Cambodia the use of Chinese inputs weakens the development potential of Chinese projects: only one-third of jobs from Chinese FDI in Laos go to Laotians, while Cambodia's Chinese-owned textile factories use imported materials.[77] In Latin America there have been protests demanding greater input from local firms. Malaysia has cancelled $22 billion worth of BRI projects after complaints of inflated prices. Pakistan has received over $50 billion in BRI loans, the world's highest figure, focused on the China-Pakistan Economic Corridor (CPEC), a vast scheme of pipelines, railways, highways and power plants from Xinjiang to the port of Gwadar. But two-thirds of its projects remain incomplete, the Karakoram highway to Gwadar carries very little traffic, and Pakistan has complained about the limited opportunities for Pakistani firms and workers. Gwadar port is under-utilised, Pakistan has been unable to service its loans, and a Chinese firm has taken over the running of the port.

The serious environmental impacts of Chinese BRI projects are also widely criticised by activists and protesters. In Ecuador, China's firms engaged in the oil industry have left a trail of environmental devastation while also violating the rights and disrupting the established patterns of social relations of indigenous peoples. In Gambia, China combined debt cancellation and investment in agriculture and fisheries in return for fishing rights and the establishment of fish processing plants. Local people complain of huge pollution and the illegal dumping of waste, while over-fishing has decimated fish stocks in a country where half the population depends on fish for half its protein intake.[78] The processing plants produce fish protein that is shipped to China to feed Tilapia that are then sold in Gambia, increasing the pressure on local producers.

Trade along the Belt and Road between China and the Global South has mushroomed: with Latin America from $12 billion in 2000 to $445 billion in 2021; with Africa from $10 billion in 2000 to $251 billion in 2021.[79] But this trade replicates traditional North-South patterns and perpetuates the South's dependence on primary product exports, imports of higher-value manufactures, and structural weakness in the global economy.[80] Brazil, one of Latin America's most industrialised countries, illustrates the problem: between 2010 and 2015, 84 percent of its exports to China were primary products, while 97 percent of its imports from China were manufactures which undercut Brazilian production and so harmed Brazil's prospects for deeper industrial development.[81]

Trade with China in the commodities boom in the early years of the twenty-first century helped finance the "Pink Tide" governments' modest increases in welfare spending and income redistribution. But when the boom ended in 2015-16 Latin American growth slowed and the exchange rates of local currencies fell, sometimes by 25 percent. Even under the Workers' Party governments of Lula and Dilma Rousseff, the commodities boom perpetuated industrial weakness and consolidated Brazil's specialisation in primary production and the centrality of extractivist capital to its political-economy.[82] In Argentina, when officials criticised Chinese exports for undercutting local production and imposed anti-dumping measures, China blocked imports of Argentinian soy oil, a processed product, but not the soybeans that its own agribusiness processes. Chinese pressure has contributed to the reprimarisation of Argentina's economy.[83] The picture is similar in Africa. Chinese imports minerals and metals – in some years up to 75 percent of imports by value is constituted by oil and petroleum – and exports processed foods, consumer goods and low or medium technology manufactures that have flooded markets in some countries and undercut local production.[84] After the global commodity price collapse the value of African exports to China fell by 40 percent and the exchange rates of African currencies collapsed.

Beijing's "win-win" propaganda obscures the class relations at the heart of its relations with the Global South. It also obscures the wider context of the relative marginalisation of large parts of the Global South. Africa again offers an illustration. The $83 billion of FDI inflows to Africa in 2021 were dwarfed by the $619 billion going to the developing economies of Asia, and the $647 billion to the developed economies.[85] Africa receives only about 5 percent of global FDI annually, and only 3 percent of China's. And, while US capital has been in retreat, in 2018 Dutch ($79 billion), French ($53 billion) and UK ($49 billion) transnational capitals all held larger stocks of FDI in Africa than China.[86] China is joining, rather than replacing, older imperialisms in the exploitation of Africa, which remains marginal to the dominant investment flows in the global economy. There is no new Beijing consensus emerging from shared interests between the ruling classes of the Global South. As Wei Liang has argued:

> China does not share the interests that many developing countries have in delaying full external economic liberalisation. Indeed, China instead shares with the US and the EU a desire for bold trade liberalisation in developing economies, allowing easier market access to Chinese exports.[87]

That China is part of the imperialist problem rather than its solution is underlined by its role in the politics of countries in the Global South. South African academic-activist Patrick Bond argues that China has been "even more predatory than Western corporations" in Africa and provides "support to local dictators".[88] Mugabe's regime in Zimbabwe benefitted from huge Chinese FDI in the mining sector, including in the Anjin Corporation, a joint venture between China and the

Zimbabwean military. In return for access to Zimbabwe's diamonds, Anjin gifted $98 million to build a new defence college for Mugabe's army.[89] China also reportedly financed Mugabe's hiring of the Israeli firm Nikuv International Projects to fix the 2013 election in his favour, while Chinese firms have been accused, as elsewhere, of violating Zimbabwean workers' rights.

The BRI is rapidly reaching the limits imposed by global capitalism and inter-imperialist rivalry. Between 2010 and 2020 China rose from almost nowhere to become the largest official creditor, lending more to the poorer countries than all other countries and international financial institutions combined. Today, the growing mass of non-performing BRI loans and the sharp deterioration in recipients' payment positions suggest that the BRI "has become a financial millstone for Beijing and its biggest banks".[90] According to the AidData report mentioned above, there have been "more project suspensions and cancellations during the BRI era" than in the pre-BRI era as recipient governments respond to concerns about over-pricing by China, planning delays and cost over-runs. Many states have demanded a renegotiation of their BRI-related debts, three-quarters of which are at commercial rates, reduced the scale of projects, demanded the inclusion of technology transfer and use of local content clauses, and complained about the conditions attached to China's lending. The BRI has provoked local opposition, and the entire project is floundering: BRI lending collapsed to $4 billion in 2019, from a peak of $75 billion in 2016.[91] Its problems are unlikely to end soon, raising doubts over China's capacity to extend its geopolitical influence on the back of economic inter-dependencies.

The US and its allies have responded to BRI infrastructure spending with a number of initiatives. In 2018 the Better Utilisation of Investment Leading to Development (BUILD) act promoted US loans to the private sector in the Global South. In 2019 the US established the International Development Finance Corporation to support infrastructure projects via low interest rate loans, albeit that its $60 billion funding is puny relative to the BRI. But as US-China tensions rise and the strategic turn towards tighter containment of China gathers pace, the scale and scope of US initiatives are expanding. In June 2021 the

G7 announced the Build Back Better World (B3W) initiative, revised the following year as the "Partnership for Global Infrastructure and Investment", which pledged US$600 billion by 2027 for infrastructure projects in developing countries. China is under mounting pressure to respond to Western pressures on the BRI. The recent expansion of the BRICS group is part of its response.

China and the BRICS

In 2001 Jim O'Neill, then head of global economic research at the investment bank Goldman Sachs, wrote a paper, "The world needs better economic BRICs", that identified Brazil, Russia, India and China as promising investment opportunities for Goldman Sachs' clients. The choice was somewhat arbitrary, but O'Neill argued that the four BRICs contained 25 percent of world territory and 40 percent of its population and predicted that all would be in the top five of the world's national economies by 2050. Despite the absence of common geostrategic interests, beyond the general demand for greater influence and representation for the Global South in the IFIs (World Bank, IMF, WTO) and global economy, in 2006 the four began to cooperate more closely and in 2009 the BRIC group was formed. South Africa joined in 2010, transforming the BRIC into BRICS.

The BRICS group is not a coherent bloc. In 2020 Chinese and Indian troops fought in minor border skirmishes; India leans increasingly westward and is more aligned with the US than at any time in its independent history; Brazilian capitals compete with those from South Africa in southern Africa; and, fearing a dilution of their own influence, China and Russia have resisted the claims of the other three BRICS countries to permanent membership of the UN Security Council. Nevertheless, the rivalries within the group have not prevented cooperation to increase the BRICS' influence within the world system. Western suspicion towards the BRICS, China in particular, suggest for some leftist commentators that the BRICS' promotion of south-south cooperation represents a form of anti-imperialism or, more minimally, a democratising trend in the global system. The evidence does not support this view.

In the postwar period the states of the Global South demanded greater global influence and an international economic framework that promoted development. These demands were amplified by the end of colonial rule in Africa, the Caribbean and Asia and by the 1970s the Global South was demanding a New International Economic Order (NIEO), including political regulation of the global economy, codes of conduct for transnational corporations, and commodity price agreements to benefit raw material producing countries. By the end of the decade the West had taken advantage of the global economic crisis and debt crisis facing much of the Global South to subvert these demands and promote their opposite – deregulated global markets. Codes of conduct for capital never materialised, but codes of good governance and market friendliness were imposed on the world's weaker states. The BRICS periodically complain that the IFIs disregard the interests of the Global South, but they simultaneously promote the policies of these institutions. Far from challenging established power and policies, the BRICS promote a pro-business agenda and "lubricate, legitimise and extend neoliberal political economy" within their own economies and regions.[92] South-south cooperation now means little more than increased opportunities for transnationals from the Global South in the Global South. The BRICS group is not anti-imperialist: it "aims not to overturn tables at the proverbial temple, but to collaborate in holding them up".[93]

The BRICS are not simply transmission belts for neoliberalism however. The concept of sub-imperialism developed by the Brazilian Marxist Ruy Mauro Marini in the 1960s and 1970s allows for a more dialectical understanding of the BRICS' relationship to the wider world system.[94] Marini sought to situate the growing importance of regional powers in the overall framework of US imperialism as its slow relative decline forced it to enlist the support of subordinate, but regionally powerful, allies. The key sub-imperialisms at that time included Argentina, Brazil, South Africa, Saudi Arabia, Israel, Iran, and Iraq. These were not mere agents of the US but had a relationship of what Marini called "antagonistic cooperation" with the dominant imperialism, sharing its overall project of protecting the capitalist world system while also promoting their own interests, sometimes in opposition to those of the US. China and Russia are not dependent in the same way as the other BRICS countries and cannot be described as sub-imperialist, and for these others the balance between antagonism and cooperation is not constant. Nevertheless, the concept of sub-imperialism is useful in highlighting that all the BRICS countries negotiate and manage their insertion into the inter-imperialist system, balancing between support for and subtle subversion of neoliberalism as they protect their own interests and those of their major companies.

China in particular has benefitted enormously from substantial adherence to the rules of the Washington Consensus and IFI membership to strengthen its position in global trade and production. But it has simultaneously challenged those rules by protecting Chinese firms, and channelling resources to state-owned banks and SOEs, particularly in what state managers identify as strategically important sectors. Their activities are geared towards production for profit in global and domestic markets, but the protection of the beneficiaries of state support from short-term commercial criteria allows them to adopt long-term geostrategic and developmental perspectives in line with Chinese state interests. Their contribution to China's development and growing power has enabled it to expand its influence and become the major challenge to US power and Western pre-eminence. There may not be an emergent Beijing Consensus around a more statised growth model across the Global South that is gradually replacing the Washington Consensus, as some have suggested, but there is resistance and challenge within the prevailing inter-imperialist system. The growth of the BRICS and of their regional influence, particularly of China, is deepening global friction and antagonisms.

The launch of the BRICS' New Development Bank (NDB) in 2014 illustrates the combination of antagonism and cooperation designed to secure systemic reproduction. The NDB initially attracted criticism from some Western strategists and commentators as a threat, but the World Bank and IMF ultimately supported it as an adjunct to their own operations. Meanwhile, there are fears in the Global South that its subordination to the interests of the five BRICS states, particularly China, means its lending will perpetuate the Global South's concentration on energy and low technology primary exports. But if the BRICS group does not represent a systematic challenge to neoliberalism, lacks geopolitical coherence, perpetuates the dependency of much of the Global South and is dominated by China, it is far from insignificant.[95]

The BRICS group comprises important centres of production and capital accumulation and states with substantial regional influence, and could develop into a more integrated grouping. Although there is only a remote possibility that it might eventually form a geopolitical bloc like NATO/the West, Western imperialism could face greater difficulties in its dealings with members and face varying degrees of exclusion from strategically important minerals and other inputs as well as marginalisation from strategic decision making. Its significance is underlined by the forty-odd expressions of interest in joining the BRICS from across the Global South over the last decade and the announcement at the August 2023 BRICS summit of six new members – Saudi Arabia, Iran, Ethiopia, Egypt, Argentina and the United Arab Emirates (UAE).[96]

The new BRICS+ group highlights the shifting hierarchies of power and changing geopolitical patterns of a dynamic world system. Comparing the new members with the sub-imperialisms listed above reveals the danger facing the West of a long-term decline in its global influence. Iran, a key US ally before the 1978 revolution, has switched sides; Saudi Arabia and Egypt, both long-term US allies, have moved towards greater contestation of US interests, even without fully endorsing China's geostrategic interests. That four new members are key players in the Middle East region reinforces the challenge to US influence that was already apparent when a China-brokered rapprochement between Iran and Saudi Arabia, whose rivalry had destabilised the region for decades, was announced in March 2023. Both countries' officials claimed that "deteriorating relations with the United States was one of the main reasons for their shift in policy".[97] The West's problems were further reinforced in late-2023 by Israel's war on Gaza. Russia was the main beneficiary from the BRICS group: it bolstered its relations with Iran (sponsor of Hamas) in order to secure the supply of Iranian drones for its Ukraine offensive, and with the Arab world (notably the UAE and Saudi Arabia) and retreated from its twenty-year modus vivendi with Israel. Widespread condemnation of Israel and the US, Israel's main sponsor, in the Global South also encouraged a Russian diplomatic offensive there.

China's relations with the Global South explored above are likely to prohibit a full consolidation of its influence in the form of a strategic alliance, while in the medium term Western power resources (military, financial, etc) are likely to allow it to claw back influence. Even so, BRICS expansion is likely to enhance China's global power and provide, as is surely the intention, insurance against possible further economic decoupling from the West. Decoupling, although limited (see above), is a symptom of an intensified China-US rivalry that is nowhere more intense than in China's backyard.

US-China Rivalry in Asia

China's deepening influence in its immediate neighbourhood proceeded relatively smoothly in the first decade of the twenty-first century. The "good neighbour" strategy led to solidaristic actions after the Asian crisis, the ASEAN+3 arrangements tied the rest of Asia more closely to China's economy, and territorial disputes with neighbours were either shelved or resolved. But by 2010, recognising that its neighbours were more dependent on China than vice versa, China had become more assertive. The 2010s saw increased tensions in the South China Sea, including a conflict with the Philippines over territorial claims.[98] When the latter won a ruling from the International Maritime Organisation, China simply rejected it.

China's Asian influence was boosted in 2016 when the China-led Asian Infrastructure Investment Bank (AIIB) was established despite US objections and efforts by the Obama government to stop its allies from joining. This project reflected Asian unease at IMF mismanagement of the 1997-8 Asian crisis, including US rejection of Japan's proposed Asian Monetary Fund as a threat to the IMF, over which it exercises an informal veto due to the weighting of votes. US failures over the AIIB prompted former Treasury Secretary Lawrence Summers to argue that it might represent "the moment the United States lost its role as the underwriter of the global economic system".[99] Although the AIIB's capital base of $100 billion was fully half that of the World Bank, Summers' claim was an over-statement:

the World Bank and IMF both work with the AIIB, including as co-financers of some projects, and recognise it as a compliment to the global financial institutions. But it highlighted the concerns of many US geostrategists over China's increasing influence.[100] These concerns deepened in 2017 when the newly elected Trump withdrew the US from the TPP, which excluded China and was designed to link the eleven non-US signatories, who together with the US represented 40 percent of world GDP, more closely with the US economy. Tariffs between the signatories were due to end by 2025 and the TPP's rules of origin limited tariff-free trade to goods manufactured fully in member economies or using components from other members. Clauses on labour and environmental standards and SOEs were also directed at China. Trump's US withdrawal under his America First agenda was based on a calculation that the size of the US market and its military power provided adequate leverage over the TPP signatories and that existing bilateral agreements provided a better defence of US interests than being tied down in a rules-based multilateralism.

TPP's 2020 replacement, the fifteen-member Regional Comprehensive Economic Partnership (RCEP), reinforced US fears about China's importance for Asian regional economic integration. The RCEP does not include the US but is the world's largest-ever free trade agreement, covering 30 percent of the world's population and GDP, and includes ASEAN's ten members, China, Japan, South Korea, Australia, and New Zealand. Nor does it involve the sorts of commitments that the TPP included – on labour standards, the environment and state ownership, for instance – that have created difficulties for China's trade negotiators in the past. It is, however, little more than a multilateral codification of existing bilateral trade agreements, involves modest tariff reductions and is only expected to add 0.2-0.4 percent to regional output.[101] Although it presents no threat to the Washington consensus – Premier Li Keqiang described it as a "victory of multilateralism and free trade" – the RCEP underlines that China's neighbours will not be easily prised from its economic embrace. But the economic interdependence of the rest of Asia with China, far from obliterating rivalry or diminishing regional fears of China's power, raises them to a higher level.[102]

Alongside interdependence a dangerous intensification of military rivalry is underway in Asia.

Chinese troop numbers have halved to 2 million over the last twenty-five years, largely due to a redirection of spending to advanced weapons and communications systems. A key modernisation concerns aircraft carriers, an important vehicle for global power projection. Between 2012 and 2022 China launched its first three carriers, a fourth is planned and two more are under consideration. The power-projection capabilities of this fleet are enhanced by China's first overseas naval base, in Djibouti on the Horn of Africa. China's military modernisation provides a pretext for Western military specialists to warn the world about Chinese expansionism. What is the evidence?

In the last fifteen years China has been engaged in a massive militarisation of the South China Sea, including by building new installations on the numerous reefs and islets in the 90 percent of the sea that it claims as its own territorial waters.[103] But wider Western claims distort reality. China's first overseas base compares to the 800 the US military have (200 in Japan and South Korea combined). Against China's fleet of up to six aircraft carriers (commissioned, under construction or planned) the US has thirty-seven. Adding those of its allies takes the figure to sixty-eight. The same disparities exist in total arms spending: according to the Stockholm International Peace Research Institute (SIPRI), China's rose from $20 billion in 1989 to $293 billion in 2021, but the US total for 2021 was $801 billion in 2021.[104] The US remains capable of military power projection on a vastly greater scale than China, while its allies' spending tips the balance further in its favour. A third of global arms sales in the first two decades of the twenty-first century came from the US while China averaged just 4 percent. SIPRI's latest figures, for 2018-2022, show that NATO countries accounted for two-thirds of global arms sales (the US figure is 40 percent) and China just 5.2 percent.[105]

The US's global network of military bases form what Bruce Cummings calls an "archipelago of empire", into which the US is determined to tie non-China Asia. It has stoked Asian concerns to reinforce its military presence in the region since Obama's 2011 pivot. Military support for long-established regional allies, like Australia and Japan (where the US has 55,000 troops), has increased. In 2017 the Terminal High Altitude Area Defence (THAAD) system was sited in South Korea (which has the world's sixth largest army and 28,000 US troops stationed there), ostensibly focused on North Korea but almost certainly also directed at China. Taiwan has also received increased aid ($18 billion under Trump and over $3 billion under Biden by mid-2023). There have been hundreds of joint naval operations involving the Japan-based US Seventh Fleet and allied navies in the seas around China since 2011 to demonstrate US capacity to contain China's naval power.[106]

US claims about Chinese expansionism are a weapon of mass deception designed to obscure the reality of US and NATO expansion. The US is deepening and expanding its military alliances and cooperation across Asia. The Quadrilateral Security Dialogue (QUAD), launched by the US, Australia, Japan and India in 2007, soon fell into abeyance but was resurrected in 2017. The US Secretaries of State and Defence, Antony Blinken and Lloyd Austin, have spoken of enlarging the QUAD by including South Korea and other Asian allies, as well as NATO states such as France and Britain. NATO is also likely to expand its influence in Asia: leaders from Australia, Japan, New Zealand and South Korea participated at a NATO summit for the first time in June 2022. The end-of-summit statement said that China was a "challenge to our interests, security and values". US NATO allies (Britain, France, Germany, the Netherlands and Canada) have all sent warships to the South China Sea since 2021. The Australia-UK-US alliance, AUKUS, was established in 2021 to increase military cooperation in a range of high-tech areas, including electronic warfare and AI, and will also provide support for Australia's nuclear submarine programme.[107]

Against the increasing numbers of states arranged against it, China's only security alliance is the Shanghai Cooperation Organisation (SCO), involving China, Russia, the Central Asian states, Pakistan and India, which is moving closer to the US. But this is not a conventional military alliance or mutual defence pact, but a grouping of states whose ruling classes share an interest in combatting potential religious radicalism. In military matters China is largely isolated. The US aims to keep it isolated. Its Indo-Pacific strategy aims "not to change the PRC, but to shape the strategic environment in which it operates, building a balance of influence in the world that is maximally favourable to the United States, allies and partners, and the interests and values we share".[108] In practice this means that for all that US military power on a global scale is vastly superior to China's, its focus in the short-to-medium term is on China's capacity to challenge the US in Asia, and in particular in the seas around China. Here, a key military hot spot is Taiwan.

History provides rationalisations for both the incorporation of Taiwan into China and its independence. Before the victory of the Qing over the Ming dynasty in 1644, Formosa (as Taiwan was then called) was an unimportant island largely populated by indigenous Austronesian peoples, who today comprise around 2 percent of the population, the other 98 percent being Han Chinese. Ming forces fled to Taiwan, intending to use it as a base to re-take China, but after their defeat in 1684 the Qing dynasty incorporated Taiwan into China, where it remained despite regular rebellions of both indigenous people and settlers until 1895 when it was ceded to Japan after the Sino-Japan war. After Japan's defeat in 1945, Taiwan returned to Chinese control, but GMD rule provoked a major rebellion, albeit to secure autonomy within China, in 1947. The GMD invaded and brutally crushed the rebellion. In 1949 over 1 million GMD troops, functionaries, and supporters decamped to Taiwan after their defeat in the civil war and they dominated politics and state for the next fifty years. Their descendants represent approximately 15 percent of today's population but are disproportionately represented in senior state positions. Aside from the nostalgic hankerings of many "mainlanders" (the GMD arrivistes' descendants), the psychological ties of most Taiwanese with China have weakened over centuries.

Taiwan-China relations were further complicated after 1949 by wider international relations. During the Cold War the GMD regime was dependent on US economic aid and military guarantees. In 1955 the two signed a mutual defence pact and Taiwan received

$5.6 billion in US aid during the Cold War (the whole of Africa received just $7 billion).[109] Taiwan's role as a pawn in the US strategy to contain "communism" had one major benefit for the island: inclusion in the US's Asian security zone contributed to its economic miracle in the 1950s and 1960s and its emergence as one of the Asian Tiger economies. But, as in chess, geopolitical pawns may be surrendered for tactical gain. In 1971, as Nixon and Kissinger pursued improved relations with China, Taiwan was expelled from the UN, which recognized Beijing instead. In 1979 the US broke diplomatic relations with Taiwan and has subsequently accepted in practice Beijing's "one China" policy (which states that the "renegade province" of Taiwan is part of China) without formally endorsing Chinese sovereignty over Taiwan. US military aid continued but was substantially reduced. Today, only a dozen states have diplomatic relations with Taiwan.

Since 1949 the status quo position has been that China will not seek unification so long as Taiwan does not declare independence. This allowed Taiwan to live a semi-sovereign existence (with a separate political system, currency, armed forces, etc) under unofficial US protection and, in the post-Mao reform era, produced mutual benefits from trade and investment. Taiwanese capital invested in China on a huge scale after 1990, becoming the largest overseas investor by 2000. Total Taiwanese FDI in China is around $200 billion, China's headline export, the Apple iPhone, is manufactured by the Taiwanese company Foxconn that employs a million Chinese workers, and a million Taiwanese people live in China. Taiwanese students are encouraged by low fees to study at Chinese universities, and Taiwanese firms receive incentives and tax-breaks to establish business operations in China. But increased economic ties have not moderated military tensions, in part by contributing to China's economic rise and military modernisation. As a result, Taiwanese capital is a key player in the intensifying high-tech and military rivalry between the West and China. Encouraged by the pro-independence Democratic People's Party government's "New Southbound Policy" adopted in 2016, Taiwanese capital has begun reorienting on other Asian countries. If decoupling does occur it will be a long-drawn-out process: the stock of Taiwan's overseas FDI has declined from a high point of 62 percent of the Taiwanese total in 2014 but had only fallen to 53 percent by 2022.[110] But that decline is a Taiwanese expression of the tougher US stance on Taiwan.

US geostrategy has been moving against China for a decade and in 2021 the CFR reported that Taiwan is "becoming the most dangerous flash point in the world for a possible war" between the US and China.[111] High-level contacts between Taiwan and the US have increased as the US deepens its support for Taiwan as a bulwark against China's growing military power in Asia. Trump's phone conversation with Taiwanese president Tsai Ing-wen in 2017 was the first between the two countries' leaders since before 1979. On Biden's fourth day in office, the US declared its unwavering commitment to Taiwan. US speaker Nancy Pelosi visited Taiwan in August 2022, and in April 2023 Tsai visited US House of Representatives speaker Kevin McCarthy. These contacts provoked fury in China, and on each occasion China responded with demonstrations of its military might. Immediately after China's April exercises ended, the US started its largest ever joint exercises with the Philippines, involving 18,000 troops.

The US shift on Taiwan dovetails with its increasing military engagement in the region (AUKUS, NATO involvement, etc, see above). It has long adopted a "strategic ambiguity" over Taiwan, keeping China guessing about whether it would defend Taiwan militarily in the event of conflict across the Taiwan Strait, but in May 2022 Biden became the first US president to declare US military support for Taiwan in the event of a Chinese invasion. The US routinely condemns Chinese incursions into Taiwanese airspace, but US incursions are on a colossal scale: in 2020 there were over ten per day in the first half of the year.[112] If China did invade Taiwan, a US failure to ditch any remaining ambiguity and respond militarily would constitute a huge strategic defeat and weaken its dominance of its global military allies.

Despite increased US support for Taiwan and China's increasing bellicosity, neither a Taiwanese declaration of independence nor an adventurist Chinese invasion seem likely in the immediate future.

But the US military and geostrategic elites have taken advantage of Russia's surprise invasion of Ukraine in 2022 to warn of possible parallels with Chinese moves against Taiwan. These warnings are designed to corral the rest of the West behind US leadership and restore its centrality to global geopolitics.[113] Conversely, Beijing fears that NATO's expansion in Europe and arming of Ukraine may embolden it to provide additional military support for Taiwan. Should Western military pressure on China intensify, Xi has warned that "no one should underestimate the resolve, the will, and the ability of the Chinese people to defend their national sovereignty and territorial integrity".[114] The danger of military miscalculations is higher than at any time since China joined the WTO in 2001.[115]

A new Cold War?

Capitalism's dynamic nature, rooted in competition, generates new products and production processes (and therefore changes in the strategic importance of particular inputs) and new centres of capital accumulation. Inter-imperialist rivalry is similarly dynamic: changes in the relative power of major imperialist states impact on their capacities to shape the economic and strategic environment facing others and therefore on their global influence. Rivalry generates a permanent preparation for war and a permanent danger of miscalculation and adventurist attacks, but it does not produce a permanent economic and geopolitical free-for-all or permanent war. The balance between conflict and cooperation is not fixed, and in the era of globalisation capitalist planning bodies like the World Economic Forum and the IFIs indicate the common interests of the world's dominant capitalist classes in, for example, opening up and structurally adjusting the economies and states of the Global South. Rivalry is the permanent backdrop to cooperation, however, forcing states to develop strategies for managing their relations with others.[116] The US-China relationship is an asymmetrical inter-imperialist rivalry.

As the world's foremost capitalist power, the US is subject to what international relations scholar Doug Stokes calls "dual national and transnational logics": it promotes both US capitalist interests and the reproduction of the capitalist world system, which requires that rivalry be accompanied by cooperation.[117] During the Cold War, US power moderated rivalry between its weaker allies. It traded hegemonic concessions (access to the US market, military aid and security guarantees, etc) in return for its allies' commitments to anti-communism, arms purchases from the US, market access for US capital, and measures to support seigniorage (using the dollar in trade settlements and holding dollar-denominated assets). The US is still the dominant, but not unchallenged, power in the IFIs and the scale of US power still exercises a gravitational pull on the rest of the world, the BRICS+ states included. But as its relative decline grinds slowly on, it remains reliant on its allies to contain China's rise. Does that US-led containment mean that we are in a new Cold War, as some claim?

The West's military expansion, moves towards decoupling, and pressures on Chinese companies have a whiff of cold war, but the analogy falls in a number of key respects. China has no military buffer zone along the lines of the USSR's East European empire. It has no equivalent of what Hung calls the "dollar-security nexus", and while BRICS expansion reinforces Beijing's global influence, the enlarged group does not constitute a strategic alliance of the sort that Washington has built.[118] There are no spheres of influence that each superpower largely refrains from overt interference in. There is no clash of universalist ideologies (freedom and democracy versus communism) with the capacity to mobilise millions of supporters worldwide and through the prism of which everything (politics, economics, art and culture, sport, etc) was viewed in the Cold War. China cannot count on the support of sizeable Communist Parties in key Western countries and the Global South. There are no proxy wars in which the two superpowers arm the different sides but from which they stand formally aloof. And as we have seen, in many respects China, along with the other BRICS, broadly upholds the Washington Consensus even while subverting it at the margins. Nor is there a sharp East-West economic separation: China and the West share a common dependency on the relatively integrated world economy. Decoupling may slowly erode this, but for now the two sides are deeply interdependent.

The phrase "new Cold War" may be journalistic and academic shorthand for the intensification of conflict, but US and Western strategists use it for a more menacing purpose.[119] In the Second Cold War, Reagan's rhetoric about the "evil empire" was used to restore US leadership of the West in the face of relative economic decline and after the defeat in Vietnam.[120] Today, the US promotes a Cold War narrative to limit allies' pursuit of their own interests in relations with China, encourage its military and technological isolation, and corral allies under its leadership. One component of the narrative, and a pretext for the extension of US power in Asia and Europe, is that an emergent China-Russia axis threatens Western interests. The potential parallels between Russia's invasion of Ukraine in February 2022 and Chinese moves against Taiwan reinforced this narrative. The evidence is not compelling.

Rivalry with the West led to improved China-Russia relations long before the invasion. In 2017-18 Russian arms sales to China increased substantially after Russia set aside concerns over Chinese reverse-engineering and cloning of its advanced military hardware. Three weeks before the invasion, Xi and Putin signed a strategic declaration involving friendship with "no limits", but in practice the limits have been quite narrow. China has increased oil imports from Russia, but eight months into the war Xi raised concerns with Putin about the conduct of the war and despite Russian requests for arms China had provided very little military equipment, except non-lethal material.[121] Shortly after the war started China convinced both the AIIB and the BRICS' NDB to suspend their activities with Russia. The scale and duration of NATO's commitment to its Ukraine proxy and Israel's invasion of Gaza in October 2023 strengthened China's support for Russia, and in December 2023 Xi announced to Russian Prime Minister Mikhail Mishustin that China will continue to seek "high-level' political and economic ties with Moscow.[122] There are advantages for China of an extended war in Ukraine: it increases Russia's dependence on China and diverts US and NATO attention and resources away from Asia. But the Ukraine war also presents problems for China. It remains on most measures a long way behind the US and does not want the war to produce significant gains for

Ukraine, which would strengthen NATO. More generally, geopolitical instability poses a threat to continued trade and investment ties with the West on which it depends to close the gap. In this context, if a China-Russia axis is being established it is not only in its infancy but more an axis of convenience than a strategic partnership. Indeed, in some areas they are strategic rivals: China's increasing influence in central Asia via the BRI and arms spending, encroaches on Russia's traditional area of influence.

The blurred lines between the West and the supposed China-Russia axis also suggest that global geopolitics are more fluid than the idea of a new Cold War implies. India provides an illustration. India is a QUAD member, has shifted its strategic orientation towards the West in response to increasing Chinese power, and in the same week as US Secretary of State Antony Blinken's frosty visit to Xi in June 2023, Biden and Indian Prime Minister Narendra Modi agreed to deepen the 2009 "global strategic partnership" via deeper cooperation in technology, commerce, and defence. Yet, during the Ukraine war India has substantially increased its imports from Russia: from $6.6 billion to $32.8 billion between April-December 2021 and the same period in 2022.[123] Building on close Cold War relations with the USSR India signed a Strategic Partnership with Russia in 2000, participates in joint military exercises, and sources around 50 percent of its arms imports from Russia. It has refused to condemn Russia over Ukraine. India's relations with Russia have broad similarities with China-Russia relations, yet while there has been no inflammatory talk of an India-Russia axis and little Western criticism of India's relations with Russia, corralling India behind a relatively united Western response to Russia and China will not be straightforward.[124]

It is not inconceivable that a new Cold War could develop, but the Cold War analogy is for now misplaced. This is not a cause for celebration, however, for, in the words of British foreign minister Douglas Hurd at the time of the break-up of Yugoslavia, the Cold War was "unfriendly but stable".[125] Today the world is becoming more dangerous. The tensions between China and the West may be punctuated intermittently by high-level talks that produce modest agreements on a limited range of issues. When Biden and Xi met at the Asia-Pacific Economic Cooperation Summit in November 2023, Biden claimed that the talks were "some of the most constructive and productive discussions we've had", while Xi said "Planet Earth is big enough" for both superpowers.[126] But they achieved little of substance. The restoration of US-China military communications, closed after Pelosi's August 2022 visit to Taiwan, is significant and may limit the possibility of miscalculations. But China's agreement to limit exports of the ingredients for opioid production and promise to explore the loan of more pandas to the US are the sort of thing that make satire superfluous. Iran and North Korea were not discussed, there was no progress on Taiwan or the military use of AI, and Biden refused to lift restrictions on US high-tech exports to China. Biden's reference to Xi as a "dictator" in his post-talks press conference emphasised that US-China relations are currently closer to antagonism than cooperation.

Conclusion

The relatively benign geopolitical conditions in which China developed after 1978 have disappeared. The West claims that it is responding to China's assertiveness and the increasing military threat it poses while China counters that its behaviour and military capabilities are a reaction to mounting Western pressure and bellicosity. China's interests are more regionally concentrated than those of the US, yet far from diluting the US-China rivalry this concentration makes it potentially more destabilising. Christopher Layne, an astute conservative geopolitical analyst, argues that the US attempt to maintain its position of primacy in Asia "makes the prospect of a hot war ever more likely".[127] Unable to afford the hegemonic concessions of the Cold War, unwilling to make them to its nearest challenger, yet determined to hold on to the privileges attached to the dollar's reserve status, the scale of its economy, its technological leadership, military might and system of alliances, the US has moved from Obama's pivot, through Trump's America First agenda, to Biden's "get tough with China" strategy outlined during the 2020 US presidential election. Getting tough over economic competition requires the US to "build a united front of US allies and partners to confront" China.[128] Xi meanwhile has surrounded himself by military cadres and promotes a harder nationalism in the face of external challenges and internal questioning of CCP legitimacy. The tendencies towards conflict will deepen in the economic crisis that looks increasingly likely, early signs of which are swirling over China's property sector and youth jobs market.

The two sides are far from equal, but the world's second most powerful imperialism does not provide a progressive alternative. China and the US are locked into a system of inter-imperialist rivalry which flows from capitalism itself and imparts its murderous and destructive logic onto all the world's states. It is a logic with a permanent tendency towards conflict and, therefore, preparation for conflict, towards which obscene amounts of resources are directed. The world desperately needs cooperation on the inter-locking crises facing all of humanity (climate emergency, health crises and future pandemics, economic and financial crises, etc).[129] The rivalry between the monstrous powers at the top of the world's imperialist hierarchy hinders that cooperation, indeed contributes to the very crises that require cooperative solution. Capitalist America and capitalist China are, however asymmetrically, both part of the problem facing the world's 99 percent.

Conclusion:
Prospects for change

Since Mao's death, China's economic system has been transformed. But there was no rupture, no counter-revolution against Maoist socialism. The transformation resulted from a sideways move from state capitalism to a hybrid of state and private capitalism that has since become a central component of the global capitalist economy. China's capitalism is not an exact copy of Western-inspired neoliberalism, but it is broadly consistent with the globally dominant neoliberal model of economic management. Deng's reforms unleashed a powerful internal growth potential but its realisation was dependent on the mutual reinforcement of internal and external dynamics: tens of millions of workers migrated to the SEZs where they combined with foreign and Chinese capital to produce a vast mass of surplus-value embodied in exports for the world market. Economic modernisation was accelerated by the regime's insistence that foreign capital share its technological superiority via joint ventures with Chinese firms and, over time, many private firms and SOEs, now usually part-privatised and listed on the world's major stock exchanges, have joined the ranks of the world's largest corporations.

China's economic rise is now presented as a threat to Western capitalism, but in the last forty years it has played a major role in sustaining it. The opening of the reform era provided what David Harvey calls a "spatial fix", a new space of accumulation and new source of surplus and profit for a sclerotic Western capitalism battered by three severe crises between 1973 and 1993.[1] Later, China's stimulus package after the 2008 financial crisis helped the global economy return to (relatively weak and debt-fuelled) growth. China's rulers' interests overlapped with those of the wider system to such an extent that Hung argued in 2016 that China was "a key force in helping perpetuate US global dominance".[2] But today the internal and external conditions that enabled China's rulers to strike a balance between their own interests and those of the wider system have begun to disappear. China must now contend with the exhaustion of its forty-year growth model and with the consequences of its elevation to the position of major challenger to US global power as a consequence of the success of that model. The state-capitalist ruling class today operates under increasingly severe constraints.

Pressure from the West is forcing a reorientation of the economy towards domestic growth – weakening the already declining dependencies on FDI and exports and providing a degree of insurance against external economic turbulence and threat. But this demands a significant redistribution of income from rich to poor through increases in wages and/or welfare spending. In the abstract, demographic change is driving in this direction: the population is ageing, the number of working-age people has begun a significant long-term decline, and the supply of low-wage rural-urban migrants that fuelled the boom has collapsed. But redistribution contradicts the interests of the party-state elite, and without major struggle higher wages, pensions and social security payments are unlikely. Cutting the rate of capital accumulation to reduce the subordination of consumption to accumulation is equally problematic: it would slow China's industrial and technological catch-up with its rivals, hinder the increase in China's labour productivity, and threaten long-term competitiveness and exports.

Adding to these long-term structural problems is the more immediate challenge of increasing signs of economic crisis. Confounding ruling-class hopes for a post-lockdown economic rebound, the 2022 growth rate of 3 percent was the lowest since the mid-1970s, the first time in forty years that China grew below the international average. While other major economies are grappling with inflationary pressures, China has been gripped by deflation since July 2023. The property sector is particularly weak, property prices have fallen substantially and the largest property developer, Evergrande, was frantically fighting a liquidation order in a Hong Kong court in January 2024. The difficulties in the property sector are impacting on the wider economy: building material sales fell 7 percent in the first half of 2023, fuelling the deflationary pressures. Since late-2022 company revenues and profits have fallen, often quite sharply, according to data from the National Bureau of Statistics.[3] Meanwhile foreign capitals' declining confidence in their Chinese operations was reflected in large reductions in levels of reinvestment and substantial repatriation of profits in 2023.[4] Youth unemployment is now well over 20 percent.[5]

What can China do to address these long-term and short-term crisis tendencies? The long history of capitalism provides no grounds for optimism. Speculative asset-price booms are inevitably followed by crashes, and while general economic crises can be postponed or moderated by the expansion of debt, this merely postpones the problem and risks a more severe crash in the following years. And China is in a very weak position to expand debt. Debt is a huge problem across all sectors of the economy and total debt as a percentage of GDP reached a record 280 percent in early 2023.[6] Its weakness was illustrated by its response to the Covid pandemic in 2020. In 2008 its stimulus package was officially 8 percent of GDP, but bank lending took that to over 20 percent. On the back of ballooning debt, this time round China's stimulus was far smaller than those of other major economies: the US stimulus amounted to some 25 percent of GDP, the UK's was 18 percent and the EU's was 11 percent, while China's was a feeble 4.7 percent.[7] Worse still, we saw in chapter two that injections of debt have a decreasing impact on the real economy.

In 2018 I wrote: "debt and slower growth weaken the state's capacity to address problems by throwing resources at them. Nor can capital rely on fresh supplies of cheap labour in the future. If and when the developing stock market and housing bubbles burst, as they surely will, the impact on China and the rest of the world economy will be very great indeed".[8] This assessment was rooted in Cliff's *State Capitalism in Russia*, which accurately predicted a long stagnation as a key feature of crisis under state-capitalism. Hung's warning in 2016 of a vast "uncoordinated, redundant, and unprofitable expansion of productive capacity" is just as relevant today and China's zombie SOEs emphasise the extent of the problem.[9] My assessment was also based on Marx's general theory of capitalist crisis and, today, the twin tendencies towards stagnation and falling profit rates flowing from China's exposure to global rhythms of accumulation are now coming together. The consequences of over-accumulation are inescapable and driving the Chinese economy towards a crisis that will not be confined to China and that will exacerbate the inter-imperialist rivalry with the West.

The digital economy accounts for 40 percent of China's GDP and the US drive for high-tech decoupling is designed to undermine China's competitive position.[10] Corralling the rest of the world behind its own imperialism will not be straightforward and the US faces resistance from Asian firms that retain deep economic links to China and have taken advantage of the export restrictions imposed on other Western firms by increasing their own sales to China. Nevertheless, the US is committed to a strategy of reinforcing its military presence in Asia and intensifying the military encirclement and containment of China.

The US and its Western allies are also seeking to take advantage of an emerging resistance to China's Belt and Road Initiative. The conditions attached to many BRI loans and infrastructure agreements have been renegotiated at the insistence of recipient states. The extractivist logic of the BRI has also been criticised. As Hung already noted in 2016, "China's investment in these countries and its importing of their natural resources are driven by the same capitalist logic and national interest that drove the expansion of Western powers into the developing world...[and] China is starting to be perceived in some developing countries as a new colonial power".[11] As that perception strengthens, the West is attempting to restore influence in the Global South with initiatives that mirror the BRI's infrastructure spending.

China is considerably weaker than the West but forms a partial bulwark that prevents US and Western power from simply steam-rolling others. Its position was reinforced in 2023 by the expansion of the BRICS in August, and its influence in the strategically important Middle East in particular is likely to be enhanced by the inclusion of Saudi Arabia, Iran, Egypt and the UAE in the group. The events of late-2023 and early-2024 are likely to further increase China's influence. Israel's assault on Gaza provoked widespread condemnation of Israel's Western backers, particularly the US, and in early-2024 many states in the Global South supported the South African case against Israeli genocide in the International

Criminal Court. Not a single Western state expressed its support. The US and UK bombing of Houthi positions in Yemen in January 2024 is likely to reinforce the turn towards China: presented as a means to avoid the escalation of Israel's assault into a wider regional war, the bombings were themselves an escalation and as Mohamad Bazzi wrote "the US and its allies are resisting the clearest path for de-escalation across the region: putting pressure on Israel to end its invasion and accept a ceasefire".[12] The absence of Saudi Arabia and the UAE, two of the US's closest Middle Eastern allies, from the naval coalition put together by the US in December 2023 to stem Houthi attacks on shipping in the Red Sea underlines the shifting balance in the region.

But acting as a counter-weight to US power does not make China progressive. A rebalancing of the global imperialist system may provide some with the satisfaction that the world's foremost bully is losing influence to its main rival. But for the international Left and global working class the enemy of my enemy is not my friend. China is itself a major imperialist power, represses internal dissent and opposition and its state institutionalises and operates a system of massive exploitation. Any pretence that it represents a progressive alternative to the US evaporated long ago. The international Left should reject Western propaganda on China and refuse to line up with the West, but its critique of the West must not involve silence on China's internal capitalism or external imperialism. Socialist internationalism is founded on the common interests of the world's workers and oppressed: it should support their struggles whether they take place in Shenzhen or Chicago.

Like ruling classes the world over, China's rulers combine instruments of coercion and consent to maintain their rule. The quest for consent produces occasional concessions to popular demands, including the (widely evaded) 2008 labour law, action on environmental degradation, and minimum wage increases. But consent is always underpinned by control over the state's coercive power.[13] Facing a wave of protests and strikes the ruling class under Xi's leadership has turned decisively towards coercion since 2015. Ruling-class anxieties about the developing crisis ensure that repression shows no sign of ending. Indeed, new "enemies" have been found: the sinicisation of mosques that is most marked in Xinjiang also includes transformation of a thousand mosques in Hui areas, despite the Hui having no recent history of separatism, speaking Mandarin, and there being no history of terrorism among them.[14] Every person in China is a potential protester and faces a dense network of surveillance, internet censorship and police violence.

Yet, protests and strikes persist. The disfiguring of a mosque in Najiaying in Yunnan province and its replacement by a sinicised mosque in June lead to protests by thousands of people. Protesters braved police violence in the aftermath of the "great Foxconn escape" and in solidarity with Uyghur Muslims in late-2022. Despite the fierce crackdown in Hong Kong in recent years, which has now forced both the HKCTU and liberal Civic Party to disband, protests took place in solidarity with the Urumchi fire victims. 2023 saw a small recovery in strikes as well as widespread references to the "lying flat" *(tangping)* social movement of young people. In some ways reminiscent of the hippies of the 1960s (including dropping out in picturesque Himalayan beauty-spots like Dali in the south-west), this movement has turned its back on consumerism and workplace stress in a country with one of the highest annual working hours in the world. The pampered leadership has criticised this trend, and the multi-millionaire Xi Jinping has told those facing unemployment that they should "eat bitterness" (ie accept the sort of sacrifice endured on the Long March). Dropping out is a symptom of a society heading for trouble, not a solution, but the rejection of official ideas, allied to the combativity and courage of strikers and protesters, contains seeds of hope for the future.[15] But what sort of future?

Some observers set their sights low. Echoing arguments that reflect official views, they suggest that Chinese society is not ready for democracy and further development demands a paternalistic, ethical Confucian leadership acting on behalf of society that is in keeping with Chinese "traditions".[16] But the CCP leadership will not be softened by appeals to Confucian ethics, which in any case combine appeals to moral virtue and the just treatment of the ruled with demands for stability, deference to enlightened rulers and hierarchy. China's business-friendly regime is deeply intertwined with the mega-rich and has turned to increased repression as it has tightened its grip on power and further squeezed the space for reforms and democratisation as the early signs of the coming crisis have emerged. Uyghur oppression, domestic violence, and the relocation of production to inland provinces with lower wages will not be halted by moral arguments.

Like all ruling classes, China's rulers will mobilise racism and religious difference to divide. They will use gender and sexuality, making the female body a site of political strategy, demonising trans people and "abnormal", "Western" or "decadent" sexualities, and promoting a return to "traditional" values and practices. They will deepen the appeals to national identity and unity, one of the hallmarks of Xi's regime, in order to suppress dissent and blame foreigners (along with the undeserving poor) for social ills. Many may be seduced, at least for a time, but the roots of party-state legitimacy have been watered for four decades by economic growth, and slower growth is beginning to shrivel those roots. Repression will intensify but the scale of the coming crisis is likely to force millions into a new wave of protest and struggle with the potential to break down differences and unite the masses around their common interests. In the struggles to come China's workers and protesters will rediscover forms of grassroots organisation seen in earlier struggles (from Tiananmen in 1989, through the 2007-2016 strike wave to the "white paper" protests of 2022). Struggle erupts even in the most inhospitable circumstance, but if they are to break through the repressive armour of Chinese state power, they will also need to develop new forms of national coordination and organisation.

The stakes are high. Capitalism's competitive dynamic produces environmental devastation, vast inequality and obscene excess and waste. It also drives the world towards war. David Harvey noted two decades ago the "increasingly fierce international competition as multiple dynamic centres of capital accumulation compete on the world stage in the face of strong currents of over accumulation". These dynamics have since intensified and Harvey's prediction that geopolitical confrontations would erupt "in the form of trade wars and currency wars, with the ever-present danger of military confrontations" has proved terrifyingly accurate.[17]

Only the collective power of the working class can democratise change and create a society based not on the appropriation of the labour-power of billions of workers for profit (whether by private or public firms) but on the satisfaction of their needs. The potential of this collective power is revealed in every strike and in every protest and movement of the oppressed. But potentials that are not embodied in organisation can disappear almost as soon as they appear, consigned to personal reminiscence and resigned sadness over what might have been. Building a revolutionary socialist party is a daunting task, but the experience of failed revolutions since the success of the Russian Revolution in 1917 demonstrates that such a party, rooted in the struggles of workers and the oppressed and preserving the history, experience and memory of those struggles, is indispensable for success. If China's workers can build a revolutionary party, however unlikely it might seem today, then the twenty-first century can be a century of successful workers' revolutions. World society, even the planet, depends on it.

Endnotes

····················

Introduction

1 These final words of Tony Cliff's talk at the closing rally of the Marxism Festival in London in July 1989 forcefully (and movingly) reminded his audience that the working class is an international class.

2 The clash between claim and reality brings to mind the old Soviet joke: "under capitalism there is exploitation of people by other people, but in the USSR we have completely reversed this".

3 Xi Jinping, "Opinion on strengthening the work of the Unified Front within the private economy of the new era", *Chinese Communist Party Politburo* (Beijing, 15 September 2020 (in Mandarin)), cited in Doyon (2021).

4 Huang Yasheng, *Selling China: Foreign Direct Investment During the Reform Era* (Cambridge: Cambridge University Press, 2003). In this book "local" refers to both provincial governments and lower levels of government including cities, counties, townships and villages.

5 Engels made essentially the same point about nationalised property, dismissing the argument that state ownership is necessarily socialist. If every nationalisation is socialist, he argued, then Napoleon "would rank among the founders of socialism" after his nationalisation of the tobacco trade. See Frederick Engels, *Anti-Duhring (Herr Eugen Duhring's Revolution in Science)* (Peking: Foreign Languages Press, 1976) p359.

6 Neoliberalism is a problematic concept. In general terms it refers to the promotion of private interests expressed in market exchanges over state economic intervention and welfare support. But in the groupings of rich countries (the OECD, G7, etc) state spending as a percentage of GDP is higher today than at the start of the neoliberal era in the late-1970s. Since then many countries have introduced minimum wages and despite decades of welfare retrenchment all retain public pensions and welfare systems that bear some resemblance to pre-existing systems. Nevertheless, the neoliberal offensive is real. Much state spending is on subsidies and other supports for capital; many state activities have been outsourced to private businesses; public housing and other state assets have been privatised; housing, health, pensions, social protection and education are increasingly subject to market processes and funding constraints. The language of consumerism and individual rights predominates over that of social rights and public provision. Over forty years the neoliberal right (aided by social-democratic and labour parties) has, for now at least, succeeded in shifting the boundary between what should be provided by the state and what should be left to the private sector. But this shift, part of a project to de-politicise the capitalist state, is no mere technocratic fix. It is part of a ruling-class offensive to protect private property and restore profitability against the threat from the labour movement. The changes mentioned above have therefore coincided with widespread attacks on trade union rights. Nevertheless, in broad terms capitalist production and social reproduction would be more difficult if there were a more aggressive dismantling of state power. In this book neoliberalism is used, with these caveats in mind, to denote the promotion of the interests of capital and to attack the collective interests of labour.

7 Ho-fung Hung, *The China Boom. Why China will not Rule the World* (New York: Columbia University Press, 2016), pp3-4.

8 Eli Friedman, "Foxconn's Great Escape", *Asian Labour Review: A Journal for Labour Movements across Asia* (8 November 2022). https://labourreview.org/foxconns-great-escape/

9 Arthur Kaufman, "China's Anti-Lockdown Protests and the Quest for Inter-Ethnic Solidarity", *China Digital Times* (2 December 2022). https://chinadigitaltimes.net/2022/12/chinas-anti-lockdown-protests-and-the-quest-for-inter-ethnic-solidarity/

10 Simon Gilbert, "China, the Uyghurs and the Left", *International Socialism* 172 (Autumn 2021) pp48-50.

11 Democracy Now!, "From Xinjiang to Shanghai, Protests Grow in China over COVID Restrictions After Fatal Apartment Fire" (28 November 2022). https://www.democracynow.org/2022/11/28/protests_erupt_china_strict_zero_covid/ See also Yun Dong "The Uprising in China: resisting lockdowns, repression, and precarity", *Spectre Journal* (30 November 2022). https://spectrejournal.com/uprising-against-lockdowns-and-precarity-in-china/

12 Promise Li, "Socialists should support the popular resistance in China", *The Call* (30 November 2022). https://socialistcall.com/2022/11/30/socialists-should-support-the-popular-resistance-in-china/

13 Jun Cai et al "Modeling transmission of SARS-CoV-2 Omicron in China", *Nature Medicine* (volume 28 2022). https://www.nature.com/articles/s41591-022-01855-7

14 Keith Zhai and Yang Jie "Letter from Apple Supplier Foxconn's founder prodded China to ease zero-Covid rules", *Wall Street Journal* (8 December 2022). https://www.wsj.com/articles/letter-from-top-apple-supplier-foxconn-prodded-china-to-ease-zero-covid-rules-11670504366. All Foxconn's plants reveal close ties to local authorities. Its Pixian plant is in a vast business park built by a company owned by Chengdu city authorities, who forced 10,000 families to relocate in 2010 to make way for the park. Because the park is designated as a trade zone, Foxconn pays no taxes there. The streets in the Pixian plant have names such as Tian Run Lu (Heaven Profit Road). See Jordan Pouille, "China's company towns", *Le Monde Diplomatique* (July 2012).

15 Revolutionary Communists in China "Statement on protests", *Rebel* (3 December 2022). http://www.rebelnews.ie/2022/12/03/revolutionary-communists-in-china-statement-on-protests/

16 Christian Sorace and Nicholas Loubere, "Biopolitical Binaries (or how not to read the Chinese protests)", *Made in China Journal* (2 December 2022). https://madeinchinajournal.com/2022/12/02/biopolitical-binaries-or-how-not-to-read-the-chinese-protests/

17 Western firms, meanwhile, refused to share mRNA technology with China.

18 Covid-related repression started before the WHO declared the pandemic. In January police forced Li Wenliang, the Wuhan doctor who alerted the world to the virus before his death from Covid in February 2020, to sign a letter saying that alerting colleagues was dishonest and "gravely disturbed social order".

19 Yuri Prasad, "China's rapid growth was paid for in the blood of the poor", *Socialist Worker* (7 December 2022).

20 Tony Cliff, *State Capitalism in Russia* (London: Bookmarks, 1988). Cliff, writing under his given name, Ygael Gluckstein, also wrote *Mao's China* (London: Allen and Unwin, 1957), a substantial analysis of the early years of post-revolutionary China. An excellent analysis of Mao's China from a state capitalist perspective is provided by Nigel Harris, *The Mandate of Heaven: Marx and Mao in Modern China* (London: Quartet Books, 1978). Charlie Hore, *The Road to Tiananmen Square* (London: Bookmarks, 1991) is an accessible analysis of twentieth-century China up to the 1989 massacre.

21 Tony Cliff, introduction to *The Nature of Stalinist Russia* (1948, distributed in duplicated form), cited in Chris Harman, introduction to Cliff (1988) pp16-17.

22 Private property should not be confused with personal property. In the context of the world system as a whole, state property is private as it is possessed exclusively by national state managers who exclude non-nationals (and, outside the realms of ideology, virtually all national citizens too) from exercising any influence over its use.

23 Ma Jian interview, *The Guardian* (3 November 2018). https://www. theguardian.com/books/2018/nov/02/ ma-jian-interview-exiled-chinese-writer-free-speech-dissidents-novel

Chapter 1
The 1949 revolution, Maoism and the post-Mao transition

1 Notably the 1850-64 Taiping Rebellion which aimed to modernise the Chinese state and society.

2 Imperialism and Western racism went hand in glove. The widespread belief that there were signs barring "Chinese and dogs" from Shanghai's waterfront park is probably mistaken, but the park regulations from 1894 to 1928 included variations on the 1903 wording: "No dogs or bicycles are admitted" and "No Chinese are admitted, except servants in attendance upon foreigners". See Robert A. Bickers and Jeffrey N. Wasserstrom, "Shanghai's 'Dogs and Chinese Not Admitted' Sign: legend, history and contemporary symbol", *The China Quarterly* (volume 142, 1995).

3 Harold Isaacs, *The Tragedy of the Chinese Revolution* (Stanford: Stanford University Press, 1961) p85. The Comintern admitted the GMD as a "sympathising party" at this time, with only Trotsky voting against when the Soviet Communist Party leadership approved the decision. Trotsky also opposed making Chiang Kai-shek a member of honour of the Comintern.

4 Isaacs, p64.

5 Duncan Hallas, *The Comintern* (London: Bookmarks, 1985) p121.

6 These putschist manoeuvres were an early sign of a change in Comintern strategy in mid-1928. The first period (1919-1924) was one of revolutionary advance in the wake of the Russian Revolution. The second period reflected the ebbing of the revolutionary tide and capitalist re-stabilisation. Then, against all the evidence, the Comintern now proclaimed that it had entered a third period, of sharpening imperialist contradictions, the rise of fascism, and deepening economic crisis. No united front work could be countenanced with the social-democratic parties that, notwithstanding the threat from actual fascism, were presented as social fascists and the main enemy of the left. This lurch to wild ultra-leftism isolated the communists within the world's labour movements, allowed the mainstream left to attack and isolate them, and ultimately fatally undermined the fight against fascism.

7 Karl Marx, "The Eighteenth Brumaire of Louis Bonaparte", in *Karl Marx: Selected Works* (volume 2) (London: Lawrence and Wishart, 1942) p415.

8 Hallas, ch7.

9 Michael Dillon, *China. A Modern History* (2nd edition) (London: I B Tauris, 2021) p291.

10 Nigel Harris, contribution to the debate on "The revolutionary role of the peasants", *International Socialism* 1st series (December 1969/January 1970) p22. https://www.marxists.org/history/etol/ writers/harris/1969/12/peasants.htm

11 Michael Löwy, *The Politics of Combined and Uneven Development* (London: Verso, 1987) pp213-4. Löwy nevertheless concludes that China, like Vietnam, Cuba, etc, were bureaucratic states of proletarian origin.

12 Lin Piao and Mao cited in Gluckstein, pp212-13.

13 Gluckstein, p193.

14 See Graham Hutchings, *China 1949: Year of Revolution* (London: Bloomsbury, 2021), cited in "Seizing the moment, cautiously", *Economist* (23 January 2021) p49.

15 Gluckstein, p194.

16 Shen Zhihua, "Revisiting Stalin's and Mao's Motivations in the Korean War", Wilson Centre Blog Post. https://www.wilsoncenter.org/blog-post/revisiting-stalins-and-maos-motivations-korean-war

17 Richard Whelan, *Drawing the Line: The Korean War 1950-53* (London: Faber and Faber, 1990), pp152-3.

18 Agricultural produce was also used to pay for imports of industrial equipment from the USSR.

19 Gluckstein, p124.

20 Hung (2016) p38.

21 Gluckstein, p190.

22 Harris (1978), p43.

23 Gluckstein, p201.

24 Gluckstein, p203.

25 On the labour code see Harris (1978), p91.

26 Gluckstein, pp41-2.

27 Harris (1978), p48.

28 Yang Jisheng (CCP member and ex-editor of the *Xinhua* state news agency) gives a figure of 36 million in *Tombstone* (London: Penguin, 2013), the key text on the famine.

29 Mao's diminished position was demonstrated in 1961 by the staging of an allegorical play about a sixteenth-century emperor who removed subordinates who had the temerity to criticise his cruelty.

30 Harris (1978) p60.

31 This section draws on Hore (1991) ch4.

32 Mao Zedong, "A Letter to the Red Guards of Tsinghua University Middle School" (1 August 1966). https://www.marxists.org/reference/archive/mao/selected-works/volume-9/mswv9_60.htm

33 Harris (1978) p62.

34 Harris (1978) p60.

35 Wu Yiching, *The Cultural Revolution at the Margins: Chinese Socialism in Crisis* (Cambridge, Mass.: Harvard University Press, 2014). Kindle edition, loc 534.

36 Ralf Ruckus, *The Left in China* (London: Pluto Press, 2023) is an excellent account of resistance and opposition in China since 1949.

37 Wu Yiching loc 177.

38 Jeffrey Sachs, *The End of Poverty*, (London: Allen Lane, 2005) p153. Sachs was one of the Western bourgeois economic advisors recruited to advise on the Chinese transition in the mid-1980s. He later designed the shock therapy and mass privatisation that produced economic devastation after the collapse of the USSR. See also Julian Gewirtz, *Unlikely Partners: Chinese Reformers, Western Economists, and the Making of Global China* (Cambridge, Mass.: Harvard, 2017).

39 Cited in George Gorton, "China's 'market socialism': can it work and how far can it go?", *International Socialism* 34 (Winter 1987) p68.

40 Andrew G. Walder and Gong Xiaoxia, "Workers in the Tiananmen Protests: The Politics of the Beijing Workers Autonomous Federation", *The Australian Journal of Chinese Affairs* 29 (January 1993) (now known as *The China Journal*). This article has influenced later leftist thinking on Tiananmen and provides a corrective to the dominant Western argument that the protesters were largely intellectuals and students demanding a liberal democratic China. https://www.journals.uchicago.edu/doi/abs/10.2307/2949950

41 Promise Li, "The Radical, Transnational Legacy of Tiananmen Workers", *The Nation* (3 June 2022). https://www.thenation.com/article/world/tiananmen-square-massacre-workers/

42 Willy Wo-Lap Lam, *Chinese Politics in the Era of Xi Jinping* (Abingdon: Routledge, 2015), pxi.

43 Alex Callinicos, *The Revenge of History: Marxism and the East European Revolutions* (Cambridge: Polity Press, 1991). For useful analyses of Tiananmen and its consequences see George Black and Robin Munro, *Black Hands of Beijing: Lives of Defiance in China's Democracy Movement* (London: John Wiley and Sons, 1993) and Louisa Lim, *The People's Republic of Amnesia: Tiananmen Revisited* (Oxford: Oxford University Press, 2014).

....

Chapter 2
Economic rise and emerging problems – the contradictions of authoritarian state capitalism

1 Data on the contributions of the public and private sectors must be treated with caution. Firstly, there is no single methodology for handling the relevant economic data. Thus, SOE contribution to GDP could be 23 percent or 27.5 percent, depending on methodology used. See Chunlin Zhang "How Much Do State-Owned Enterprises Contribute to China's GDP and Employment?", World Bank (2019). https://documents1.worldbank.org/curated/en/449701565248091726/pdf/How-Much-Do-State-Owned-Enterprises-Contribute-to-China-s-GDP-and-Employment.pdf Additionally, ownership is not clear-cut: SOEs and other state-linked investors had stakes in 14 percent of private firms in 2000 but this had risen to 33.5 percent

by 2019. See Edward Cunningham, "What is the future of China's private sector?", *Harvard Kennedy School* (Summer 2022). https://www.hks.harvard.edu/faculty-research/policy-topics/international-relations-security/what-future-chinas-private-sector

2 In fact there is a huge imbalance between China and the US on the purchase of licences for the use of patents owned by other firms: in 2012 China earned $1 billion from the sale of intellectual property right licences but spent $18 billion. See Lam, p169. By 2020 earnings had increased to $8 billion but spending had also surged, to $38 billion. See Andrew Cainey and Christiane Prange, *Xiconomics. What China's Dual Circulation Strategy Means for Global Business* (Newcastle: Agenda Publishing, 2023), p100.

3 Holly Chik, "China was the biggest contributor to research in top science journals last year" *South China Morning Post* (23 May 2023). https://www.scmp.com/news/china/science/article/3221533/china-was-biggest-contributor-research-top-science-journals-last-year

4 See Isabella Weber, *How China Escaped Shock Therapy: the Market Reform Debate* (Abingdon: Routledge, 2021).

5 Ho-fung Hung, "Sinomania: global crisis, China's crisis?", *Socialist Register 2012* (London: Merlin Press, 2011) p217.

6 World Bank "Foreign direct investment: net inflows". https://data.worldbank.org/indicator/BX.KLT.DINV.CD.WD?locations=CN

7 World Bank "Merchandise exports (current US$) – China". https://data.worldbank.org/indicator/TX.VAL.MRCH.CD.WT?view=chart&locations=CN

8 Hao Qi and David Kotz, "The Impact of State-Owned Enterprises on China's Economic Growth" *Review of Radical Political Economics* (52(1), 2020). Bourgeois economics' concept of diminishing returns to scale is also ideological, used to justify market competition in the face of

evidence that giant firms are often more efficient. See Peter Gowan, "*Industrial development and international political conflict in contemporary capitalism*", in Alex Anievas (ed.), *Marxism and World Politics* (Abingdon: Routledge, 2009).

9 Chunlin Zhang (2019)

10 See Hung (2016) p65.

11 Privatised assets often ended up in the hands of managers. Those allowed to buy the stock were limited to managerial cadre and share prices were set at well below their real value. See Alvin So, *Class and Class Conflict in Post Socialist China* (Singapore: World Scientific Publishing, 2013), p57.

12 Chris Harman, "The state and capital today", *International Socialism 51* (Summer 1991). http://isj.org.uk/the-state-and-capitalism-today

13 Gabriel Wildau, "China prepares fresh round of state-orchestrated megamergers", *Financial Times* (9 July 2017).

14 Tom Mitchell, "Leaders of China's big state enterprises take curious career paths", *Financial Times* (4 October 2017).

15 Xin Li and Kjeld Erik Brødsgaard, "SOE Reform in China: past, present and future", *The Copenhagen Journal of Asian Studies* 31(2) (2013) pp70-74.

16 Hou Lei, "Official: wage share decreases 22 years in a row", *China Daily* (12 May 2010). http://www.chinadaily.com.cn/china/2010-05/12/content_9841109.htm As with other economic indicators, calculations of wages as a proportion of GDP produce different results depending on criteria (before or after tax, inclusion or exclusion of social benefits, etc). But the broad accuracy of ACFTU's claim is confirmed by Hung (2016), pp152-3: wages as a proportion of GDP fell from 53 percent in 1998 to 41.4 percent in 2005.

17 Chen Weihua "Income gap, a woe for China and the US", *China Daily* (12 October 2010). https://www.chinadaily.com.cn/business/2010-10/12/content_11399437.htm; Damian Tobin, "Inequality in China: rural poverty persists as urban wealth balloons", *BBC News* (29 July 2011). http://archives.truthaboutchina.com/2011/07/inequality-in-china-rural-pove.html

18 Li and Brødsgaard, pp72-73. Based on the work of "independent social scientists" (albeit a team established by the Bank of China) Lam puts the Gini figure at over 0.6. See Lam, p.156.

19 This compares to a 2017 study by the US Federal Reserve showing that the savings of 44 percent of Americans would not cover an unexpected $400 bill.

20 Beverly Silver and Lu Zhang, "China as an emerging epicenter of world labour unrest", in Ho-fung Hung (ed.) *China and the Transformation of Global Capitalism* (Baltimore: John Hopkins University Press, 2009) p175. Unrecorded protests make the unofficial figure much higher.

21 China's then president Hu Jintao spoke about safeguarding "the legitimate rights and interests of workers". Cited in Beverly Silver and Lu Zhang (2009) p176.

22 Hung (2016) p160.

23 Hung (2016) p160. Wang Hui argues that only 8 percent of the stimulus went to welfare, with 70 percent going to infrastructure. See Wang Hui, "Global imbalances and the limits of the exchange rate weapon", in E Helleiner and J Kirschner (eds) *The Great Wall of Money* (Ithaca NY: Cornell University Press, 2014), pp118-9.

24 Wang Hui (2016) p181.

25 Under Mao, the industrialisation drive was decentralised as Mao sought to ensure that "most regions were self-contained industrial networks". The enormous duplication that this

produced was reinforced by Deng's further decentralisation: by 1997 three-quarters of provinces had their own car manufacturing industries, most of the 122 assembly lines being small and hopelessly inefficient. See Martin Hart-Landsberg and Paul Burkett, *China and Socialism* (India: Aakar, 2006) pp62-3.

26 See Wade Shepard, *Ghost Cities of China: The Story of Cities Without People in the World's Most Populated Country* (London: Zed, 2015).

27 Michel Aglietta "What's behind the yuan devaluation", *Le Monde Diplomatique* (November 2015).

28 Atif Ansar, Bent Flyvbjerg, Alexander Budzier and Daniel Lunn "Does infrastructure investment lead to economic growth or economic fragility? Evidence from China", Oxford Review of Economic Policy (Vol. 32, No. 3, Autumn 2016) pp360-390 https://www.jstor.org/stable/26363344

29 Ansar, Flyvbjerg, Budzier and Lunn, p379.

30 Ansar, Flyvbjerg, Budzier and Lunn, p380.

31 See Robert Brenner, *The Economics of Global Turbulence* (London: Verso, 2006). On the Marxist analysis of economic crises see Chris Harman, *Explaining the Crisis* (London: Bookmarks, 1999).

32 International Monetary Fund, "Global Debt Database". https://www.imf.org/external/datamapper/datasets/GDD. Other measurements differ, with some claiming that world debt now stands at 350 percent of GDP.

33 Bank for International Settlements, "Total credit to the non-financial sector (core debt)". https://stats.bis.org/statx/srs/table/f1.1

34 S&P Global Ratings agency, cited in Evelyn Cheng, "China's debt-heavy local governments look for new ways to raise cash", *CNBC* (26 March 2023). https://www.cnbc.com/2023/03/27/

chinas-local-governments-finding-new-ways-to-raise-money-amid-debt-concerns.html

35 Engen Tham, Xie Yu and Ziyi Tang, "Analysis: China's debt-laden local governments pose challenges to economic growth, financial system", *Reuters*, 10 March 2023. https://www.reuters.com/world/china/debt-laden-local-governments-pose-fresh-challenges-chinas-growth-financial-2023-03-10/

36 Bank for International Settlements, "Total credit to non-financial corporations (core debt)". https://stats.bis.org/statx/srs/table/f4.1

37 Cited in Gabriel Wildau, "Prominent China debt bear warns of $6.8tn in hidden losses", *Financial Times* (16 August 2017). https://www.ft.com/content/3bc4da08-8171-11e7-a4ce-15b2513cb3ff

38 State banks have been periodically required to turn the screws on shadow banking, but the funds entering the sector have partly come from industrial SOEs that borrow at low interest rates from state banks and then pass on funds at higher rates to the private sector.

39 People's Bank of China, "Shadow Banking", *China Financial Stability Report*, Special Topic IV, 2013, pp197-205, cited in Apostolos Apostolou, Alexander Al-Haschimi and Martino Ricci "Financial risks in China's corporate sector: real estate and beyond", *European Central Bank* (2/2022). https://www.ecb.europa.eu/pub/economic-bulletin/articles/2022/html/ecb.ebart202202_01~48041a563f.en.html

40 Shuli Ren, "Worried About Shadow Banking? Don't Look at China", *Bloomberg* (30 March 2023). https://www.bloomberg.com/opinion/articles/2023-03-30/shadow-banking-don-t-look-at-china-the-us-also-has-a-problem

41 Liao Shumin, "China Is Likely First Country to Reach 96% Urban Home Ownership, PBOC Says", *Yicai* (27 April 2020). Yicai is the financial news arm of state-owned giant Shanghai Media Group. https://www.yicaiglobal.com/news/china-is-likely-first-country-to-reach-96-urban-home-ownership-pboc-says.

42 Yougin Huang, Shenjing He S, Li Gan, "Introduction to SI: homeownership and housing divide in China", *Cities* (Vol 108, January 2021). https://www.sciencedirect.com/science/article/pii/S0264275120313159?via%3Dihub

43 According to Hung (2016) p55, this was part of the design under Deng, to tie local bureaucracies into market transformation "as a counterweight to the conservative old guard".

44 "So bad it's good", *Economist* (19 January 2019) p77.

45 Yuri Prasad, "Chinas rulers can't bank on 'market miracle' anymore", *Socialist Worker* (29 September 2021) p17.

46 Martin Farrer and Vincent Ni, "Property market meltdown puts stability at risk", *The Guardian* (20 July 2022) p31. Chinese credit rating agencies (another sign of China's accommodation to neoliberalism) generally give AAA ratings to SOEs because they are backed by the state. But in November 2020 Yongcheng Coal and Electricity defaulted on part of its debt repayment, and investors dumped its shares alongside those of other SOEs close to Henan province authorities. SOEs in other provinces have also faced debt and interest repayment problems and ten defaulted in 2020. As most SOEs are part-privatised small domestic investors are at risk of losing their savings.

47 Cited in John Authers, "Emerging market bulls charge back into the China shop", *Financial Times* (1/2 April 2017).

48 Hung (2016) figure 6.5, p162.

49 Tom Hancock, "Chinese economic Officials Debate the Growing Threat of Debt", *Bloomberg* (8 April 2023). https://www.bloomberg.com/news/newsletters/2023-04-08/chinese-economic-officials-debate-the-threat-of-debt-new-economy-saturday

50 For a longer treatment of the contradictory pressures on China's economic strategists see Minqi Li, *China and the 21ˢᵗ Century Crisis* (London: Pluto, 2016) especially ch7

51 Kaye Wiggins, Cheng Leng and Tomas Hale, "Global investment banks' profits drop in China", *Financial Times* (22 May 2023). https://www.ft.com/content/0889ab6e-e1f1-4db5-9ba6-4e4722f786c3

52 Charles Kindleberger "Dominance and leadership in the international economy: exploitation, public goods, and free rides", *International Studies Quarterly* 25(2) (1981) p248.

53 Guglielmo Carchedi and Michael Roberts, *Capitalism in the Twenty-first Century: Through the prism of value* (London: Pluto Press, 2023) p127.

54 Ho-fung Hung, "China and the lingering Pax Americana", in Patrick Bond and Ana Garcia (eds), *BRICS: An Anti-capitalist Critique* (London: Pluto Press, 2015) p255.

55 Robert Greene, "Beijing's global ambitions for central bank digital currencies are growing clearer", *Carnegie Endowment for International Peace (*6 October 2021), cited in Cainey and Prange, pp82-3. https://carnegieendowment.org/2021/10/06/beijing-s-global-ambitions-for-central-bank-digital-currencies-are-growing-clearer-pub-85503

56 Cainey and Prange, p89.

57 Trump labelled China a currency manipulator during his campaign and presidency. In fact, after de-pegging from the dollar in July 2005 the RMB

appreciated consistently, gaining 37 percent by January 2014. Only since then has it gradually depreciated, losing 11 percent against the dollar by 1 January 2023. The decline would have been faster without Xi's capital outflow restrictions and reduction of foreign reserves in an effort to maintain the RMB's exchange rate.

58 Martin Wolf, "Chinese finance is storing up trouble for the rest of the world", *Financial Times* (4 April 2017). https://www.ft.com/content/da94e4e2-1787-11e7-9c35-0dd2cb31823a

59 Zhou, whose reference to a Minsky moment was mentioned earlier in the chapter, lead China's campaign for the RMB to be accepted as a reserve currency by the IMF.

60 Valentina Romei and Rob Minto, "Chart of the week: who makes China's exports – local companies or foreign?", *Financial Times* (10 September 2012). The influence of foreign capital remains high: the figure for 2022 was 34.3 percent, according to data from the General Administration of Customs of China. http://www.customs.gov.cn/customs/302249/zfxxgk/2799825/302274/302277/302276/4127432/index.html

61 See https://english.www.gov.cn/2016special/madeinchina2025/. Fearing that grandiose claims about the development of China's domestic economy might provoke a Western backlash other leaders pressured Xi into reducing references to Made in China. The substance of the programme continues however under the dual circulation strategy.

62 See Cainey and Prange, 2023.

63 TSMC started producing 3nm chips (nanometre, or one-billionth of a metre) in 2022 while SMIC is currently producing 11nm chips. TSMC took six years to go from 10nm to 3nm and the scale of the investment required to catch up is colossal – 3nm chips have 250m

transistors per square millimetre and circuit components that are just 1/20,000[th] the breadth of a human hair. TSMC plans to invest $100bn between 2021 and 2024. See Evgeny Morozov, "Chips with everything", *Le Monde Diplomatique* (August 2021).

64 On exports-GDP ratio see World Bank data at https://data.worldbank.org/indicator/NE.EXP.GNFS.ZS?locations=CN. On foreign capitals' share of exports see C. Textor, "Foreign invested companies' share in total import and export in China 1986-2021", *Statista* (5 January 2023). https://www.statista.com/statistics/1288326/china-foreign-invested-companies-share-in-total-import-and-export/

65 Nina Xiang, "Foreign dependence the Achilles' heel in China's giant tech-sector", *Nikkei* Asia (31 January 2021). https://asia.nikkei.com/Opinion/Foreign-dependence-the-Achilles-heel-in-China-s-giant-tech-sector

Chapter 3
Xi's political project: repression and regime legitimacy

1 Lam, p60.

2 Zhang Yan "Xi's thought a development of Marxism", *China Daily UK* (10 May 2018). http://www.chinadaily.com.cn/cndy/2018-05/10/content_36172376.htm

3 Ruihan Huang and Joshua Henderson, "From fear to behaviour modification: Beijing entrenches corruption fight", *MacroPolo* (8 March 2022). https://macropolo.org/beijing-entrenches-corruption-fight/?rp=m.

4 Xinhua, "Constitution of the Communist Party of China" (28 October 2017). http://www.xinhuanet.

com//politics/19cpcnc/2017-10/28/c_1121870794.htm

5 Lam, p76.

6 Nis Grünberg, "Who is the CCP? China's Communist Party in infographics", *Mercator Institute for China Studies* (16 March 2021) https://merics.org/en/short-analysis/who-ccp-chinas-communist-party-infographics

7 Jérôme Doyon, "What's left of communism in China?", *Le Monde Diplomatique* (September 2021).

8 David Barboza, "Billions in hidden riches for family of Chinese leader", *New York Times* (26 October 2012). https://www.nytimes.com/2012/10/26/business/global/family-of-wen-jiabao-holds-a-hidden-fortune-in-china.html

9 "Xi Jinping millionaire relations reveal elite Chinese fortunes", *Bloomberg* (29 June 2012). https://www.bloomberg.com/news/articles/2012-06-29/xi-jinping-millionaire-relations-reveal-fortunes-of-elite?leadSource=uverify%20wall

10 "Xi Jinping's family is into rare earths, real estate and public contracts for a billion dollars", *PIME Asia News* (7 February 2012). https://www.asianews.it/news-en/Xi-Jinpings-family-is-into-rare-earths,-real-estate-and-public-contracts-for-a-billion-dollars-25173.html

11 See Martine Bulard, "The secretive world of the Communist Party", *Le Monde Diplomatique* (September 2012).

12 David Goodman, *Class in Contemporary China* (Cambridge: Polity Press, 2014) p79 and p88.

13 Ian Taylor, *Global Governance and Transnationalizing Capitalist Hegemony: The Myth of the "Emerging Powers"* (Abingdon: Routledge, 2017).

14 Goodman, p90.

15 Wing-Chung Ho, "The New 'Comprador Class': The Re-emergence of bureaucratic capitalists in post-Deng China", *Journal of Contemporary China* (vol. 22, issue 83, 2013).

16 Martin Hart-Landsberg, "The US Economy and China: Capitalism, Class and Crisis", *Monthly Review* (vol. 61, no. 9, 2010).

17 Goodman, p66. Here, Goodman draws on Alvin So, "The making of the cadre-capitalist class in China", in Joseph Cheng (ed.), *China's Challenges in the Twenty-First Century* (Hong Kong: Hong Kong University Press, 2003).

18 Alvin So (2013) p63. Cited in Simon Gilbert, "Class and class struggle in China today", *International Socialism 155* (Summer 2017) p158. https://isj.org.uk/class-and-class-struggle-in-china-today/

19 Verna Yu, "'The authorities will step up control': where next for China after protests?", *The Guardian* (10 Dec 2022).

20 Karl Marx and Frederick Engels "Manifesto of the Communist Party", in *Karl Marx: Selected Works* (volume 1) (London: Lawrence and Wishart, 1942) p207.

21 See Vanessa Cai, "What sidelined China's once powerful Communist Youth League?", *South China Morning Post* (9 May 2023). https://www.scmp.com/news/china/politics/article/3219931/what-sidelined-chinas-once-powerful-communist-youth-league

22 Cited in Verna Yu and Emma Graham-Harrison "The story of Xi. Some said his family's abuse by the party would forge a reformer. They were wrong", *The Guardian* (22 October 2022) p43.

23 See Claudio Katz, "Capitalist mutations in emerging, intermediate and peripheral neoliberalism", in Bond and Garcia (eds) pp73-4.

24 Ho-fung Hung, "Rise of China and the Global Overaccumulation Crisis", *Review of International Political Economy* (vol. 15, no. 2, 2008) p157.

25 The lure of political advance reinforces the dangers of financial enrichment. Officials' promotion prospects depend to a considerable extent on their region's GDP growth. As well as leading to the inflation of reported growth rates – officials in Binhai, Tianjin's financial district, admitted in January 2018 that its GDP was one-third smaller than reported – it also leads to a reluctance to reduce SOE capacity and therefore perpetuates duplication and waste production.

26 Four giant financial firms accounted for 20 percent of "irrational outflows" in 2016. Wu Xiaohui, the boss of *Anbank*, assumed (wrongly) that his marriage to Deng Xiaoping's granddaughter made him untouchable. But with many ordinary people facing financial losses in the shadow banking system the regime's concern about loss of legitimacy intensified the crackdown.

27 Qishan embodies the combination of conservative authoritarianism and liberal opening in the contemporary Chinese state, which complicates factional analysis. He supports both greater central state power and further opening to market forces and economic reform. There are echoes here of Thatcherism's combination of "the free economy and the strong state". See Andrew Gamble, *The Free Economy and the Strong State: the Politics of Thatcherism* (London: Palgrave, 1988).

28 The Chinese proverb, "kill the chicken to scare the monkey", meaning to move against one person in order to threaten others, applies here.

29 Lam, p109.

30 Cited in Tom Mitchell, "Beijing widen's anti-corruption drive", *Financial Times* (30 December 2013).

31 Ben Bland, "Hong Kong in a corner after Xi's raid on Xiao Jianhua", *Financial Times* (4/5 February 2017). https://www.ft.com/content/71a7583e-e9fb-11e6-967b-c88452263daf

32 Unintended consequences were evident soon after the crackdown began. The attacks on the culture of bribery may have actually increased costs as the mounting risks faced by corrupt officials encouraged many to "demand backhanders paid in foreign currency directly into offshore bank accounts". See Jamil Anderlini, "The political price of Xi Jinping's anti-corruption campaign", *Financial Times* (4 Jan 2017). https://www.ft.com/content/3f1938d6-d1cf-11e6-b06b-680c49b4b4c0

33 In Shenzhen for instance there are over 1,000 such committees, all adorned with party propaganda signs.

34 René Raphael & Ling Xi, "China's rewards and punishments", *Le Monde Diplomatique* (January 2019).

35 James Griffiths, *The Great Firewall of China: How to Build and Control an Alternative Version of the Internet* (London: Zed Books, 2019). Kindle edition, loc 305.

36 "Western values" are frequently mobilised by Western governments against China and other enemies of the day, but are just as frequently threatened by Western states. "Western values" are those of the (incomplete) Enlightenment project, whose content is limited by the capitalist framework in which it was elaborated but deepened by two centuries of struggle by workers, women, minority ethnic, gay and trans people, and others. For a powerful critique of such threats and defence of a radical universalism, rooted in but transcending Enlightenment values, against attacks from postcolonial theory see Vivek Chibber, *Postcolonial Theory and the Specter of Capital* (London: Verso, 2013). Chibber's focus is on postcolonial theory, but his arguments can also be applied to the CCP.

37 Lam, p85.

38 Lam, p83.

39 Wang Hui, p116.

40 Wang Hui, p111.

41 "How did Confucianism win back the Chinese Communist Party?", *Economist* (23 June 2021).

42 Confucius was criticised by all progressive Chinese movements in the twentieth century, including the May Fourth Movement of 1919. Deference is a flimsy base on which to challenge the humiliation suffered at the hands of more powerful states.

43 Some Confucian ideas were progressive for their time (he lived from 551 to 479 BCE). The Confucian proposal of an examination system for the selection of leading bureaucrats was only established under the Tang dynasty, 1,000 years after Confucius's death, but the meritocratic principle at its heart contrasts with inherited power and aristocratic privilege. Similarly, Confucius argued that rulers should be benevolent, and for reciprocity and mutual responsibilities between rulers and ruled. These ideas remain elitist and are useful tools for party-state managers to justify their own positions and present an image of reciprocity between paternalism and orderly behaviour. But, while there is no evidence of opposition movements to CCP rule that are rooted in Confucian ideas, it is not difficult to imagine how a radical reading of Confucius might be mobilised as an element of a wider challenge to the huge inequality, authoritarianism and repression under the CCP regime.

44 Emilie Frenkiel, "Xi, Shaolin monk – and emperor", *Le Monde Diplomatique* (October 2015) p5.

45 Frenkiel, p3.

Chapter 4
Workers, organisation and activism

1 See for example Chris King-Chi Chan and Pun Ngai, "The making of a new working class? A study of collective actions of migrant workers in South China", *The China Quarterly* (vol. 198, June 2009); Chris Smith and Pun Ngai, "The dormitory labour regime in China as a site for control and resistance", *The International Journal of Human Resource Management* (17(8), 2006).

2 Ching Kwan Lee "From organized dependence to disorganized despotism: changing labour regimes in Chinese factories", *The China Quarterly* (vol. 157, March 1999). See also the chapters by Lefeng Lin and Wenjuan Jia in Mingwei Liu and Chris Smith (eds) *China at Work: A Labour Process Perspective on the Transformation of Work and Employment in China* (London: Palgrave, 2016). For a focus on women workers' experiences in China's factories see C.K. Lee's *Gender and the South China Miracle: Two Worlds of Factory Women* (London: University of California Press, 1998).

3 Dexter Roberts, *The Myth of Chinese Capitalism: The Worker, the Factory and the Future of the World* (New York: Saint Martin's Press, 2020). Kindle edition, loc 478.

4 There is a parallel with postwar Italy where the labour movement of the north, already weakened by fascism, was diluted after 1945 by the migration of peasants and rural workers with no union background from the south. But a wave of strikes in 1962-63 reflected the integration of southern workers into the northern working class, and the "hot autumn" of 1969 saw the largest general strike in history up to that point. The flow of Chinese migrants has slowed dramatically and they have gained in confidence as they have become more settled. The objective conditions for independent working-class action are developing.

5 Hsiao-Hung Pai, *Scattered Sand: The Story of China's Rural Migrants* (London: Verso, 2012) is an excellent study of migrant workers and their struggles.

6 Despotism here means more than Marxism's general argument that workers under capitalism experience the despotism of the workplace, where the legal equality between buyer and seller of labour power at the level of the market becomes inequality in practice when one side of the labour contract, the worker, is put to work by the other, the boss, who controls the former's labour power during the working day.

7 Chris Smith and Mingwei Liu "In search of the labour process perspective in China", in Liu and Smith (eds), p17.

8 Regular murderous fires demonstrate that dormitory design is not based on care for the workers.

9 See Lulu Fan, "The self-organization of women workers in the informal sector of the garment industry: a study of female-led cooperative production teams in the Yangtze River delta region of China" in Liu and Smith (eds).

10 This paragraph draws on Pouille (2012).

11 The Marxist-feminist Yige Dong highlights the apparently contradictory response to the formalization of many labour contracts since a 2014 law restricted the use of sub-contracted workers in major plants. This increased workers' social rights, "at least on paper" (ie if employers do not evade the law), but many Foxconn workers preferred to stay on informal contracts and work only in the peak season. She explains this by reference to what she calls the "hybrid public-private regime of social reproduction". If workers work long overtime hours, peak-season wages at Foxconn are three or four times higher than low-season wages, which are close to the local minimum wage of around $300 a month. Meanwhile, migrant workers, particularly women, face increased demands to provide care due to the "rapid commodification of social reproduction including privatization of childcare, eldercare, and education in rural China". Poverty forces these workers into Foxconn factories while family pressure and welfare cuts force them back to rural areas to provide care, emotional support and household labour. Were the urban *hukou* available to these workers then much of the care could be provided by the social state. But social benefits are not available until workers have worked in the same city for at least fifteen years, even though social contributions are deducted from their gross pay, reducing the $300 to around $225. See Promise Li, "The Foxconn uprising in Zhengzhou" (interview with Yige Dong), *Tempest* (5 December 2022). https://www.tempestmag.org/2022/12/the-foxconn-uprising-in-zhengzhou/

12 Wejuan Jia, "The making of a dualistic labour regime: changing labour process and power relations in a Chinese state-owned enterprise under globalization", in Liu and Smith (eds).

13 Pouille.

14 Lu Zhang, *Inside China's Automobile Factories: The Politics of Labour and Worker Resistance* (Cambridge: Cambridge University Press, 2015) p167.

15 Delivery drivers killed on the streets are generally excluded from the figures because these are classified as traffic accidents. In 2015 "non-productive accidents", whatever they are, were removed from official figures. Real deaths at work are therefore far higher than official figures suggest.

16 Hao Zhang, "Employer responses to labour shortage in China: the case of the knitware industry", in Liu and Smith (eds).

17 ILOSTAT website: https://www.ilo.org/shinyapps/bulkexplorer30/?lang=en&id=CHN_A

18 The US bureau passed on its methodology to the Conference Board, from which this data is taken. See https://www.conference-board.org/ilcprogram/

19 Milton Ezrati, "The East-West wage gap not nearly as compelling as it once was", *Forbes* (30 January 2023). https://www.forbes.com/sites/miltonezrati/2023/01/30/the-east-west-wage-gap-not-nearly-as-compelling-as-it-once-was/?sh=188b9022254d

20 See "China once stressed the importance of setting minimum wages", *Economist* (21 December 2019) p89.

21 Silver and Zhang, 2009, p175.

22 Hao Ren, Eli Friedman and Zhongjin Li, *China on Strike: Narratives of Workers' Resistance* (Chicago: Haymarket Books, 2016). Kindle edition, loc 496.

23 Another category, disputes, includes cases taken through official procedures, the vast majority involving an individual or a handful of workers. They give some idea of the level of discontent but not of the number of strikes.

24 Minqi Li, *China and the 21st Century Crisis* (London: Pluto Press, 2016) p29.

25 Ren, Friedman and Li. Loc 3031.

26 Simon Gilbert, "China: a labour movement in the making?", *Socialist Review* (April 2018) p19.

27 One example of collusion is that businesses frequently fail to pay, or underpay, their contributions to social security funds controlled by local authorities.

28 Ren, Friedman and Li. Loc 473.

29 ILO Research Brief, "Institutional constraints for the extension of social insurance coverage to informal economy workers in China" (November 2020) p6. https://www.ilo.org/wcmsp5/groups/public/---asia/---ro-bangkok/---ilo-beijing/documents/briefingnote/wcms_761658.pdf

30 Geoffrey Crothall, "Trade union reform in China: an assessment", *Made in China* (vol. 5 no. 1 2020). https://madeinchinajournal.com/2020/03/02/trade-union-reform-in-china-an-assessment/

31 Very similar to Japanese unions after the defeat of the giant general unions in 1951 paved the way for 750,000 company unions. See Adrian Budd, "The crisis and contradictions of stake-holder capitalism", *Contemporary Politics* (vol. 3, no. 2, 1997).

32 Smith and Liu, p2.

33 Ren, Friedman and Li. Loc 398.

34 Ren, Friedman and Li. Loc 1354.

35 Fan, p138.

36 Ren, Friedman and Li. Hao Ren is the original Chinese edition editor.

37 "China's Yue Yuen shoe factory workers in large strike", *BBC News* (15 April 2014). https://www.bbc.co.uk/news/world-asia-china-27033186

38 See Han Dongfang, "A Chinese alternative" *Le Monde Diplomatique* (December 2014) p10.

39 Pratap Chatterjee, "Yue Yuen shoe factory backs down after workers strike for pensions", *Corpwatch* (3 May 2014). https://www.corpwatch.org/article/yue-yuen-shoe-factory-backs-down-after-workers-strike-pensions

40 Ren, Friedman and Li. Loc 277.

41 Han Dongfang.

42 Han Dongfang.

43 Chris King-chi Chan and Elaine Sio-ieng Hui, "Direct elections in workplace trade unions in China: implications for the changing labour regime", in Liu and Smith (eds) p263.

44 Yunxue Deng, "Collective bargaining in the auto parts industry in Guangzhou", in Liu and Smith (eds) p331.

45 Ren, Friedman and Li. Loc 868.

46 Wen, "The End of an Era: Labor Activism in Early 21st Century China", *Chuang* online (24 April 2023). https://chuangcn. org/2023/04/the-end-of-an-era-labor-activism-in-early-21st-century-china/

47 "Holding China's trade unions to account", *China Labour Bulletin* (17 February 2020). https://clb.org.hk/en/content/holding-china%E2%80%99s-trade-unions-account

48 Chris King-chi Chan and Elaine Sio-ieng Hui, "The development of collective bargaining in China: from 'collective bargaining by riot' to 'party-state-led wage bargaining", *The China Quarterly*, 217, 2013.

49 Wen.

50 *China Labour Bulletin* (2020).

51 Crothall 2020.

52 Labour NGOs should be regarded differently to the Western NGOs that have been criticised as (often unwitting) agents of neoliberalism and imperialism. James Petras argues that they have been used to plug holes in social welfare that have resulted from the imposition of structural adjustment by the international financial institutions. NGO projects, often devised to deliver Western states' aid programmes, operate in collaboration with local states and therefore undermine and demobilise protest movements aiming to challenge, rather than cooperate with, those states. They also pose a problem for democratisation movements by removing welfare debates and policies from the public domain. Worse, they perpetuate relations of neocolonialism and dependence on powerful external forces, whose aid programmes are based on the interests of the donor rather than the recipient. Thus, NGO talk of popular "empowerment" in the Global South is misplaced at best and an ideological smokescreen at worst. Finally, programmes fit the neoliberal model of disaggregated market-driven societies by operating at the local level rather than addressing the societal level. None of this means that NGO programme workers are not generally opposed to neoliberalism and act out of a genuine humanistic motivation. See James Petras, "NGOs: in the service of imperialism", *Journal of Contemporary Asia* (29 (4), 1999). Arundhati Roy makes a similar argument in *Capitalism: A Ghost Story* (London: Verso, 2015) chapter one. Regarding labour NGOs in China, Ren, Friedman and Li's *China on Strike* argues that they "have no democratic basis on which to represent workers. In some cases, NGOs try to contain struggle to the legal terrain, thereby restricting the development of the workers' movement", Loc 3554.

53 Wen.

54 Women play a key role in industrial relations scholarship in China. Women make up a large proportion of migrant workers, and the majority of labour activists and the students who work with them, either inside workplaces or from the outside, are women.

55 Wei Lizhi, "Feminists in danger, workers in support", *libcom.org* (13 March 2015). https://libcom.org/article/free-womens-day-five-statements-chinese-workers-and-students

56 "Shutting the gate", *Economist* (14 September 2019) p.59.

57 "Let the People Themselves Decide Whether We're Guilty", *Chuang* (14 June 2018). https://chuangcn.org/2018/06/eight-leftists-analysis/

58 Kevin Lin, "New sites of struggle in a changing China", *Socialist Review* (September 2019). https://socialistworker.co.uk/socialist-review-archive/new-sites-struggle-changing-china/

59 Wen.

60 Ren, Friedman and Li. Loc 3556.

61 C. Textor, "Distribution of the gross domestic product (GDP) across economic sectors in China from 2012 to 2022", *Statista* (29 September 2023). https://www. statista.com/statistics/270325/distribution-of-gross-domestic-product-gdp-across-economic-sectors-in-china

62 Lu Luyi and Li Tingyu, "Picking Quarrels", *Chuang* (Issue 2, no date). https:// chuangcn.org/journal/two/

63 Au Loong-yu "What is the nature of capitalism in China? On the rise of China and its inherent contradictions", *Europe Solidaire Sans Frontières* (May 2014). https://www.europe-solidaire.org/spip. php?article35764

64 The phrase was first used by the French writer Romain Rolland. See Francesca Antonini, "Pessimism of the Intellect, Optimism of the Will: Gramsci's Political Thought in the Last Miscellaneous Notebooks", *Rethinking Marxism: A Journal of Economics, Culture and Society* (Vol 31, issue 1, 2019). https://www.tandfonline/ doi/full/10.1080/08935696.2019.1577616

65 C. Textor, "Distribution of the workforce across economic sectors in China from 2012 to 2022", *Statista* (29 September 2023). https://www.statista.com/ statistics/270327/distribution-of-the-workforce-across-economic-sectors-in-china/. The events of May 1968 in France included the largest general strike in history to date and contained the potential for socialist revolution. Service workers comprised 52 percent of total employment at the time.

66 Wang Hui, p196.

67 Wang Hui, p187

68 Gilbert, 2017, pp162-4.

69 Wen.

70 996:ICU means working 9-to-9 for 6 days a week, eventually sending workers to the intensive care unit (ICU). See Wang Xuegiao and Tom Hancock, "Overdoing it: the cost of China's long-hours culture" *Financial Times* (17 January 2019). https://www.ft.com/content/ d5f01f68-9cbc-11e8-88de-49c908b1f264

71 On Mengzhu see Wen. On recent strikes see "Food delivery riders strike for increased pay per delivery", *China Labour Bulletin* (18 May 2023). https://clb.org. hk/en/content/food-delivery-riders-strike-increased-pay-delivery

72 "Surge in manufacturing protests in China", *China Labour Bulletin* (16 May 2023). https://clb.org.hk/en/content/ surge-manufacturing-protests-china-deserves-international-attention. See also Amy Hawkins, "Surge in strikes at Chinese factories after Covid rules end", *Guardian* (21 May 2023). https://www.theguardian. com/world/2023/may/21/surge-in-strikes-at-chinese-factories-after-covid-rules-end

73 Antonio Gramsci, *Selections from Political Writings 1921–1926* (London: Lawrence and Wishart, 1978) p240.

74 Antonio Gramsci, *Selections from Prison Notebooks* (London: Lawrence and Wishart, 1971) p168.

75 Antonio Gramsci, 1971, p333.

76 Minqi Li, p7.

77 Ching Kwan Lee, *Against the Law* (Berkeley: University of California Press, 2007), p239.

Chapter 5
Oppressions and resistance

1 Chuang, "introduction" to Wen.

2 See Chen Shaohua and Martin Ravallion, "Reconciling the conflicting narratives on poverty in China", *Journal of Development Economics* (vol. 153, November 2021). https://www.sciencedirect.com/science/ article/abs/pii/S0304387821000857

3 In 1953 Mao published an article in *The People's Daily* that argued that common prosperity would result from collective ownership. On "common prosperity" see Cainey and Prange, pp54-58.

4 Cited in Cainey and Prange, p56.

5 Chaguan column "The politics of poverty", *Economist* (19 September 2020) p56.

6 This paragraph draws on "Clarifying the battle lines", *Economist* (20 June 2020) p71.

7 Sonali Jain-Chandra, "Chart of the Week: Inequality in China", IMF Blog (20 September 2018). https://www.imf.org/en/Blogs/Articles/2018/09/20/chart-of-the-week-inequality-in-china

8 Barry Naughton, *The Chinese Economy: Transitions and Growth* (Cambridge, Mass.: MIT Press, 2007) p218. Arundhati Roy's data suggests that Modi's India is a close second. She writes that "the sixty-three richest people have more money than the 2018-19 Union Budget for 1.3 billion people" and that "while hundreds of millions lost their jobs" during the Covid pandemic "India's billionaires increased their wealth by 35 per cent". Arundhati Roy, *Azadi: Fascism, Fiction and Freedom in the Time of the Virus* (expanded edition) (London: Penguin Books, 2022) p219.

9 Gilbert, 2017, p156.

10 W G Runciman, *Relative Deprivation and Social Justice* (London: Routledge and Kegan Paul, 1966).

11 Shaohua and Ravallion, p1.

12 Chaguan column, "System, heal thyself", *Economist* (29 August 2020) p47.

13 Lam p156.

14 "China's social security system", *China Labour Bulletin* (18 August 2021). https://clb.org.hk/content/china%E2%80%99s-social-security-system

15 Laura He, "Chinese cities are so broke, they're cutting medical benefits for seniors", CNN (23 March 2023). https://edition.cnn.com/2023/03/31/economy/china-pension-protests-aging-society-intl-hnk/index.html

16 The State Council, The People's Republic of China, "Seventh National Census Key Data (2021)". http://www.gov.cn/xinwen/2021-05/11/content_5605871.htm

17 Karl Marx, "Marx to Meyer and Vogt" 9 April 1870, in *The Correspondence of Marx and Engels* (London: Martin Lawrence, 1934) pp289-90. https://www.marxists.org/archive/marx/works/1870/letters/70_04_09.htm

18 Cited in Simon Gilbert, "Workers and the national question", *Socialist Review* (September 2018) p21.

19 See Tsering Shakya, *Dragon in the Land of the Snows: A History of Modern Tibet since 1947* (London: Pimlico, 1999).

20 Lam p36. Xi Jinping's father, who had a strong friendship with the Dalai Lama and favoured peaceful reconciliation, was a notable exception. Some on the left today oppose Tibetan aspirations in the belief that allegiance to the Dalai Lama symbolises Tibetan backwardness or feudalism. In reality national oppression and the relative weakness of economic development combine to strengthen the position of the Dalai Lama in the thinking of ordinary Tibetans. It is not clear whether these critics of Tibet have made a careful comparison of Buddhist and Confucian thought and concluded that officially sanctioned Confucianism and China's official Confucius Institutes mark a progressive advance on Tibetan Buddhism.

21 On the struggle for Tibetan independence see Tsering Woeser, *Tibet on Fire: Self-immolations against Chinese Rule* (London: Verso, 2016) and Wang Lixiong and Tsering Shakya, *The Struggle for Tibet* (London: Verso, 2011).

22 See Martine Bulard, "Losing Tibetanness", *Le Monde Diplomatique* (December 2019).

23 Sinicisation means to make something more Chinese or to bring something under greater Chinese influence.

24 Baogang He and Yingjie Guo, *Nationalism, National Identity and Democratization in China* (Abingdon: Routledge, 2018).

25 Huo Siyu, "Main data from 7th National Population Census of Xinjiang Uygur Autonomous Region", *Global Times* (14 June 2021). https://www.globaltimes.cn/page/202106/1226112.shtml

26 Gardner Bovingdon, "Autonomy in Xinjiang: Han nationalist imperatives and Uyghur discontent", (Washington: East-West Center, 2004). https://www.eastwestcenter.org/publications/autonomy-xinjiang-han-nationalist-imperatives-and-uyghur-discontent

27 Amnesty International reports that there were around 190 executions between January 1997 and April 1999. "China: gross violations of human rights in the Xinjiang Uyghur autonomous region", *Amnesty International* (31 March 1999). https://www.amnesty.org/en/documents/asa17/018/1999/en/. See also Rémi Castets, "China's internal colony", *Le Monde Diplomatique* (March 2019).

28 Gilbert (2021) p50.

29 There have been instances of terror attacks, albeit on a small scale. These include a 2013 car-bomb in Tiananmen Square and a 2014 knife attack in Kunming.

30 Darren Byler, *Terror Capitalism: Uyghur Dispossession and Masculinity in a Chinese City* (Durham, NC: Duke University Press, 2021).

31 Enshen Li, "Fighting the 'Three Evils': a structural analysis of counter-terrorism legal architecture in China", *Emory International Law Review* (vol. 33, issue 3, 2019). https://scholarlycommons.law.emory.edu/eilr/vol33/iss3/1

32 Castets.

33 In Linxia Prefecture in Gansu province the local CCP boss sought to justify anti-Muslim measures as an attempt to "lessen the burden" on believers by reducing the "frequency, duration and scale of religious activities". See "China's repression of Islam is spreading beyond Xinjiang", *Economist* (26 September 2019). https://www.economist.com/china/2019/09/26/chinas-repression-of-islam-is-spreading-beyond-xinjiang

34 Nathan Ruser, James Leibold, Kelsey Munro and Tilla Hoja, *Cultural Erasure: Tracing the Destruction of Uyghur and Islamic Spaces in Xinjiang*, Australian Strategic Policy Institute (24 September 2020). https://www.aspi.org.au/report/cultural-erasure#:~:text=and%20case%20studies-,Mosques,188%20remained%20undamaged%20(35.3%25)

35 "China: draconian repression of Muslims in Xinjiang amounts to crimes against humanity", *Amnesty International* (10 June 2021). https://www.amnesty.org/en/latest/news/2021/06/china-draconian-repression-of-muslims-in-xinjiang-amounts-to-crimes-against-humanity/

36 See Xiao Qiang, "The road to digital unfreedom: President Xi's surveillance state", *Journal of Democracy* (vol. 30, no. 1, 2019). https://www.journalofdemocracy.org/articles/the-road-to-digital-unfreedom-president-xis-surveillance-state/

37 Tara Francis Chan "How a Chinese region that accounts for just 1.5% of the population became one of the most intrusive police states in the world", *Business Insider* (1 August 2018). https://www.businessinsider.com/xianjiang-province-china-police-state-surveillance-2018-7?r=US&IR=T

38 Children in other minority-language enclaves, in Inner Mongolia and elsewhere, have also been exposed to a patriotic education, taught in Mandarin.

39 "Break their lineage, break their roots", *Human Right Watch* (19 April 2021). https://www.hrw.org/report/2021/04/19/break-their-lineage-break-their-roots/chinas-crimes-against-humanity-targeting#_ftn122. Much is made of Xi's anti-extremism camps by Western states, but according to John Bolton, Trump's one-time hardline national security adviser, in 2019 Trump told Xi that the Uyghur camps were "exactly the right thing to do". Anon., "Before leaving office, Mike Pompeo accused China of genocide", *Economist* (23 January 2021) p48.

40 Castets.

41 Austin Ramzy and Chris Buckly "'Absolutely no mercy': leaked files expose how China organized mass detention of Muslims", *New York Times* (16 November 2019). https://www.nytimes.com/interactive/2019/11/16/world/asia/china-xinjiang-documents.html

42 The Uyghur intellectual Ilham Tohti argues that for Beijing Uyghurs' "backward" culture made them ill-suited to modernisation and reform, but as Han immigration increased and local people and cultures were marginalised, the conditions were created for increased support for self-determination. Tohti was a moderate who rejected separatism and favoured reconciliation, yet was given a life sentence for separatism in 2014! See his *We Uyghurs Have No Say* (London: Verso, 2022).

43 Beijing's security concerns have an international dimension. China depends on transport and energy infrastructures in Xinjiang and neighbouring central Asian republics to guarantee supply and extend its economic influence westwards. It has enlisted these countries, along with Russia and others, in the Shanghai Cooperation Organisation. Its member-state ruling classes share a common interest in combatting potential religious radicalism and many of its joint manoeuvres have been against "terrorist networks", which China fears could cross more fully into Xinjiang. The anti-Chinese protests in Kazakhstan in 2019, against Chinese firms' land purchases as well as over Xinjiang repression, underline the persistent threat of instability in central Asia.

44 "What happens when China's Uighurs are released from re-education camps", *Economist* (7 March 2020). https://www.economist.com/china/2020/03/05/what-happens-when-chinas-uighurs-are-released-from-re-education-camps.

45 On Hong Kong protests and relations with China see Mary-Françoise Renard, "Hong Kong's shrinking democracy", *Le Monde Diplomatique* (June 2022).

46 See Lam Chi Leung, "We've already won", *Socialist Review* (November 2014).

47 Lam Chi Leung.

48 On the 2014 and 2019 protests see Au Loong-yu, *Hong Kong in Revolt: The Protest Movement and the Future of China* (London: Pluto Press, 2020).

49 Anon., "Hong Kong protesters vow to stay on the streets despite Carrie Lam concession", *Guardian* (4 September 2019). https://www.theguardian.com/world/2019/sep/04/hong-kong-will-scrapping-extradition-bill-end-the-protests

50 Alex Hern, "Apple bows to Chinese pressure and removes podcasts from store", *Guardian* (13 June 2020). https://www.theguardian.com/technology/2020/jun/12/apple-removes-two-podcast-apps-from-china-store-after-censorship-demands. Other apps have suffered a similar fate, underlining the links between Western high-tech companies and the Chinese state. In 2020 Zoom suspended human rights activists' accounts after pressure from China's Cyberspace Administration.

51 Au Loong-yu, "Hong Kong: spontaneity and the mass movement", *Socialist Review* (November 2014); Au Loong-yu, "Victory in defeat for Hong Kong movement", *Socialist Review* (January 2015); Lam Chi Leung 2014.

52 This paragraph draws on the UNISON union's webpage "Showing solidarity with Hong Kong's independent trade unions", https://www.unison.org.uk/news/article/2023/10/showing-solidarity-with-hong-kongs-independent-trade-unions/. See also Kevin Lin, "A New Chapter for Hong Kong's Labour Movement?", *Made in China Journal* (8 March 2022). https://madeinchinajournal.com/2022/03/08/a-new-chapter-for-hong-kongs-labour-movement/

53 Leo Tang, "As long as there are people, we can continue to write our own stories", *Lausan* (17 October 2021). https://lausan.hk/2021/we-can-continue-to-write-our-own-stories

54 "Almost nobody in Hong Kong under 30 identifies as 'Chinese'", *Economist* (26 August 2019).

55 Sally Kincaid, "Women in China: what has changed?", *Socialist Review* (June 2018).

56 "Migrant workers and their children", *China Labour Bulletin* (6 September 2023). https://clb.org.hk/en/content/migrant-workers-and-their-children

57 Fan, p140.

58 Wesley Liu, "Harmony is most precious, either for a family or a society", *China Daily* (26 September 2016). https://www.chinadaily.com.cn/hkedition/2016-09/26/content_26892710.htm

59 Ethan Michelson, *Decoupling: Gender Injustice in China's Divorce Courts* (Cambridge: Cambridge University Press, 2022), p18. https://www.cambridge.org/core/books/decoupling/sisyphus-goes-to-divorce-court/7BCE8F61211516D549110B18ADB20321

60 Cited in "Though muffled, China's #MeToo movement still has support", *Economist* (16 December 2020).

61 Fok Yit Wai, "The short life of patriotic idol Jiangshan Jiao", *Think China* (24 February 2020). https://www.thinkchina.sg/short-life-patriotic-idol-jiang-shanjiao. For a wider academic analysis, including of reproductive politics, see Jingxue Zhang "Within the discrepancy and rupture: China young women's resistant reproductive consciousness", (University of Texas, 2020). https://repositories.lib.utexas.edu/bitstream/handle/2152/87058/ZHANG-THESIS-2020.pdf

62 Jing Zeng "You say #MeToo, I say #MiTu: China's online campaigns against sexual abuse", in Bianca Fileborn and Rachel Loney-Howes (eds.), *#MeToo and the Politics of Social Change* (Cham, Switzerland: Palgrave Macmillan, 2019) p78. https://www.researchgate.net/publication/335850974_You_say_MeToo_I_say_MiTu_China's_online_campaigns_against_sexual_abuse

63 Jing, p80.

64 Leta Hong Fincher, *Leftover Women: The Resurgence of Gender Inequality in China* (London: Bloomsbury Academic, 2023).

65 Pak Yiu, "China LGBTQ community hangs tough in dissent amid repression", *Nikkei Asia* (20 February 2024). https://asia.nikkei.com/Spotlight/Asia-Insight/China-LGBTQ-community-hangs-tough-in-dissent-amid-repression

66 Jessie Lau, "'It's difficult to survive': China's LGBTQ+ advocates face jail and forced confession" *Guardian* (15 January 2024). https://www.theguardian.com/global-development/2024/jan/15/its-difficult-to-survive-chinas-lgbtq-advocates-face-jail-and-forced-confession

67 Bill Browning, "China bans 'sissy men' from television in latest crackdown", *LGBTQNation* (3 September 2021). https://www.lgbtqnation.com/2021/09/china-bans-sissy-men-television-latest-crackdown/

68 Xintian Wang, "China's government is targeting 'sissy' men, with devastating consequences", *gal–dem* (26 January 2022). https://gal-dem.com/china-sissy-men-lgbtq/

69 Lucetta Kam, "Why the struggle for same-sex marriage in China will continue, despite civil code setback", *South China Morning Post* (26 July 2020). https://www.scmp.com/comment/opinion/article/3094520/why-struggle-same-sex-marriage-china-will-continue-despite-civil

70 Stephanie Yingyi Wang, "Fare thee well Beijing LGBT Centre", *Made In China* (January–June 2023). https://madeinchinajournal.com/2023/06/08/fare-thee-well-beijing-lgbt-centre/

71 Vanessa Cai, "Chinese university students disciplined over rainbow flags file lawsuit against Education Ministry", *South China Morning Post* (22 February 2023). https://www.scmp.com/news/china/politics/article/3211077/chinese-university-students-disciplined-over-rainbow-flags-file-lawsuit-against-education-ministry

72 Wang, 2023.

73 Wang, 2023.

74 This section draws on Adrian Budd, "China's environmental catastrophe", *International Socialism* 176 (Autumn 2022), a review of Richard Smith, *China's Engine of Environmental Collapse* (London: Pluto Press, 2020).

75 The EU expects to only halve the carbon emissions of its peak year, 1990, by 2030 and to achieve net-zero by 2050.

76 Berkeley Earth, "Killer air" (August 2015). https://berkeleyearth.org/wp-content/uploads/2015/08/Press-Release-Killer-Air-August-2015.pdf

77 Greenpeace East Asia, "Nearly half of Chinese provinces miss water targets, 85% of Shanghai's river water not fit for human contact", (press release) (1 June 2017). https://www.greenpeace.org/eastasia/press/1459/nearly-half-of-chinese-provinces-miss-water-targets-85-of-shanghais-river-water-not-fit-for-human-contact/

78 Richard Smith, pvii.

79 Vaclav Smil, *Making the Modern World: Materials and Dematerialization* (Chichester: John Wiley & Sons, 2014) p92.

80 "Share of energy consumption by source, China", *Our World in Data.* https://ourworldindata.org/grapher/share-energy-source-sub?time=1990..latest&country=~CHN. Chinese companies are also building hundreds of coal powered plants around the world, thereby perpetuating the global dependence on fossil fuels.

81 *Our World in Data.*

82 Dam-building impacts outside China too. China has constructed a dozen dams on the Upper Mekong river for irrigation and hydro-electric power generation. Downstream – in Thailand, Laos, Cambodia and Vietnam – water levels have become dangerously low, imperilling fishing and people's access to fresh water. Environmental activists fear the future of downstream societies if China does not agree to common management arrangements for the Mekong.

83 Aude Vidal "No more plastics in Southeast Asia paradise", *Le Monde Diplomatique* (May 2021). Malaysia also reacted to being a dumping ground for rich-country plastic waste, returning 4,000 tonnes of illegal imports to the sending countries in 2020. Nevertheless, it adheres to the logic of capitalist markets: in the first half of 2020 it received 33,000 tonnes from the UK alone, 81 percent more than in 2019. See Nicola Smith, "Britain sends more plastic waste to Southeast Asia despite clashes with local government", *Telegraph* (9 October 2020). https://www.telegraph.co.uk/news/2020/10/09/britain-sends-plastic-waste-southeast-asia-despite-clashes-local/

84 "The bad earth", *Economist* (10 June 2017). More generally, see Mohamed Larbi Bouguerra, "China's chemical catastrophe", *Le Monde Diplomatique* (February 2020).

85 There is a sleight of hand here too – electric vehicles have large carbon footprints while also requiring electricity produced from fossil fuels to charge their batteries.

86 Camille Bortolini, "Trade war in strategic minerals", *Le Monde Diplomatique* (July 2020). https://mondediplo.com/2020/07/08rare-metals

87 See Au Loong-yu, "A Leftist perspective on China's environmental destruction", *New Politics* (vol. 18, no. 2, 2021). https://newpol.org/review/a-leftist-perspective-on-chinas-environmental-destruction/

88 Richard Smith, p78 and p6.

89 Richard Smith, p193.

90 Richard Smith, p10.

91 See Guillaume Pitron, "Red China's green crisis", *Le Monde Diplomatique* (July 2017).

92 Cited in Au Loong-yu (2021).

93 Richard Smith, pxxii.

94 Lo Hoi-ying and Beata Mo, "China's 'blank paper' graduates fear years of remote learning and no experience make them unemployable", *South China Morning Post* (16 June 2023). https://www.scmp.com/economy/china-economy/article/3224211/chinas-blank-paper-graduates-fear-years-remote-learning-and-no-experience-make-them-unemployable

Chapter 6
China, the US and inter-imperialist rivalry

1 V I Lenin, "Imperialism: the Highest Stage of Capitalism", in *Lenin: Selected Works* (London: Lawrence and Wishart, 1969 [1917]). Nikolai Bukharin, *Imperialism and World Economy* (London: Merlin Press, 1987 [1918]).

2 See Alex Callinicos, *Imperialism and Global Political Economy* (Cambridge: Polity Press, 2009), pp41-52.

3 Carchedi and Roberts, p124.

4 Carchedi and Roberts, p118. The criticisms of Carchedi and Roberts in this chapter concern their particular arguments on China. Their book is, more generally, an important and powerful Marxist analysis of contemporary capitalism.

5 For a critique of UE's bolder claims see Michael Kidron, "Black Reformism", in *Capitalism and Theory* (London: Pluto Press, 1974). Criticising Samir Amin's model of UE, which differed to Emmanuel's, Kidron highlights other mechanisms of imperialist value transfer, including: repatriation of profits, fees and royalties; the arms trade (exchange of potentially productive resources from the South for "necessarily unproductive resources"); the South-to-North brain drain; northern capital's benefits from state spending in the South. Using these wider mechanisms Kidron calculated that South-North value transfers were four times higher than Amin's. Amin acknowledged the sort of criticism made by Kidron, writing that UE transfers are "of marginal significance to the centre", albeit that this is not the case for the Global South. See Samir Amin, *Accumulation on a World Scale* (New York: Monthly Review Press, 1974) p23. Carchedi and Roberts' own figures (pp140-1) reinforce Amin's argument on the scale of UE transfers: they estimate

that the total transfer of value through UE is just 1 percent of "imperialist" countries' and "dominated" countries' GDPs, hardly dramatic, albeit that their sample of the latter is only 11 countries.

6 Carchedi and Roberts, p143.

7 Carchedi and Roberts, p222.

8 UNCTAD, "Global foreign direct investment flows over the last 30 years" (5 May 2023). https://unctad.org/data-visualization/global-foreign-direct-investment-flows-over-last-30-years

9 Callinicos, 2009.

10 Philip Golub captures something of this in "Curbing China's rise", *Le Monde Diplomatique* (October 2019). https://mondediplo.com/2019/10/05china/ Golub argues that the widespread failure to foresee Trump's unilateralism in 2016 "overestimated the autonomy of capital and its capacity to shape policy, and underestimated the political and strategic implications of China's re-emergence". Corporate hostility towards Trump and conservative views of the national interest is not driven by an unwavering cosmopolitanism, but it does highlight the tensions between these differentiated logics.

In the postwar era Asian developmental states also illustrated the differentiation between capitals and the capitalist state. The Japanese and South Korean states in particular forcefully restructured private capitalist groups into conglomerates - zaibatsu in Japan and chaebols in South Korea – that then received wide-ranging state support to enhance their capacity to compete in world markets. State planners' long-term perspectives (including encouraging social stability and national development, addressing emerging technological trends, and locating future market opportunities) continue to coexist, and sometimes clash, with capitals' short-term interests and calculations.

11 Au Loong-yu, "Opposing US militarisation in the Asia-Pacific should not mean remaining silent on China's emerging imperialism" (interview with Federico Fuentes), *Links.org* 2 December 2023. https://links.org.au/au-loong-yu-hong-kong-opposing-us-militarisation-asia-pacific-should-not-mean-remaining-silent

12 Harris, 1978, p215.

13 Harris, 1978, p213.

14 Philip Golub, 2019.

15 Cited in David Sanger, "A grand trade bargain", *Foreign Affairs*, volume 80, issue 2 (January/February 2001). www.foreignaffairs.com/articles/2001-01-01/grand-trade-bargain

16 Joseph Fewsmith, "The political and social implications of China's accession to the WTO", *The China Quarterly*, (vol. 167, September 2001) p574.

17 Bob Davis and Lingling Wei, *Superpower Showdown: How the Battle Between Trump and Xi Threatens a New Cold War* (New York: HarperBusiness 2020).

18 See Adrian Budd, "China and imperialism in the 21st century", *International Socialism* (170, Spring, 2021) p132.

19 Rival interests ensure that European states do not automatically follow the US, but the EU has also adopted a tougher stance on China. Its 2019 strategic outlook document described China as an "economic competitor" and "systemic rival". See European Commission, *EU-China: a Strategic Outlook* (12 March 2019) p1. https://ec.europa.eu/info/sites/info/files/communication-eu-china-a-strategic-outlook.pdf

20 World Bank "Merchandise exports...". https://data.worldbank.org/indicator/TX.VAL.MRCH.CD.WT?view=chart&locations=CN

21 James Kynge, Amy Kazmin and Farhan Bokhari, "How China rules the waves" *Financial Times* (13 January 2017).

22 Lin Chun, *China and Global Capitalism: Reflections on Marxism, History and Contemporary Politics* (London: Palgrave Macmillan, 2013), p58.

23 Tom Mitchell, "China struggles to win friends over South China Sea", *Financial Times* (13 July 2016).

24 James Hoge, "A global power shift in the making: is the United States ready?", *Foreign Affairs* (vol. 83, issue 4, July/August 2004); Robert Kaplan, "How we would fight China", *The Atlantic* (June 2005). www.theatlantic.com/magazine/archive/2005/06/how-we-would-fight-china/303959 Arvind Subramanian, "The inevitable superpower: why China's dominance is a sure thing", *Foreign Affairs* (vol. 90, issue 5, September/October 2011) p68. www.foreignaffairs.com/articles/china/2011-08-19/inevitable-superpower

25 Barack Obama, "Remarks by the President in State of the Union Address" (20 January 2015). https://obamawhitehouse.archives.gov/the-press-office/2015/01/20/remarks-president-state-union-address-January-20-2015

26 Geoff Dyer, "Beijing's elevated aspirations", *Financial Times* (10 November 2010).

27 BBC News, "Full Text: China's new party chief Xi Jinping's speech" (15 November 2012). www.bbc.com/news/world-asia-china-20338586

28 Ye Zicheng, *Inside China's Grand Strategy: the Perspective from the People's Republic* (Lexington: University Press of Kentucky, 2011) p72.

29 Cited in Shi Jiangtao, "Are China-US relations drifting closer towards war?", *South China Morning Post* (20 July 2020). https://www.scmp.com/news/china/diplomacy/article/3093823/are-china-us-relations-drifting-closer-towards-war

30 Robert Blackwill and Ashley Tellis, *Revising US Grand Strategy Toward China* (Council on Foreign Relations, 2015). Lawrence Shoup, "Dangerous circumstances": the Council on Foreign Relations proposes a new grand strategy towards China", *Monthly Review* (vol. 67, issue 4, September 2015) p12.

31 Blackwill and Tellis, p4.

32 White House, *National Security Strategy of the United States of America* (Washington: 2017), p3. https://tinyurl.com/yrtkhdwk

33 US Congress, "HR5515: John S. McCain National Defense Authorization Act for Fiscal Year 2019". https://www.congress.gov/bill/115th-congress/house-bill/5515/text

34 Intellectual property theft is a long-standing Western complaint but intellectual property rights are increasingly protected in China as its firms increase their share of global patent applications.

35 Joe Biden, "Why America must lead again", *Foreign Affairs* (March/April 2020). https://www.foreignaffairs.com/articles/united-states/2020-01-23/why-america-must-lead-again

36 Overseas firms have a stronger presence in China than Western propaganda suggests: across major consumer categories in 2017 foreign firms' penetration averaged 40 percent, against 26 percent in the US. See Jonathan Woetzel, Jeongmin Seong et al, "China and the world: inside the dynamics of a changing relationship", *McKinsey and Company* (1 July 2019). https://www.mckinsey.com/featured-insights/china/china-and-the-world-inside-the-dynamics-of-a-changing-relationship. Meanwhile trade data can obscure complex global relationships. China has become a regional economic hub, accounting in 2021 for a quarter of the exports from Taiwan, South Korea, Japan, and ASEAN (Association of South-east Asian Nations). If the value of imported components incorporated into China's exports to the US (previously exported directly to the US) is excluded, the US deficit with China falls

considerably. Indeed, in 2022 China's total trade surplus of $857bn was largely as a result of surpluses with the EU (c.$400 bn), US ($367bn) and India (c.$100). China does not run large surpluses with the rest of the world.

37 Kishore Mahbubani "Fight to be world leader", *Le Monde Diplomatique* (April 2019), p11. https://mondediplo. com/2019/04/08us-china. Mahbubani's *Has China Won?* (New York: Hachette, 2020) is a readable and balanced analysis of US-China relations from the standpoint of Singapore's West-leaning political elite.

38 Trump also imposed tariffs on Canadian and EU exports. Even before then Trump had provoked German Chancellor Angela Merkel's 2017 argument that Europe could no longer rely on the US. https:// www.theguardian.com/world/2017/ may/28/merkel-says-eu-cannot-completely-rely-on-us-and-britain-any-more-g7-talks

39 China is not alone. In 2020 I asked a mainframe computer engineer if Western claims about Huawei's capacity to send data to China's security state were justified: he answered "of course – we know they can because we [in the West] do".

40 US claims to extra-territorial jurisdiction include sanctions against foreign firms that dealt/deal with the USSR, Cuba, Libya, Iran etc or which use the $US to settle trade contracts. This was applied to any supplier of Huawei, from whatever country, using technology bought from America, whenever it was bought. Sanctions weaken geopolitical rivals and strengthen US firms in competition with those from allied countries. The format is clear – use legal instruments associated with the sanctions regime to impose harsh fines on EU firms, for instance, allowing US firms to acquire them cheaply when the share price falls. French companies have been especially hard hit. On US sanctions and extra-territoriality see Ibrahim Warde "Trump's Iranian diktat", *Le Monde Diplomatique*

(June 2018) and Jean-Michel Quatrepoint "If it's in dollars, it's ours", *Le Monde Diplomatique* (February 2017).

41 China-bound or China-originated data was about a quarter of the global total in 2019, twice the US share.

42 Deborah James, "E-commerce and the World Trade Organisation", *Center for Economic and Policy Research* (17 November 2017). https://www.cepr.net/e-commerce-and-the-world-trade-organization/

43 Xi Jinping, "Pulling together through adversity and toward a shared future for all" (speech at Boao Forum for Asia conference), cited in Philip Golub, "Wall Street's unlikely new romance with China", *Le Monde Diplomatique* (November 2021).

44 Xi Jinping, "President Xi Jinping's message to the Davos agenda in full", *World Economic Forum* (17 January 2022). https://www.weforum.org/ agenda/2022/01/address-chinese-president-xi-jinping-2022-world-economic-forum-virtual-session/

45 The evidence of WTO breaches is weak: by early 2018 the US had made just twelve complaints to the WTO requiring a formal ruling. China complied with all and none were so serious that trade sanctions were threatened. See Philip Levy, "Was Letting China into the WTO a mistake? Why there were no better alternatives", *Foreign Affairs* online (2 April 2018). https://www.foreignaffairs. com/articles/china/2018-04-02/ was-letting-china-wto-mistake

   Chinese tech is not alone in benefitting from state support. Without massive support from the Pentagon and NASA the development of US chip technology in the 1950s and 1960s would have been far slower. In the 1980s the US accused Japan and the EU of trade distortion while simultaneously pursuing a huge industrial policy through Strategic Defence Initiative ("Star Wars") contracts, especially for IT firms.

46 Mehul Srivasta, Felicia Schwartz and Demetri Sevastopulo, "China building cyber weapons to hijack enemy satellites, says US leak", *Financial Times* (21 April 2023). https://www.ft.com/content/881c941a-c46f-4a40-b8d8-9e5c8a6775ba

47 White House, *Executive Order on Addressing United States Investments in Certain National Security Technologies and Products in Countries of Concern* (9 August 2023). https://www.whitehouse.gov/briefing-room/presidential-actions/2023/08/09/executive-order-on-addressing-united-states-investments-in-certain-national-security-technologies-and-products-in-countries-of-concern/

48 Thilo Hanemann, Mark Witzke and Yvonne Yu, "Cutting through the fog: FDI in China since COVID-19", *Rhodium Group* (13 December 2022). https://rhg.com/research/cutting-through-the-fog/

49 Nicholas Lardy, "Foreign direct investment is exiting China, new data show", *Peterson Institute for International Economics* (17 November 2023). https://www.piie.com/blogs/realtime-economics/foreign-direct-investment-exiting-china-new-data-show

50 On Japan see Martine Bulard, "ASEAN's diplomatic triumph", *Le Monde Diplomatique* (January 2021). See also Philip Golub, "US, China and global rebalance", *Le Monde Diplomatique* (June 2020).

51 Rana Foroohar "We must prepare for the reality of the Chip Wars", *Financial Times* (31 Oct 2022). https://www.ft.com/content/ef90d296-627d-4ff9-9983-ff537bdb078b

52 Bloomberg News, "China shows signs of decoupling from US as FDI, trade falls" (7 September 2023). https://www.bloomberg.com/news/articles/2023-09-07/china-fdi-into-us-plunges-to-more-than-decade-low-rhodium-says

53 US Chamber of Commerce China Centre, *Understanding US-China Decoupling* (2021). https://www.uschamber.com/assets/archived/images/024001_us_china_decoupling_report_fin.pdf

54 Cited in Andrew Hill, "The great chip war — and the challenge for global diplomacy", *Financial Times* (7 December 2022). https://www.ft.com/content/7de40326-58a9-457b-a828-edf86031883e

55 Patrick McGee and John Reed, "Apple's manufacturing shift to India hits stumbling blocks", *Financial Times* (14 February 2023). https://www.ft.com/content/0d70a823-0fba-49ae-a453-2518afcb01f9

56 Cited in Cairney and Prange, p101.

57 Bortolini.

58 Heng Weili, "Wall Street, investors reject decoupling from China", *China Daily Global* (18 March 2021). https://www.chinadaily.com.cn/a/202103/18/WS6052933da31024ad0baafd8a.html

59 Golub (2021).

60 Data in this paragraph is from Cainey and Prange, pp123-143.

61 China's technological development will in any case moderate the impact of decoupling. The World Nuclear Association reports that when its first nuclear power plant was built in the mid-1990s China was almost entirely dependent on French capital and technology but today Chinese firms contribute around 90 percent of the value of the latest plants. In textiles, Bangladesh and other Asian countries have replaced China as final producers but all have increased their imports of high-quality Chinese fabrics. On nuclear plants see https://world-nuclear.org/information-library/country-profiles/countries-a-f/china-nuclear-power.aspx

62 In real terms, this is seven times more than Marshall Plan spending.

63 Luke Patey, *How China Loses* (Oxford: Oxford University Press, 2021) p91. Patey adopts a mildly critical Western perspective on the BRI. Xi mentioned "win-win" cooperation in his Davos speech in 2017.

64 Sean Ledwith, "'The US vs China: Asia's new Cold War?' by Jude Woodward reviewed", *Monthly Review* online (2020). https://mronline.org/2020/06/02/ the-u-s-vs-china-asias-new-cold-war-by-jude-woodward-reviewed-by-sean-ledwith. Ledwith was criticising Jude Woodward, *The Us vs China: Asia's New Cold War?* (Manchester: Manchester University Press, 2017). He also criticised leftists who "dismiss legitimate struggles" in Hong Kong and Xinjiang as largely "manifestations of CIA-sponsored subversion".

65 Carchedi and Roberts, p217, p222.

66 Ammar Malik, Bradlet Parks, Brooke Russell et al, "Banking on the Belt and Road", *AidData* (September 2021). https://docs.aiddata.org/ad4/pdfs/ Banking_on_the_Belt_and_Road_ Executive_Summary.pdf

67 See also Andres Schipani, "Brazil's vulnerability is a big opportunity for Chinese investors", *Financial Times* (14 Nov 2017). This article argues that Chinese FDI in Brazil is driven by firms' need for "an outlet for excess industrial capacity in the steel, automotives and other industries". https://www.ft.com/ content/1d803686-c48e-11e7-b2bb-322b2cb39656

68 He Yafei, "China's overcapacity crisis can spur growth through overseas expansion", *South China Morning Post* (7 November 2014). https://www.scmp.com/comment/ insight-opinion/article/1399681/chinas-overcapacity-crisis-can-spur-growth-through-overseas. China's Ministry of Industry and Information Technology has also argued SOEs are exporting excess capacity, and that building railways overseas increases demand for steel. See Jonathan Holslag, "How China's New Silk Road threatens European trade", *The International Spectator: Italian Journal of International Affairs* (vol. 52, no. 1, 2017) p49.

69 Au Loong-Yu (2023).

70 Anne-Dominique Correa, "Latin America faces tough choices", *Le Monde Diplomatique* (October 2021). CAF refers to "Corporación Andino de Fomento".

71 2011 figures from United Nations Conference on Trade and Development (UNCTAD), *World Investment Report 2018*, p38. https://unctad.org/system/ files/official-document/wir2018_en.pdf 2018 figures from United Nations Conference on Trade and Development (UNCTAD), *World Investment Report 2020*, p28. https://unctad.org/system/files/ official-document/wir2020_en.pdf

72 James Kynge, "Chinese contractors grab lion's share of Silk Road projects" *Financial Times* (24 January 2018). https://www.ft.com/content/76b1be0c-0113-11e8-9650-9c0ad2d7c5b5

73 Jean-Christophe Servant, "Zambia's borrowing economy", *Le Monde Diplomatique* (December 2019) p12. https://mondediplo. com/2019/12/09zambia

74 Deborah Brautigam, Yufan Huang, and Kevin Acker, "Risky business: new data on Chinese loans and Africa's debt problem", China-Africa Research Initiative Briefing Paper no.3 (2020) pp4-7. Most Chinese commercial loans charge a 3 percent premium, and for the poorest forty African states debt service to China is higher than that to the World Bank. See https://static1.squarespace.com/ static/5652847de4b033f56d2bdc29/ t/6033fadb7ba591794b0a 9dff/1614019291794/BP+3+-+Brautigam%2C+Huang%2C+Acker+-+Chinese+Loans+African+Debt.pdf

75 Bukharin, p26

76 For critiques of China's involvement in Africa see Justin van der Merwe, Patrick Bond and Nicole Dodd (eds), *BRICS and Resistance in Africa: Contention, Assimilation and Co-optation* (London: Zed Books, 2019); Patrick Bond and Ana Garcia (eds) *BRICS. An Anti-capitalist Critique* (London: Pluto Press, 2015); Lee Wengraf, *Extracting Profit: Imperialism, Neoliberalism and the New Scramble for Africa* (Chicago: Haymarket Books, 2018).

77 See "Viva Laos Vegas", *Economist* (1 February 2020) and Christine Chaumeau, "China's destination of choice", *Le Monde Diplomatique* (July 2018).

78 Ian Urbina, "China consumes Gambia's waters", *Le Monde Diplomatique* (June 2021) pp14-15. https://mondediplo. com/2021/06/09gambia

79 Latin America data from "What does China want from Latin America and the Caribbean?" *Economist*, (15 June 2023). https://www.economist.com/ the-americas/2023/06/15/what-does-china-want-from-latin-america-and-the-caribbean. Africa data from "Data: China-Africa trade", *China Africa Research Initiative* (April 2023). http://www.sais-cari.org/data-china-africa-trade

80 For a powerful critique of extractivism see Martin Upchurch, "Is there a new extractive capitalism?", *International Socialism* (168, Autumn 2020). https://isj. org.uk/extractive-capitalism

81 Alexis Dantas and Elias Jabbour, "Brazil and China: an assessment of recent trade relations", *Economics of Agriculture* (vol. 63, issue 1, 2016) pp319-320. See also Elias Jabbour, "China's Belt and Road Initiative (BRI) in Latin America and the case of Brazil", paper presented online at the IIPPE China Workshop (5 September 2020) http://iippe.org/iippe-china-workshop-2020-02-chinas-belt-and-road-initiative-bri-in-latin-america-and-the-case-of-brazil

82 See Adrian Sotelo Valencia, *Sub-imperialism Revisited: Dependency Theory in the Thought of Ruy Mauro Marini* (Chicago: Haymarket Books, 2017) pp144-151.

83 Luciano Bolinaga and Ariel Slipak, "The Beijing Consensus and the reprimarization of the productive structure in Latin America: the case of Argentina", *Revista Problemas del Desarrollo* (vol. 46, no. 183, October-December 2015). https://www.scielo.org.mx/pdf/prode/ v46n183/0301-7036-prode-46-183-00033-en.pdf/ More generally, China takes only 3 percent of Latin American manufactured exports. See Rebecca Ray and Kehan Wang "China-Latin America economic bulletin, 2019 edition", *Global Development Policy Centre* (2019). https://www.bu.edu/gdp/files/2019/02/ GCI-Bulletin-Final-2019-1-1.pdf

84 Jean-Baptiste Malet, "China's tomato paste colonialism", *Le Monde Diplomatique* (June 2017). https://mondediplo. com/2017/06/12Tomatoes

85 United Nations Conference on Trade and Development (UNCTAD), *World Investment Report 2022*, p8. https:// unctad.org/system/files/official-document/ wir2022_en.pdf

86 UNCTAD (2020), p28.

87 Wei Liang, "China: globalization and the emergence of a new status quo power?", *Asian Perspective* (vol. 31, no. 4, 2020) p133. See also Hung (2016) pp106-114.

88 Patrick Bond, "BRICS and the sub-imperial location", in Patrick Bond and Ana Garcia (eds) p18.

89 Farai Maguwu section on "BRICS seen from Zimbabwe", in Baruti Amisi et al, "BRICS corporate snapshots during African extractivism", in Bond and Garcia (eds) p108.

90 James Kynge, "China hit by surge in Belt and Road bad loans", *Financial Times* (16 April 2023).

91 James Kynge and Jonathan Wheatley, "China pulls back from the world: rethinking Xi's 'Project of the Century'", *Financial Times* (11 December 2020).

92 Patrick Bond, "BRICS and the sub-imperial location", p23.

93 Ana Garcia and Patrick Bond, "Introduction", in Patrick Bond and Ana Garcia (eds) p1.

94 See Ruy Mauro Marini, "Brazilian interdependence and imperialist integration", *Monthly Review* (vol. 17, no. 7, 1965); Ruy Mauro Marini, *Subdesarrollo y revolución* (5th edition) (Mexico City: Siglo XXI Editores, 1974). For recent analyses of Marini's thought see Sotelo Valencia (2017) and Amanda Latimer, "Situating Ruy Mauro Marini (1931-1997): movements, struggles, and intellectual communities", in Ruy Mauro Marini, *The Dialectics of Dependency* (edited by Amanda Latimer and Jaime Osorio) (New York: Monthly Review Press, 2022).

95 In 2022 the BRICS accounted for 26.5 percent of global GDP, but China represented nearly 70 percent of this.

96 The new right-wing president Javier Milei subsequently withdrew Argentina's application.

97 "China-brokered Saudi-Iran deal driving 'wave of reconciliation', says Wang", *Aljazeera* (21 Aug 2023). https://www.aljazeera.com/news/2023/8/21/china-brokered-saudi-iran-deal-driving-wave-of-reconciliation-says-wang

98 China used its economic power in 2012 by banning imports of Filipino bananas, which represent 25 percent of the Philippines' agricultural exports.

99 Lawrence Summers, "Time US leadership woke up to new economic era", *Financial Times* (6 April 2015).

100 The AIIB's $100 billion starting capital is significant – roughly two-thirds that of the Japan-led Asian Development Bank and half that of the World Bank – but in practice AIIB project lending is far smaller than that of China's state-owned banks. This is also true of the lending of the BRICS' New Development Bank.

101 It is widely believed that the WTO has removed most trade restrictions. In reality, there are 300 regional trade agreements in the world, with each state-capital complex negotiating the terms of its insertion into regional and global value chains. See World Trade Organisation, 2021, "Regional Trade Agreements", www.wto.org/english/tratop_e/region_e/region_e.htm#facts

102 Australia has placed itself firmly in the US military camp despite sending two-fifths of its exports to China. Australian foreign ministry data shows that total trade with China in 2021 was A$282bn, versus A$68bn with the US. https://www.dfat.gov.au/trade/trade-and-investment-data-information-and-publications/trade-statistics/trade-time-series-data. China sought to deepen Australia's vulnerability in 2019 with severe restrictions on a quarter of Australian exports to China in response to Australia's exclusion of Huawei from its 5G network.

103 The limits of the territorial claim are the so-called "9-dash line", drawn up by the GMD (originally as an 11-dash line) and simply taken over by the CCP in 1949. It is a straightforwardly nationalist claim that, in the words of the radical Filipino writer Walden Bello, says "fuck you" to the other states bordering the South China Sea. See Walden Bello "Is China an imperial power in the image of the West?", *Foreign Policy in Focus* (13 November 2019). https://fpif.org/is-china-an-imperial-power-in-the-image-of-the-west/

Bello answers "no" because he mistakenly reduces imperialism to colonial conquest. Water is the basis of another dispute between China and its neighbours. The countries along the Mekong (Thailand, Laos, Cambodia and Vietnam) have suffered falling water levels that imperil fishing and access to fresh water due to China's irrigation and hydro-electric schemes in the Upper Mekong. China has so far not agreed to common river-management arrangements.

104 Stockholm International Peace Research Institute (SIPRI), "World military expenditure passes \$2 trillion for first time" (25 April 2022). https://www.sipri.org/media/press-release/2022/world-military-expenditure-passes-2-trillion-first-time

105 Pieter Wezeman, Justine Gadon and Siemon Wezeman, *Trends in international arms transfer, 2022* (Stockholm: SIPRI, March 2023). https://www.sipri.org/publications/2023/sipri-fact-sheets/trends-international-arms-transfers-2022. The Kafkaesque absurdity of capitalist geopolitics is brought home by the data: the five permanent members of the UN Security Council, charged with keeping or restoring global peace, account for 75 percent of global arms sales.

106 Global Security, "Pacific fleet exercises". www.globalsecurity.org/military/ops/ex-pacfleet.htm

107 The "Five Eyes" intelligence-sharing alliance was established in the Cold War between the US National Security Agency, Britain's Government Communications Headquarters (GCHQ) and similar agencies in Canada, Australia and New Zealand. Under Deng Xiaoping the US established listening posts, nicknamed "big ears", in Xinjiang to eavesdrop on Soviet communications. It's now focused on China: in 2021 the US Congress intelligence sub-committee recommended expansion to include South Korea, India and Germany, and other allies, including possibly Israel. Facing Western criticism over

Hong Kong in 2020, foreign ministry spokesperson Zhao Lijian said those challenging Chinese security might "get their eyes poked out". See Philippe Leymarie, "Five eyes on the world", *Le Monde Diplomatique* (April 2022).

108 White House (Executive Office of the President, National Security Council), "Indo-Pacific Strategy of the United States" (Washington: White House, February 2022). https://www.whitehouse.gov/wp-content/uploads/2022/02/U.S.-Indo-Pacific-Strategy.pdf

109 See Tomas Tengely-Evans "Why the world is unequal", *Socialist Worker* (27 May 2020).

110 See Chad Brown and Yilin Wang, "Taiwan's outbound foreign investment, particularly in tech, continues to go to mainland China despite strict controls", *Peterson Institute for International Economics* (27 February 2023). https://www.piie.com/research/piie-charts/taiwans-outbound-foreign-investment-particularly-tech-continues-go-mainland

111 Robert Blackwill and Philip Zelokow, *The United States, China and Taiwan: a Strategy to Prevent War* (New York: Council on Foreign Relations, 2021).

112 Daniel Schaeffer, "Chine-États-Unis-Mer de Chine du Sud et riverains: en attendant Biden" (China-US-South China Sea and bordering countries: waiting for Biden), *Asie21* (15 September 2020). Cited in Martine Bulard "Is an Asian NATO imminent?", *Le Monde Diplomatique* (June 2021). https://mondediplo.com/2021/06/08bulard

113 For an excellent analysis of the Ukraine War and imperialist rivalry, see Tomas Tengely-Evans, "Death rides out: NATO, Russia and the war in Ukraine", *International Socialism* (178, Spring 2023).

114 Cited in Alice Hérait, "Taiwan strengthens ties with the US", *Le Monde Diplomatique* (October 2021). https://mondediplo.com/2021/10/07taiwan

115 The international Left should oppose any Chinese invasion of Taiwan, which would extinguish the limited (bourgeois) democracy, including trade union freedoms, that exist there. Regional bullying cannot be excused by China's rivalry with a more powerful global bully. But support for the principle of Taiwan's right to self-determination against China's great power chauvinism does not mean supporting it under circumstances where Taiwan is potentially the biggest flashpoint in the competition between the world's two largest powers. A declaration of Taiwanese independence is currently inconceivable without prior US approval and would almost certainly provoke a Chinese invasion. The US would then be forced to respond to prevent the loss of global prestige and, potentially, increase in China's global military influence. In the event of a war, that could lead to the death of millions, Taiwan would either be forcibly incorporated into China or remain "independent" only thanks to a huge US military presence. This would not be self-determination. Meanwhile, reaction would be rampant in both the US and China, increasing the possibility of a third world war.

Lenin grasped the importance of situating struggle over principles within concrete historical circumstances. Socialists, Lenin argued, "cannot be in favour of a war between great nations, in favour of the slaughter of twenty million people for the sake of the problematical liberation of a small nation with a population of perhaps ten or twenty millions!". They must continue to demand "complete national equality" while recognising that "the democratic interests of one country must be subordinated to the democratic interests of *several and all* countries". He illustrates his argument by assuming "two great monarchies" separated by "a little monarchy" that declares itself a republic and that the two great monarchies would go to war to restore the monarchy. Lenin argues that the international Left, along with the internationalist Left in the small country, "*would be against substituting a republic for the monarchy* in this case". Such a substitution "is not an absolute, but one of the democratic demands, subordinate to the interests of democracy (and still more, of course, to those of the socialist proletariat) as a whole". The demand for a republic should not disappear from the Left's programme or principles, but the Left should "not forget the elementary logical difference between the general and the particular". See V I Lenin, "The discussion on self-determination summed up" (section 7) (2016) at https://www.marxists.org/archive/lenin/works/1916/jul/x01.htm

The only progressive solution for Taiwan lies with the movement for political change in China. The overthrow from below of authoritarian state capitalism would enable a real choice between independence or reunification based on the interests of the mass of people rather than those of the Taiwanese, US and Chinese ruling classes.

116 Other Marxist theories of imperialism, like Karl Kautsky's theory of ultra-imperialism in the 1910s, contemporary theorisations of US super-imperialism and transnationalism overstate (short-term) cooperation and understate (long-term) rivalry. For a critique, see Adrian Budd, *Class, States and International Relations: a Critical Appraisal of Robert Cox and Neo-Gramscian Theory* (London: Routledge, 2013) ch6.

117 Doug Stokes, "The heart of empire? Theorising US Empire in an era of transnational capitalism", *Third World Quarterly* (vol. 26, no. 2, 2005) p230. https://core.ac.uk/download/pdf/90154.pdf/ The cooperation that exists is structured by states' relative powers: as Peter Gowan argued about EU-US relations, they combine subordinate "cooperation with some elements of friction and competition". Peter Gowan, *The Global Gamble:*

Washington's Faustian Bid for World Dominance (London: Verso, 1999) pviii. Marini's "antagonistic cooperation" is a useful way to capture the dialectic of cooperation and conflict.

118 Ho-fung Hung, "…Pax Americana", p256.

119 Gilbert Achcar, *The New Cold War: the US, Russia and China from Kosovo to Ukraine* (London: Westbourne Press, 2023) is an exception, a serious piece of Marxist analysis of US global power (largely focused on US-Russia relations).

120 Even when facing the USSR, the US protected its own interests by inflicting damage on allies. Concerned about its trade deficit with Japan in the 1980s the US imposed high tariffs on consumer electronics and forced Japan to revalue the Yen by 50 percent over two years at the Plaza Accord in 1986. This was a key cause of the long-term stagnation of the Japanese economy.

121 Jack Lau and Shi Jiangtao, "China offers Russia 'strong support on core interests' as Xi Jinping and Vladimir Putin meet for first time since Ukraine invasion", *South China Morning Post* (15 September 2022).https://www.scmp.com/news/china/diplomacy/article/3192630/xi-jinping-and-vladimir-putin-speak-person-first-time-russia?module=inline&pgtype=article

122 Kawala Xie, "Deeper China-Russia relations a 'strategic choice' by both sides, Xi Jinping tells Russian Prime Minister Mishustin", *South China Morning Post* (20 December 2023). https://www.scmp.com/news/china/diplomacy/article/3245774/deeper-china-russia-relations-strategic-choice-both-sides-xi-jinping-tells-russian-prime-minister

123 Nuriya Kapralou, "Russia aims to widen trade with India as energy ties boom", *Nikkei Asia* (3 April 2023). https://asia.nikkei.com/Economy/Trade/Russia-aims-to-widen-trade-with-India-as-energy-ties-boom

124 Many countries in the Global South, dependent on Russian energy and wheat supplies, sympathetic to Moscow's concerns about NATO enlargement and having experienced Western domination, have also refused to condemn Russia but not faced US threats and criticism. See Martine Bulard, "China's delicate balancing act", *Le Monde Diplomatique* (April 2022).

125 Douglas Hurd, "Foreign Policy and International Security", *Boundary and Security Bulletin* (Durham: International Boundaries Research Unit, July 1993). https://www.durham.ac.uk/media/durham-university/research-/research-centres/ibru-centre-for-borders-research/maps-and-databases/publications-database/boundary-amp-security-bulletins/bsb1-2_hurd.pdf

126 Alexandra Sharp, "The big takeaways from the Biden-Xi APEC Meeting", *Foreign Policy* (16 November 2023). https://foreignpolicy.com/2023/11/16/biden-xi-apec-meeting-talks-dictator-communication-channels-fentanyl-pandas-ai/

127 Christopher Layne, "Coming storms: the return of great-power war", *Foreign Affairs* (vol. 99, no. 6, November/December 2020) p47. https://www.foreignaffairs.com/articles/united-states/2020-10-13/coming-storms

128 Biden (2020), pp70-1.

129 See Alex Callinicos, *The New Age of Catastrophe* (Cambridge: Polity Press, 2023) for a powerful Marxist analysis of these inter-locking crises.

Conclusion
Prospects for change

1 See David Harvey, *Spaces of Hope* (Edinburgh: Edinburgh University Press, 2000) chapter 2; David Harvey, *The Limits to Capital* (London: Verso, 1999) chapter 13.

2 Hung (2016) p174.

3 Joe Cash, "China's industrial profits growth slows, keeps stimulus calls alive", *Reuters* (27 November 2023). https://www.reuters.com/world/china/chinas-industrial-profits-fall-78-jan-oct-2023-11-27/

4 See Robin Wigglesworth "How much FDI is China actually attracting", *Financial Times* (27 November 2023). https://www.ft.com/content/47fc5fc5-0606-465e-bb37-61da1f67cabb

5 So serious has the problem of youth unemployment become that in June 2023 the party-state did what all responsible authorities rooted in Stalinism would do – it stopped publishing the data.

6 Bloomberg, "China's debt-to-GDP ratio rises to record 279.7% on credit boom" (8 May 2023). The data doesn't include bank loans to local government financing vehicles. https://www.bloomberg.com/news/articles/2023-05-08/china-s-debt-to-gdp-ratio-rises-to-record-279-7-on-credit-boom

7 Einar H. Dyvik, "Value of COVID-19 fiscal stimulus packages in G20 countries as of May 2021, as a share of GDP", *Statista* (29 August 2023). https://www.statista.com/statistics/1107572/covid-19-value-g20-stimulus-packages-share-gdp/

8 Adrian Budd, "New strains on state capitalism", *Socialist Review* (May 2018).

9 Hung (2016), p152.

10 From a weaker position China reciprocates in the tech-war. In mid-2023 it barred the US chip-maker Micron Technology from Chinese markets on national security grounds. This is largely a gesture of defiance. Micron's relatively low-level chips can be replaced by Chinese production reasonably easily, while more advanced chip-makers, such as Intel, Qualcomm and Nvidia, whose products are currently vital for China's production of advanced IT and electronics, escaped restrictions.

11 Hung (2016), p175.

12 Mohamad Bazzi, "Why bombing Yemen is a grave mistake", *Guardian* (13 January 2024).

13 It is often argued that the Italian Marxist Antonio Gramsci emphasised the consensual aspects of bourgeois class rule. As a socialist revolutionary he was rightly interested in how the ruling class tries to mobilise consent in order that the revolutionary party be better able to challenge it. But consent was secondary to force in the arsenal of ruling class power, which is "characterised by the combination of force and consent, which balance each other reciprocally, without force predominating excessively over consent." For the ruling class "the attempt is always made to ensure that force will appear to be based on the consent of the majority". Antonio Gramsci, *Selections from the Prison Notebooks* (London: Lawrence and Wishart, 1971) p80.

14 A Hui-led uprising in 1856, provoked by pogroms against Hui by Han immigrants, removed Qing control over large parts of Yunnan until 1873. See David Atwill, *The Panthay Rebellion* (London: Verso 2023).

15 Dropping out was temporary for most hippies. For every Abbie Hoffman, who maintained his radical views throughout his life, there were several Jerry Rubins, whose *Growing (up) at Thirty-Seven* (New York: M Evans, 1976) provided a pathetic justification for his business activities. Apple, in which Rubin was an early investor, no doubt delighted in the counter-culture veneer Rubin provided on its way to becoming the world's largest company.

16 Jean-Louis Rocca "China's mandarin
   democracy", *Le Monde Diplomatique*
   (March 2017).

17 David Harvey, *The New Imperialism*
   (Oxford: Oxford University Press, 2003)
   p124.

Further reading

There is a huge and rapidly growing literature on China, much of it expressing Western concerns about China's growing power. The books in this category often betray their intent by references in their titles to China taking over the world or being a threat of some sort – to democracy, to Western values, etc. Works such as these, designed for Western businesses or state managers and strategists, contain nuggets of information but provide little in the way of serious analysis. Mainstream books are not entirely without merit, however, and readers seeking a deeper understanding of China would benefit by first reading a good general history such as Michael Dillon's *China: a Modern History* (2nd edition) (London: I B Tauris, 2021).

Fortunately there is also a growing body of critical scholarship on China that aims to provide the tools to understand the nature of the party-state regime, the central dynamics of China's emerging power and the prospects for resistance to it. Some of them are listed below under headings organised in line with the sequence of the chapters of this book.

1925-27 Chinese Revolution

- Isaacs, Harold, *The Tragedy of the Chinese Revolution* (Stanford: Stanford University Press, 1961).

Mao and the Mao period

- Harris, Nigel, *The Mandate of Heaven: Marx and Mao in Modern China* (London: Quartet Books, 1978).

- Hore, Charlie, *The Road to Tiananmen Square* (London: Bookmarks, 1991).

- Yang, Jisheng, *Tombstone* (London: Penguin, 2013).

Tiananmen protests and massacre

- Black, George, and Robin Munro, *Black Hands of Beijing: Lives of Defiance in China's Democracy Movement* (London: John Wiley and Sons, 1993).

- Lim, Louisa, *The People's Republic of Amnesia: Tiananmen Revisited* (Oxford: Oxford University Press, 2014).

China's economy

- Hung, Ho-fung, *The China Boom: Why China will not Rule the World* (New York: Columbia University Press, 2016).

- Hung, Ho-fung (ed.) *China and the Transformation of Global Capitalism* (Baltimore: John Hopkins University Press, 2009).

- Li, Minqi, *China and the 21st Century Crisis* (London: Pluto, 2016).

Politics under Xi Jinping

- Lam, Willy Wo-Lap, *Chinese Politics in the Era of Xi Jinping* (Abingdon: Routledge, 2015).

Workers in contemporary China

- Lee, Ching Kwan, *Gender and the South China Miracle: Two Worlds of Factory Women* (London: University of California Press, 1998).

- Lee, Ching Kwan, *Against the Law* (Berkeley: University of California Press, 2007).

- Liu, Mingwei and Chris Smith (eds) *China at Work: a Labour Process Perspective on the Transformation of Work and Employment in China* (London: Palgrave, 2016).

- Pai, Hsiao-Hung, *Scattered Sand: the Story of China's Rural Migrants* (London: Verso, 2012)

- Ren, Hao, Eli Friedman and Zhongjin Li, *China on Strike: Narratives of Workers' Resistance* (Chicago: Haymarket Books, 2016).

- Zhang, Lu, *Inside China's Automobile Factories: the Politics of Labour and Worker Resistance* (Cambridge: Cambridge University Press, 2015).

Repression, protest and resistance

- Byler, Darren, *Terror Capitalism: Uyghur Dispossession and Masculinity in a Chinese City* (Durham, NC: Duke University Press, 2021).
- Gilbert, Simon, "China, the Uyghurs and the Left", *International Socialism* (no. 172, Autumn 2021).
- Hong Fincher, Leta, *Leftover Women: the Resurgence of Gender Inequality in China* (London: Bloomsbury Academic, 2023).
- Lixiong, Wang, and Tsering Shakya, *The Struggle for Tibet* (London: Verso, 2011).
- Loong-yu, Au, *Hong Kong in Revolt: the Protest Movement and the Future of China* (London: Pluto Press, 2020).
- Ruckus, Ralf, *The Left in China* (London: Pluto Press, 2023).
- Shakya, Tsering, *Dragon in the Land of the Snows: a History of Modern Tibet since 1947* (London: Pimlico, 1999).
- Smith, Richard, *China's Engine of Environmental Collapse* (London: Pluto Press, 2020).
- Tohti, Ilham, *We Uyghurs Have No Say* (London: Verso, 2022).
- Woeser, Tsering, *Tibet on Fire: Self-immolations Against Chinese Rule* (London: Verso, 2016).

Inter-imperialist rivalry

- Callinicos, Alex, *Imperialism and Global Political Economy* (Cambridge: Polity Press, 2009).
- Golub, Philip S., *East Asia's Reemergence* (Cambridge: Polity Press, 2016).
- Heydarian, Richard Javad, *Asia's New Battlefield: the USA, China and the Struggle for the Western Pacific* (London: Zed, 2015).

Journals

A new generation of writers and activists, often part of the global Chinese diaspora, is producing insightful analysis in various online and print journals. These sometimes bear the hallmarks of the academic milieux in which many of the authors work, but are nevertheless an important resource for the global left. These journals and websites include:

- *Asian Labour Review: a Journal for Labour Movements across Asia*

- *Chuang* (whose resource page contains further important sources)

- *Dove and Crane Collective* (radical members of the Chinese diaspora in the US "working against US-China conflict")

- *Gongchao* (which focuses mainly on workers' and other struggles)

- *Lausan* (a contribution to the "tradition of Hong Kong's leftist activists, writers and organisers")

- *Made in China* (covering "all facets of politics and society in mainland China and the Sinophone world at large")

- *China Labour Bulletin* is a vital source for up-to-the-minute information on and analysis of workers' struggles.

- *The China Quarterly* and *Journal of Contemporary China* are academic journals that frequently contain important articles.

Index